LOST
GULFPORT

LOST GULFPORT

JOHN CUEVAS

THE History PRESS

Published by The History Press
Charleston, SC
www.historypress.com

Cover images provided by Paul Jermyn.

First published 2018

Manufactured in the United States

ISBN 9781467140225

Library of Congress Control Number: 2018940074

CONTENTS

Acknowledgements 7
Introduction 9

The Highway through Downtown 17
The Way It Was, 1950–1964:
A Walking Tour of Downtown Gulfport 23
Home and Business Profiles 39
Attorneys, Doctors, Morticians and Insurance Sales 40
Buses, Trains and Automobiles 43
Bookstores, Drugstores and Gift Shops 49
Churches and Civic Organizations 55
Clothing and Accessories 58
Cookies, Candy and Stone Ice Cream 75
Department Stores, Furniture Stores and Five-and-Dimes 87
Famous Houses 96
Federal, County and City Services 104
Home Improvement and Real Estate Sales 110
Hotels, Banks and Office Buildings 112
Movie Theaters, Sports and Other Fun Things 122
Music, Photographers and Television Shops 134
Newspapers and Printing Companies 136
Restaurants, Bars and Hamburger Stands 138
Miscellaneous Businesses 159

Epilogue 161
Bibliography 163
Index 167
About the Author 175

ACKNOWLEDGEMENTS

In an effort to construct a map of downtown Gulfport during its golden age, I have gathered input from several friends and acquaintances, not only to help me with the map but also to contribute their memories of living on the coast during the '50s. This book would not have been possible without their input. I would like to acknowledge several of those who helped.

My thanks to Betty Shaw for sharing her knowledge of Gulfport's history and to Linda Goesling for her help with my research. Along with Karl Fasold, Linda helped put together the history of the Fasold family's jewelry businesses on the coast.

Gary Sinopoli, Joe Salloum, Chris Farmer, Anneas J R Moses, Judy D'Angelo, Rebecca Hilton, Nels Anderson and others contributed valuable information about businesses in Gulfport.

I cannot say enough about Dan Ellis for his excellent, in-depth research on Gulfport and other cities along the coast. I don't believe there is anyone who has worked harder or dug deeper into the history of our wonderful Gulf Coast. His recent book, *Gulfport: "Celebration City,"* was not only a great source of information but also an inspiration to me.

It has been my real pleasure to work with Mayme, Jill and Danna, the Stone sisters, whose father, Dan, started the most beloved store in Gulfport, the Stone Ice Cream Company. Together, the three sisters collected the wonderful story of their loving family and the business to which their father devoted his life.

Paul Jermyn was the single largest contributor of photos for this book. Over the years, his vintage collection has enhanced many articles and books about the coast. We are all indebted to him for his passion in preserving these old photographs, as well as his willingness to share these great images. My deepest thanks to Paul.

The highlight of this book is the walking tour of downtown Gulfport. Creating the map of stores as they existed in the '50s was a formidable task, as one can imagine. I could not have created the map without the help of Anneas J R Moses, Linda Goesling and, in particular, Wayne Saucier. Without Wayne's remarkable knowledge and assistance, a complete map would not have been possible. Wayne, I can't thank you enough.

INTRODUCTION

Although still rural in many respects, Gulfport stood out as the cosmopolitan area of south Mississippi. In relative terms, it was not New Orleans or Mobile, but it was the next best thing. Before the advent of shopping malls and strip shopping centers, Gulfport, like other American cities of the period, was concentrated in a central downtown area. People from all the surrounding towns came to Gulfport to shop and conduct business. In a 2002 article in the *SunHerald*, jewelry store owner Karl Fasold recalled, "'Til 9 o'clock at night, there were so many people on the sidewalk that you had to watch where you walked. This was the only shopping area around, so they all come down to Gulfport."

During the '50s and early '60s, the city was experiencing rapid growth. According to Harrison County census records, the population that was only 8,000 in 1925 had expanded to 25,000 in 1948, and by 1955, the city was ranked as the seventh-largest city in Mississippi with a population of 28,100. In 1950, the business district was growing, with three more stores added along 25th Avenue and eleven new stores built along 13th Street, the main street of town; the latter handled one of the heaviest concentrations of traffic in the state.

By the summer of 1951, the four-lane Highway 90 that ran parallel to the beach had been completed between Gulfport's eastern limits and the city of Long Beach on the west. Before Interstate 10, the widened Highway 90 was the most direct route between Mobile and New Orleans. The poet Rena Lloyd Humphreys, from Greenwood, Mississippi, proclaimed Gulfport

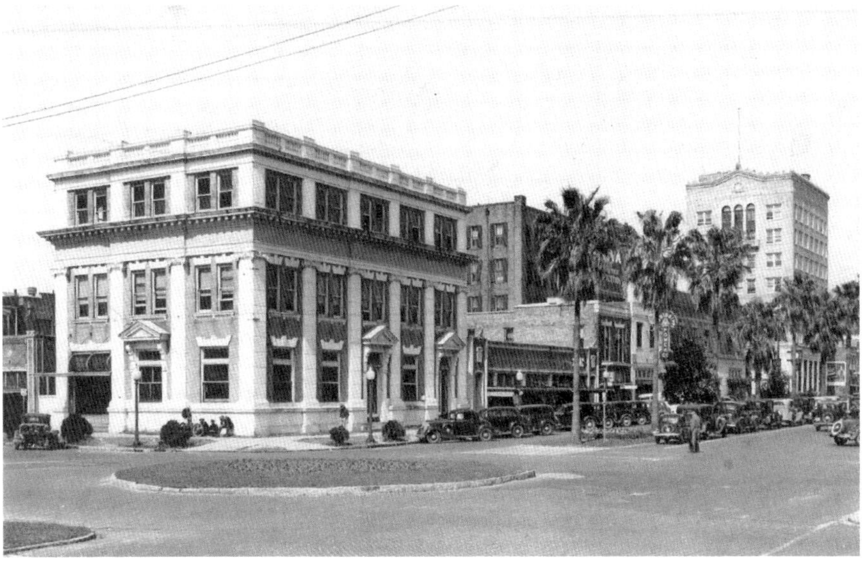

In 1950, the business district was growing, with three more stores added along 25th Avenue and eleven new stores built along 13th Street, the main street of town. *Paul Jermyn Collection.*

the "City of Destiny." The first line of her poem, "Gulfport, where your ship comes in," became the slogan of the city for more than sixty years. By the late 1950s, the city limits stretched from Lewis Avenue to the west to Courthouse Road on the East, from the beach on the south and up Highway 49 to the Phillips' Milk of Magnesia Plant on the North.

Gulfport was not like other small towns. The city had stores and services usually found in larger cities. In addition, Gulfport had commerce as well as nightlife. When other small towns closed down at dark, Gulfport and the cities along the coast were just beginning to rock. The nightclubs, bars, strip clubs, illegal booze and open gambling kept the coast towns open into the early hours.

Over time, small businesses cropped up along the Pass Road between Gulfport and Biloxi. The hodgepodge of small stores and shops that developed was a combination of new and aging structures thrown together with little concern for architectural appeal. A conglomeration of small, inauspicious buildings also developed along Highway 90 from Biloxi to Bay St. Louis. Small tourist cottages, service stations, souvenir shops and local restaurants were common. As the decade continued, ordinances were passed for the purpose of restricting signs and structures in an attempt to make the

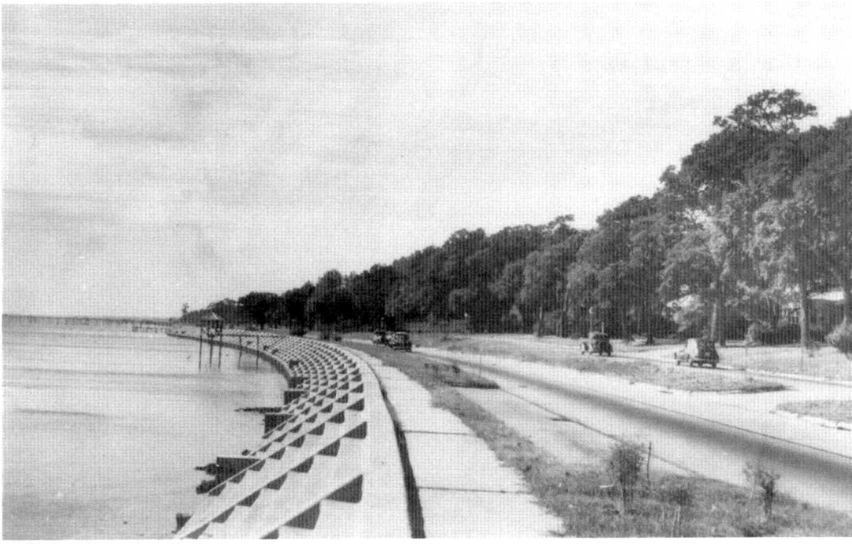

Before Interstate 10, the widened Highway 90 was the most direct route between Mobile and New Orleans. *Paul Jermyn Collection.*

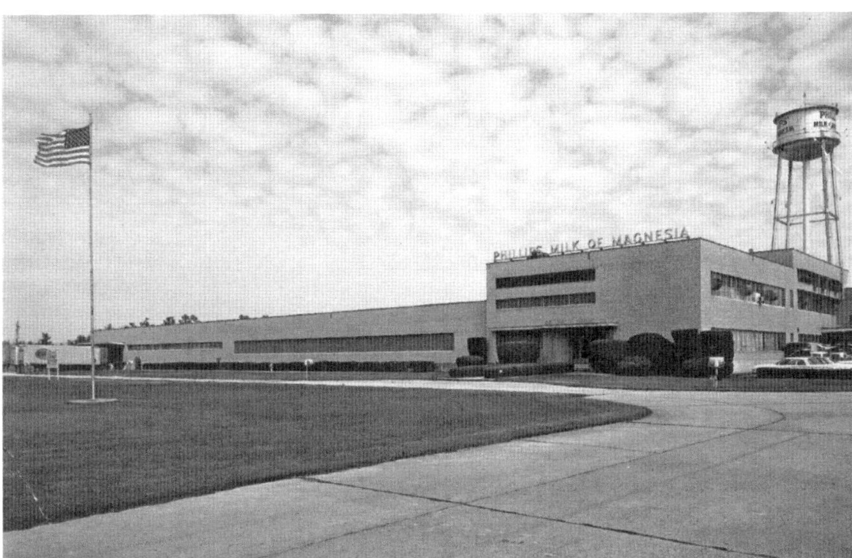

By the late 1950s, the city limits stretched up Highway 49 north to the Phillips' Milk of Magnesia Plant. *Paul Jermyn Collection.*

sites more attractive, with little result. Eventually, some of these mom and pop businesses were beginning to be pushed out by national franchises such as McDonald's and Kentucky Fried Chicken. At first, these new buildings were not much different from the local stores. They were identifiable but were not overly attention-grabbing, aside from McDonald's golden arches. In the '60s, the drive-in concept of restaurants gave way to the idea of family dining, as fast-food companies began encouraging customers to eat inside.

By the early '60s, the concept of enclosed shopping malls around the country had begun to move the clusters of stores lined up along the roads and highways into one environmentally controlled location. The original purpose was to create a downtown in the suburbs. Malls were intended to be like public squares where people would gather to shop, dine, hold civic meetings and enjoy entertainment.

On September 26, 1963, Edgewater Plaza Shopping City, the Mississippi Gulf Coast's first fully enclosed shopping mall, was opened on property adjacent to the Edgewater Gulf Hotel. There were twenty original stores, with Gayfers Department Store from Mobile as the primary anchor. On opening day, hundreds poured into the new mall.

Enclosed malls were never intended to take business away from downtown merchants, but that is exactly what happened. It was originally thought that the malls would actually be an aid to city shopping. It was hoped, in fact, that if any businesses would be harmed, it would be the cheap strip stores that were everywhere on the coast. It's hard to imagine now where they thought the people who swarmed into the Edgewater Plaza Shopping City would come from. The new mall drew the people who found shopping and parking in Gulfport too inconvenient. In addition to providing free one-stop parking, the enclosed, air-conditioned environment at the mall made shopping a pleasure. Now the consumer could park and shop for just about anything he or she wanted within walking distance and all under one roof.

In 1965, the construction of Interstate 10 began. Once completed, the highway fundamentally eliminated the major flow of traffic into the downtown area. That same year, the City of Gulfport began the widening of 25th Avenue. In so doing, the city eliminated all the parking along the main thoroughfare in the shopping district of Gulfport. No one in charge seemed to recognize the importance of street parking in the downtown area to retain the shoppers, who were now turning to Edgewater Plaza for their buying needs. The removal of downtown parking without providing alternatives led to the perception that shopping in Gulfport was not worth the effort. In addition, the once lovely avenue with palm trees and flowers was transformed into a multi-laned, blacktopped thoroughfare that quickly whisked potential shoppers from the new I-10 expressway past the downtown merchants onto Highway 90 and away from the city.

As downtown Gulfport withered, the mall expanded. In 1971, the adjacent Edgewater Gulf Hotel was demolished to make room for additional merchants. Two of the major retailers in Gulfport that had hung on until the end, Sears and J.C. Penney, were finally forced to leave downtown, driving two more nails in the city's coffin.

Sears opened in the expanded wing of the mall in 1972, closing its main store on 25th Avenue in Gulfport. In 1979, when J.J. Newberry, one of the mall's original twenty stores, closed, J.C. Penney moved into the space, closing its downtown location. McCrory's, Gulfport's iconic five-and-dime, also moved to the mall.

The Edgewater Plaza Shopping City was so successful that the mall had turned into a place name. The developers saw the social and financial benefit in leading people to identify with the mall, so once the new addition was completed in 1973, the name of the mall was changed from the original, Edgewater Plaza Shopping City, to simply the Edgewater Mall.

According to the *Mobile Register*, Interstate 10 from U.S. Highway 49 in Gulfport to Mississippi Highway 57 in Jackson County opened on March 25, 1976. The new interstate ran parallel with Highway 90 (Beach Boulevard), so travelers from Mobile to New Orleans were now able to bypass the beach road, avoiding the traffic lights and bumper-to-bumper traffic. The road that created the vibrant young city of Gulfport by routing traffic into the downtown area was no longer the route of choice. Even the local residents found the use of the new interstate to be far more convenient. The interstate highway system created ghost towns all over the country that had once been vibrant communities. Gulfport was one of the interstate's many victims.

I consider the golden age of Gulfport from about 1950 to the early '60s. The generation during that era had a hunger for the future. Although we had a preoccupation with tailfins and rockets, we had a sense that we were the future. Our visions might have seemed overly innocent in retrospect, but as we entered the '60s, we saw many of our aspirations fulfilled. Americans beat out the Russians by being the first country to land a man on the moon and return him safely to the earth. Many parents were able to send their children to college for the first time and give them many of the things they never had. We found ourselves with leisure time, unlike youngsters of previous generations. We had our own spending money. We drove our own cars. And we were a growing force of societal change.

As we moved from the innocence of the '50s, the '60s were transforming everything. The changes were so dramatic as to make the '50s look embarrassingly naïve and shallow. Even the typical American family was changing in ways we never could have imagined. Defined in our day as a mom, dad, brother and sister, the families were beginning to look quite different. It is now more common to find that mom and dad are divorced (or may have never married), the daughter is the CEO of a new IT company, the son is gay and the mother has tied herself to a tree to save the environment.

We have come to realize how much of what we knew no longer exists. So much is gone—not just the objects and places we remember, but the environment that gave us the conditions for arguably one of the greatest periods in America's history. Although we can't go back, I consider it a blessing to have been part of the golden age of Gulfport. It was an era when we saw a sleepy coastal town become the second-largest city in Mississippi. It was a fantastic journey, and we were all along for the ride.

Now that we are older, and hopefully much wiser, we look back with gratitude to Clarence Welch, the "Pop Corn King"; Mrs. Ethelynd Baxley and her radio drama; Effie Gridley and Jackie Hines at the GRC; Ma Rippy and her skating rink; Mr. Broussard and his afternoon concerts; Señor Lopez and his hot tamale cart; the Dog House Jr. for its scrumptious hamburgers; Stone Ice Cream for the greatest frozen treats ever; Jones Brothers' Drug Store for the use of its telephone; and all of the many others for making our young lives so much richer.

It is easy to forget how vibrant Gulfport was during its golden age. So much of the city has changed. Many of our special places are now rubble. Our beloved high school is now a federal building, the store where we bought our first suit or prom dress is now a neighborhood bar and Katrina has leveled the places where some of us had our first dance. The Gulfport we knew no longer exists. The truth is that we ignored the importance of many of those special places, not realizing at the time how much they really meant to us. The moment we last walked out the door, they could have closed and we would not have noticed. Different stores have opened and closed in the same spot over the years, but we did not see how the slow transformation was dramatically changing the town we loved.

The biggest mistake many of us made was not stopping to live each moment of those glorious years to its fullest. That is very clear now that those moments are gone. We were in such a rush to get on to the next thing—school, college, marriage, family and career. We got so caught up in living that we didn't notice the changes taking place. But no matter how much time passes, no matter how many places have come and gone, there are some memories that remain with us forever. During that time, the town was alive with popular stores and eager shoppers as travelers poured into the city. Many of those who remember Gulfport the way it was reminisce about their favorite restaurants, stores and shops.

Sadly, downtown Gulfport of the golden age no longer exists. Hurricanes Camille (1969) and Katrina (2005) wiped away many of the buildings, leaving vacant lots, while shopping malls and Interstate 10 siphoned the businesses away from what was once a busy downtown area. As we have gotten older, some of us who grew up in Gulfport reflect on the way it was "in the good old days."

In trying to recall those honey-colored days, I realized that there was nothing available that accurately portrayed the city the way we knew it. There are some excellent history books about Gulfport, but none concentrated so specifically on the places we remember most. For that reason, I have compiled a map of downtown Gulfport the way it was when we were growing up.

So, go back in time with me as I take you on a walking tour of Gulfport during the '50s and early '60s, going block by block, naming each store and business. After the tour, I'll give a brief synopsis of some of the more memorable places. I have also included many photos of the people and places from that time. Hopefully this book will serve as a reference for historians, as well as a source of nostalgia for the local people who still recall with fondness the "lost" Gulfport of the golden age.

THE HIGHWAY THROUGH DOWNTOWN

The Great Southern Hotel, a prominent landmark in Gulfport for almost fifty years, sat directly in the path of Highway 90. Gulfport's growth benefited from the circuitous route around the hotel. Heavy traffic between Mobile and New Orleans was forced through the heart of downtown, resulting in a high-volume flow of potential business.

In 1902, Captain Joseph T. Jones, Gulfport's cofounder, built the Great Southern Hotel on two acres of land facing 13th Street to the north and the Mississippi Sound to the south. Jones, who lived in Buffalo, New York, built the luxurious hotel as a getaway for northerners looking to escape the winter cold. He also used the hotel as his private residence while he was on the coast overseeing the construction of Gulfport.

Located only a few hundred yards from the Gulf, the large three-story building had a distinctive look with its dark olive paint, white trim, gray shutters and red tile roof. There was no other building like it anywhere on the coast. This state-of-the-art hotel offered unprecedented amenities for the time. There was a private telephone in each of the 250 guest rooms, hot and cold running water and a bath for every two rooms; the hotel also had its own sewerage system. An artesian well provided the water, and a power plant built just for the hotel supplied steam heat and electricity. Guests enjoyed relaxing on large comfortable chairs in the spacious lobby, which featured tall columns and a beamed ceiling made of antique oak. The tile floors were laid out in a beautiful black-and-white pattern that complemented the exquisite décor of the hotel. There was a billiard room off of the lobby

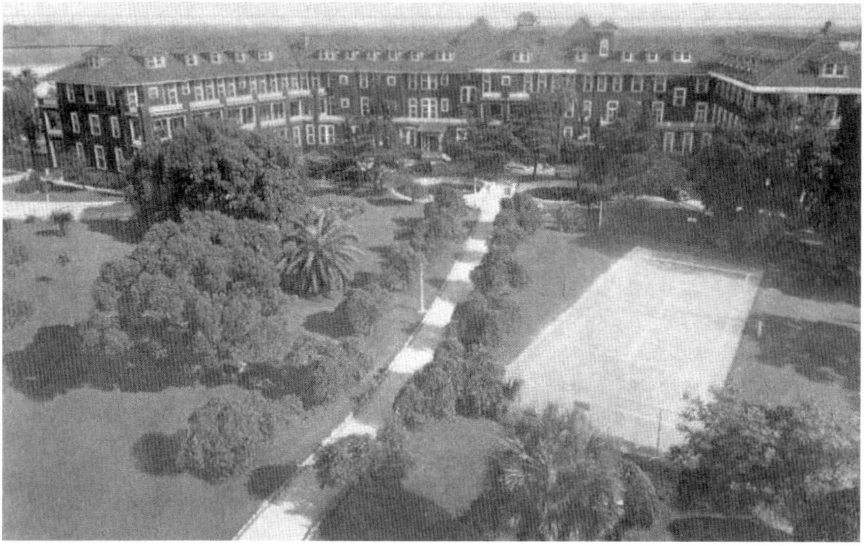

The Great Southern Hotel was a prominent landmark in Gulfport for almost fifty years. *Paul Jermyn Collection.*

and a grand dining room finished in Flemish oak. The hotel had its own orchestra providing music for dinner and dancing, as well as a small coffee shop for breakfast or an afternoon snack.

Guests could stroll about the grounds and enjoy the palm tree–lined walks or sit on the open verandas, sipping a glass of refreshing iced tea while enjoying a beautiful sunset over the Gulf. Captain Jones constructed a long pier that led from the hotel to the newly built Gulfport Yacht Club. For those who preferred not to make the walk, or possibly weren't physically able, the hotel provided a tram to the clubhouse at the end of the pier.

The front lawn was beautifully landscaped with sheltering palms and other ornamental trees and bushes. Two circular ponds stocked with large colorful goldfish provided a serene setting next to the hotel tennis court. As an added convenience, a horse-and-buggy rental service was available for those visitors needing transportation.

In 1908, Donald Ross, a preeminent golf course designer, was hired to create a nine-hole golf course for the hotel. Ross had designed almost four hundred courses throughout his career, helping to pioneer the golf industry in the United States. Known as the Great Southern Golf Club, it was located on the beach a short distance from the hotel and was the first golf course in Mississippi. The golf course is still in use today.

To get around the Great Southern Hotel, traffic had to be funneled off the beach road. The route through town headed east toward New Orleans beginning from Highway 90 onto 15th Street heading west past the Gulfport High School and then left on 21st Avenue; right onto 14th Street; past the Hancock Bank, M. Salloum's and other major merchants; left at the El Mecca Hotel on 27th Avenue; right onto 13th Street; and left onto 30th Avenue toward the beach, where it reconnected with Highway 90, continuing west toward Long Beach and beyond.

As traffic increased on Highway 90, it was no longer practical for the highway to meander through downtown Gulfport in such a circuitous way. The once glorious hotel that had been the pride of the coast, and one of the reasons for the city's growth, now sat in the way of the city's progress. By the late 1940s, newer hotels like the Buena Vista and the Edgewater Gulf were competing for tourist dollars. The aging Great Southern struggled to survive during the Great Depression and was almost forced to close throughout the '40s. In 1947, it was dealt a tragic blow after being virtually destroyed by the massive hurricane of that year that devastated the coast. It was decided that a straight road that cut out the hassles of traffic lights and frequent stops was necessary, and the old hotel was standing in the way. In 1951, sadly, the Great Southern Hotel fell victim to the city's growth.

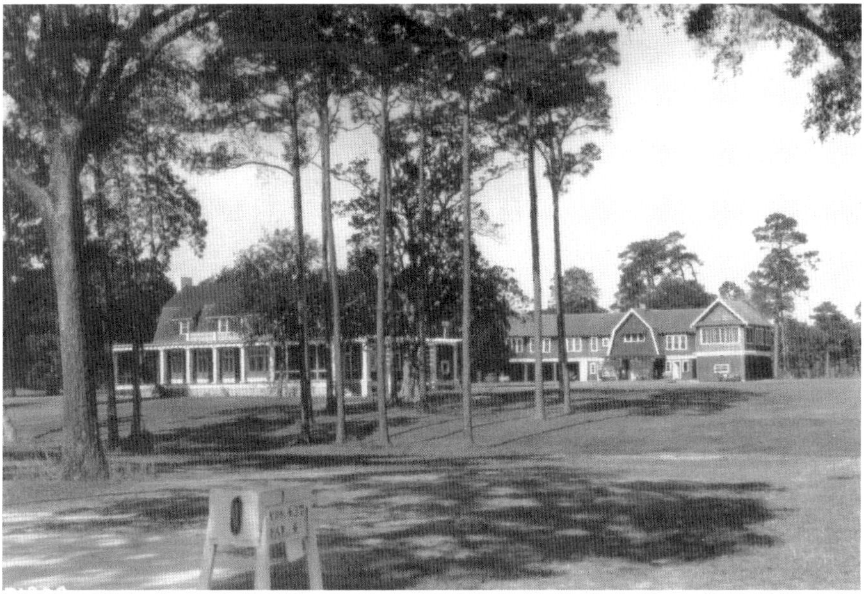

The Great Southern Golf Club was located a short distance from the hotel and was the first golf course in Mississippi. *Paul Jermyn Collection.*

With the removal of the old hotel, the four-lane highway was completed by the summer of that year. U.S. Highway 90 now ran straight between Gulfport's eastern limits and the city of Long Beach on the west. No longer having to wind through the streets of town, the new road was the most direct route between Mobile and New Orleans.

The increased traffic in downtown turned Gulfport into a lively shopping center. Sidewalks were full of people strolling in and out of popular merchants like Marshall's Cards and Books, Northrop's, J.C. Penney, M. Salloum's, Anderson's Men's Wear, Woolworth, McCrory's, Sears and other great stores. We shopped the latest furniture styles at J.C. Clower Furniture Company, we stood watching in fascination at the mechanical displays in the window of Joseph Fasold's Jewelry store, we kept up with the newest fashion trends at Lerner's and Hurd's Style Shop, we were drawn to the smell of buttered popcorn drifting onto the sidewalk from the Paramount Theatre and we stood transfixed in front of the window of the Western Auto store as we watched the newfangled thing called television. The times were exhilarating, and shoppers could feel the energy in the air—it was electric.

On Saturdays, we would often go into town with our mothers. While they shopped, we would enjoy a hamburger at the Woolworth lunch counter or a hot dog at the Dog House Jr. and, afterward, a snowball at the Pop Corn King or a milkshake at McCrory's—so many great memories of a great time and place.

During the golden era, oyster shell roads were still common throughout the city. Oysters are so plentiful along the coast that they were an inexpensive solution for road surfacing. The shells would eventually be crushed under the weight of the traffic, leaving a smooth surface that was almost noiseless. The shells would also harden like cement when wet, making the streets better for travel than other types of roads at that time. There were some problems, however. Although the shells seemed to harden, they were still soft and didn't hold up. Not only did the shells have to be continuously replaced, but the dust from the crushed shells was also almost as bad as the dust from dirt roads.

Paving bricks were the answer. By the mid-1880s, bricks were being widely used throughout the country, bringing an end to the mud of dirt roads and the dust of oyster shells. By 1900, a type of paving brick had been developed that was cheap to produce and almost indestructible. Although the bricks were durable, the time it took and the amount of labor needed to lay them discouraged their use. Because the cost of labor made them expensive to repair, blacktop or concrete was poured directly on top, using the old paving bricks as a solid base. In the 1950s, most of the main roads in downtown Gulfport were covered over with asphalt, although the brick streets on some of the less-traveled roads were still visible. Before they were paved over, remnants of the tracks of the now defunct trolley system were still clearly evident on some of the old brick roads.

THE WAY IT WAS, 1950–1964

A Walking Tour of Downtown Gulfport

There were no formal boundaries for the downtown area, but the maps here represent the center of commerce in Gulfport during the '50s and early '60s. There were many other stores, churches and businesses north of the railroad tracks, especially along 25th Avenue and the Pass Road, that certainly deserve recognition, and some will be mentioned later.

The tour will cover each downtown street, starting at the lower left corner of Block A on the first map and moving clockwise around the block, returning to the starting point. Then, it will continue to each of the other blocks, finally ending the tour with Block V. A number identifies the merchant and the location on each block. The names of the merchants are listed in order. Those merchants listed without a block identification number were located outside the downtown district and do not appear on the downtown map.

While great effort has been made to present an accurate picture of downtown Gulfport in the '50s, there is always the possibility of error with a project of this scope. It is also important to understand that within this period, several businesses either moved or were closed. Some readers, therefore, might remember certain parts of the city differently depending on the year.

It should also be mentioned that one of the major factors that changed the face of much of old Gulfport was a government program called urban renewal. Urban renewal started in the '60s throughout the country and was intended to rejuvenate downtown areas that had been destroyed by the interstate highway system. The purpose was to restore areas but not to manage them. It was the first formal program intended to redevelop cities by attracting new development and removing deteriorating commercial buildings. There was a fear that the areas that were already blighted may cause surrounding areas to also become blighted.

Municipalities often undertook large-scale clearance of business districts. Gulfport closed 26th Avenue between 14th Street and the railroad and demolished the stores in order to clean up some of the deteriorating conditions. Many cities found that they couldn't attract private reinvestments in the cleared sites. In Gulfport, the Hancock Bank took over the 26th Avenue area, turning it into One Hancock Plaza in 1981.

Downtown Gulfport
1950s–early 1960s

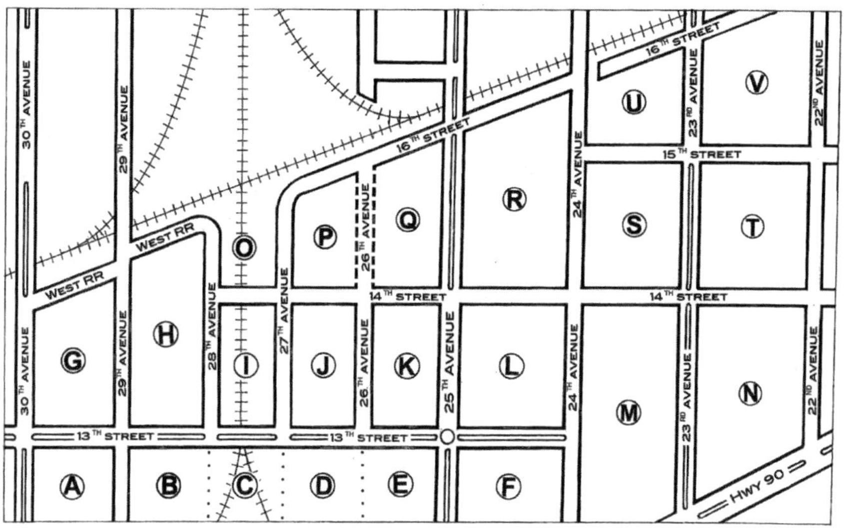

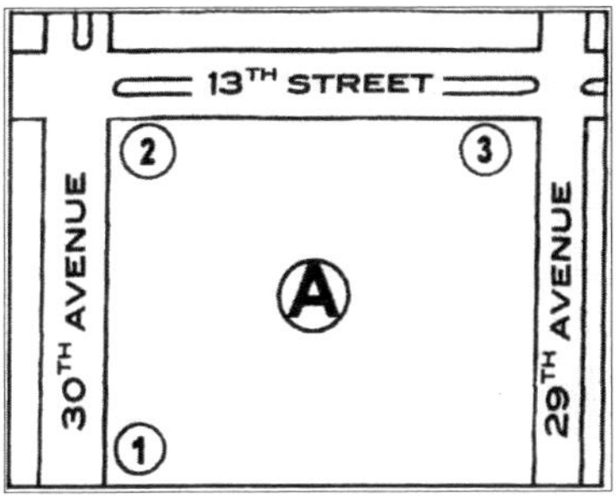

Block A
1. The Power Plant (A-1)
2. The Merchants Company (A-2)
3. Billups Service Station (A-3)

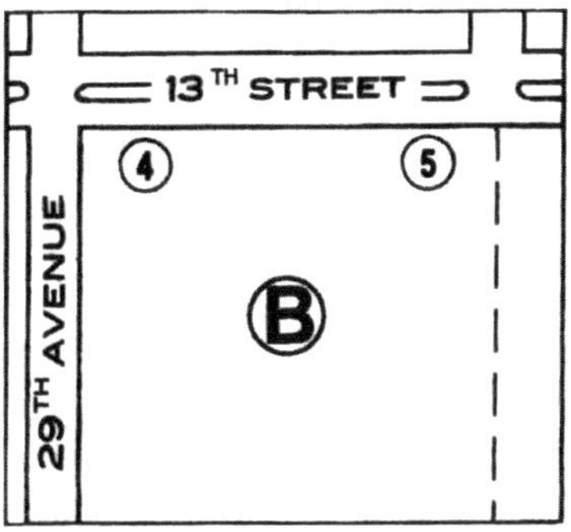

Block B
4. The Gulfport Ice Company (B-4)
5. Hamilton Brothers Plumbing (B-5)
   (Later) Coast Co-op Farm Store & Farm Bureau Insurance (B-5)

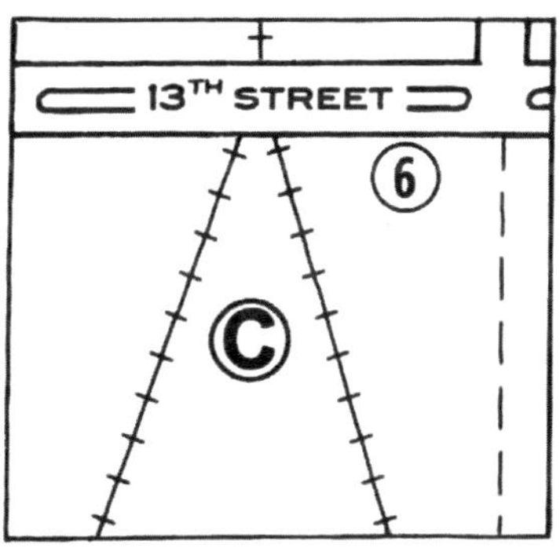

Block C
6. Nunnally Ford (C-6)
   (Later) Braun Ford (C-6)
   (Later) Bubba Oustalet Ford (C-6)
   (Later) Butch Oustalet Ford (C-6)

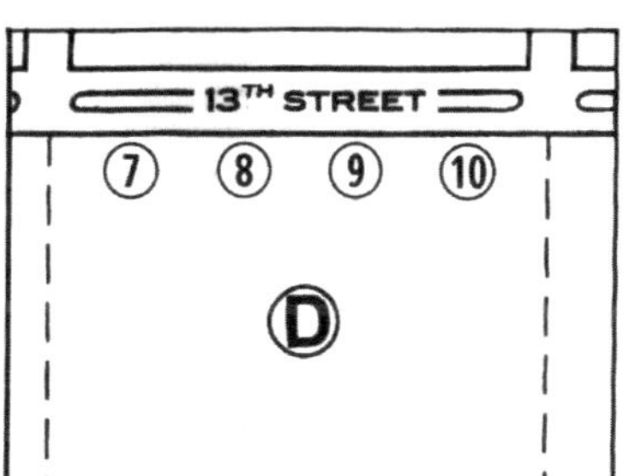

Block D
7. The Legion Theatre (D-7)
8. Gulf and Ship Island Railroad Building (D-8)
9. McCrory's Five and Dime (D-9)
10. City Bus Service (D-10)

Block E

11. Butler's Shoes (E-11)
12. Lerner Shops (E-12)
13. Kinney Shoes (E-13)
14. Singer Sewing Machine Company (E-14)
15. Schwobilt Men's Wear (E-15)
    (Later) Elmer's Mens Wear (E-15)
16. Rex Hats (E-16)
    (Later) The American Plan Corporation (E-16)
17. Keith Jewelry (E-17)
    (Later) Busch Jewelry Store (E-17)
18. Albright & Wood Drugs (E-18)
19. Harp's Bakery (E-19)
    (Later) Elmer's Mens Wear (E-19)
20. Campbell Appliance Company (E-20)
    (Later) The Purple Lantern (E-20)
21. Be-Wise Food Store (E-21)
    (Later) The Purple Lantern (E-21)
22. Gulf National Bank (E-22)

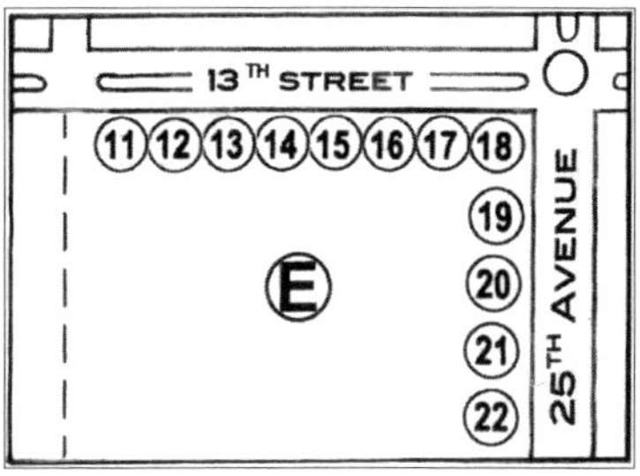

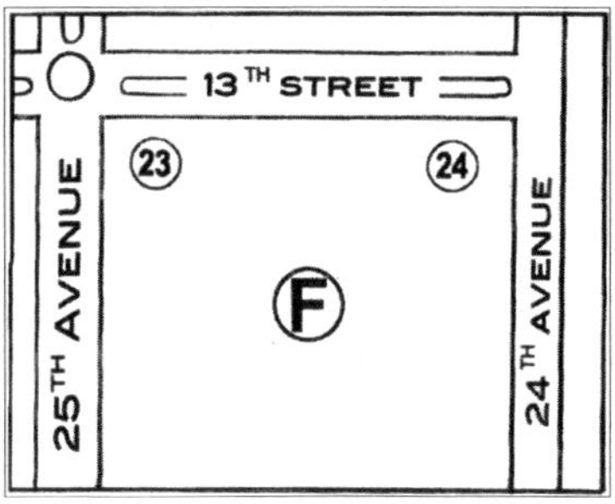

Block F

23. Gulfport Post Office (F-23)
24. The First Presbyterian Church of Gulfport (F-24)

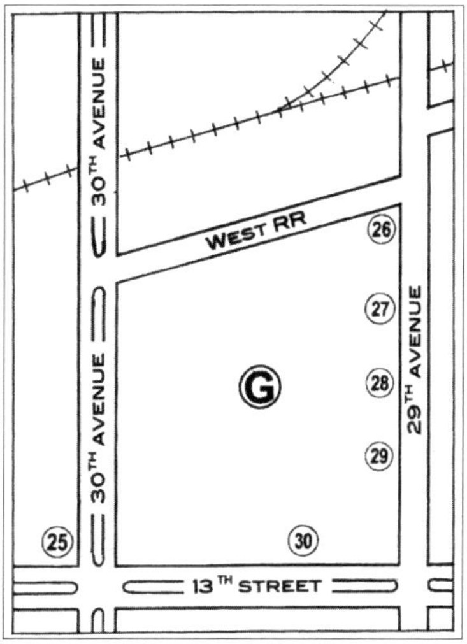

Block G

25. Brown's Sporting Goods (G-25)
    (Later) Sportsman's Corner (G-25)
26. L&N Railroad Freight Building & Yard (G-26)
27. The Gulfport Laundry Building (G-27)
28. George Saucier Home (G-28)
29. Lloyd Eubanks Home (G-29)
30. The Coast Coca-Cola Bottling Company (G-30)

Businesses on 29th Avenue, north of the railroad tracks

The Swift Company
Cottam Company
Gulf Amusement
Baria Sales
Wigley & Culp Wholesale
FEB Distribution Company

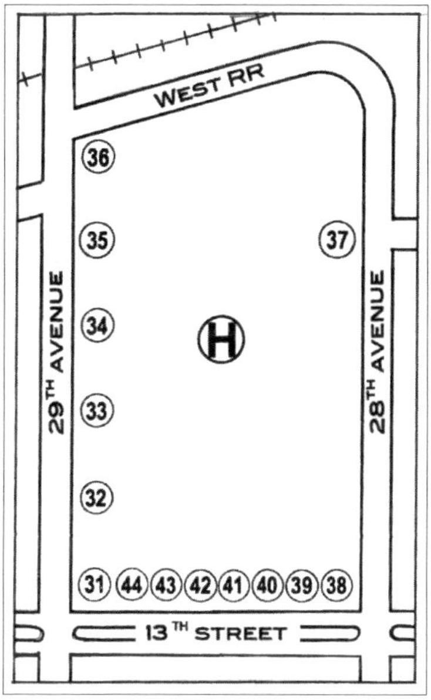

Block H

31. Washington Pecan Company (H-31)
32. Hardy Meat Company (H-32)
33. O.K. Transfer and Storage Company (H-33)
    (Later) Fayard Moving and Transportation Corporation (H-33)
34. American Legion Wrestling Arena (H-34)
35. Coca-Cola Company's storage building (H-35)
36. Bourgeois Building Supplies (H-36)
37. Master Brake and Tire Company (H-37)
38. Lane Hotel (H-38)
39. Lane Hotel Coffee Shop (H-39)
40. Gremillion's Barber Shop (H-40)
41. Mack's Barber Supply Company (H-41)
42. National Cash Register Company (H-42)
43. Katie's Café (H-43)
44. Pete's Electric Service (H-44)
    (Later) Johnson's Auto Repair (H-44)

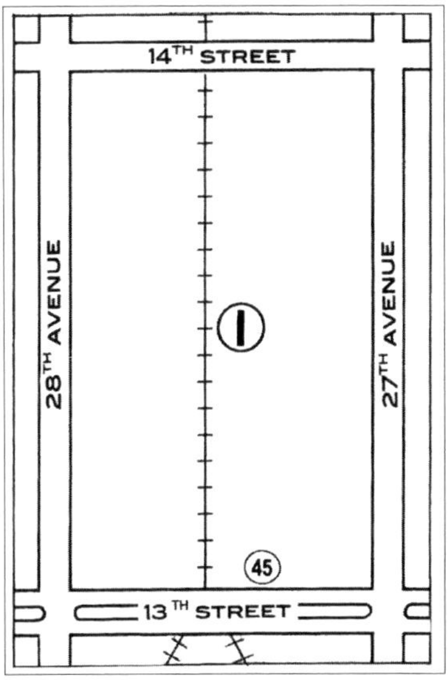

Block I

45. A&P Supermarket (I-45)

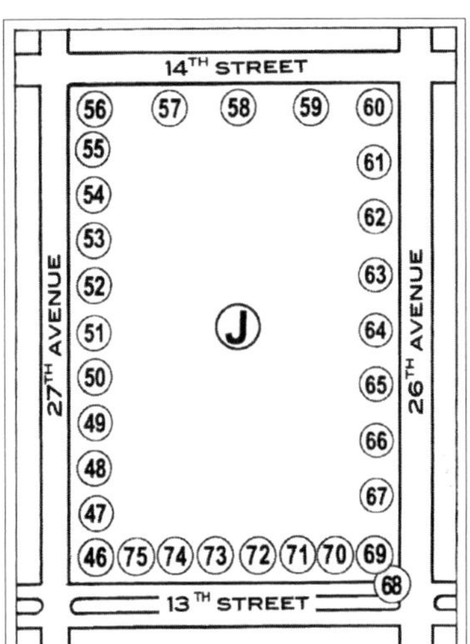

Block J

46. Barber's Hardware (J-46)
47. The Town & Country Shop (J-47)
48. Myrick Real Estate (J-48)
49. Stacey's Women's Wear (J-49)
50. A.E. Morlan Jewelry and Watch Repair (J-50)
    (Later) Broussard's Music Store (J-50)
51. J.C. Clower Furniture (J-51)
52. Life of Georgia Insurance (J-52)
53. Harp's Bakery (J-53)
    (Later) The Sunlite Bakery (J-53)
54. Southern Bible Store (J-54)

Block J (continued)

55. Fasold's Jewelry (J-55)
    (Later) Lyon Jewelry Store (J-55)
56. El Mecca Hotel and Café (J-56)
57. Jay's Barbershop (J-57)
58. Robertson's Men's Wear (J-58)
59. Agar Realty (J-59)
    (Later) Fasold's Optometry (J-59)
60. Northrop's (J-60)
    (Later) M. Salloum Department Store (J-60)
61. J.C. Penney (J-61)
62. J.C. Clower Furniture Store (J-62)
63. Dr. Lee B. Daron & Dr. Starr, Optometrists (J-63)
64. Zollman's Music (J-64)
65. Fasold's Jewelry (J-65)
    (Later) Jordan's Newsstand (J-65)
66. Charcoal Grill (J-66)
67. Brumfield Drugs (J-67)
68. Lopez Tamale Cart (J-68)
69. First National Bank (J-69)
    (Later) Reed's Dress Shop (J-69)
70. E.J. Younghans Novelty Shop (J-70)
    (Later) Barber's Hardware (J-70)
71. Ear, Nose and Throat Clinic (Upstairs) (J-71)
72. Helwick Radio & TV (J-72)
    (Later) Brumfield Drugs (J-72)
73. Jack's Barber Shop (J-73)
74. Quality Bakery (J-74)
    (Above Quality Bakery) Oberlies Radio Repair (J-74)
75. Southern Restaurant (J-75)
    (Later) Russell Finance (J-75)

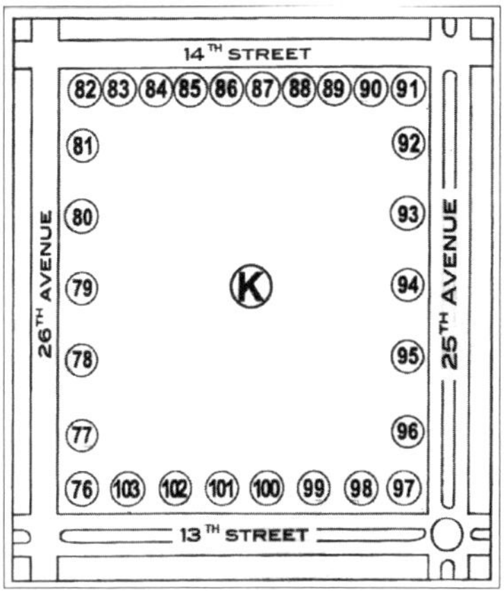

Block K

76. The Splendid Café (K-76)
(Later) The Darling Shop (K-76)
77. Walgreen Drugs (K-77)
(Later) Grant Drugs (K-77)
78. Dixie Theatre (K-78)
(Later part of) F.W. Woolworth (K-78)
79. The Strand Theatre (K-79)
(Later) The Paramount Theatre (K-79)
80. Bradley Jewelry (K-80)
(Later) Karl's Jewelry (K-80)
81. Merchant's Restaurant (K-81)
(Later) Paramount Restaurant (K-81)
(Later) Raul's Restaurant (K-81)
(Later) Commodore Restaurant (K-81)
(Later) Palace Restaurant (K-81)
82. Jones Brothers' Drug Store (K-82)
83. Deluxe Shoeshine and Hat Cleaning (K-83)
84. Sale Studio (K-84)
85. The Shoe Hospital (K-85)
(Later) Barber and Thatcher Books (K-85)
(Later) Marshall's Books and Gifts (K-85)
86. Cooper's Jewelry (K-86)
(Later) Marshall's Books and Gifts (K-86)
87. Smith-Todd Hardware (K-87)
88. Office Supply Store (K-88)
89. Hewes Office Building (K-89)
90. Stratakos Candy Company (K-90)
91. Day Drug Store (K-91)
(Later) The Toggery (K-91)
92. Mississippi Power Company (K-92)
93. Toomer's Gift Shop (K-93)
94. Kerr Real Estate (K-94)
95. Auto-Lec Store (K-95)
96. 4-H Market (K-96)
97. Gulf National Bank (K-97)
(Later) Gryder Shoes (K-97)
98. The Pop Corn King (K-98)
99. Auto-Lec (K-99)
(Later) Shamis Ladies Fashions (K-99)
(Later) Marshall's Books and Gifts (K-99)
100. Frank's Place (K-100)
101. Household Finance Corporation (K-101)
102. Splendid Café (102)
(Later) The Arrow Grill (K-102)
103. Splendid Hotel (K-103)
(Later) R.O. Besse Jewelers (K-103)

Block L

104. Sears (L-104)
105. Brumfield's Department Store (L-105) (Later) Hewes Brothers Department Store (L-105)
106. The Anderson Theatre (L-106) Karl Fasold's Jewelry Store (L-106) (Later) Gulf Theatre (L-106) (Later) Coast Hardware (L-106)
107. Young Ages Children Wear (L-107)
108. Glenn's Drug Store (L-108) (Later) Tripplet-Day Drug Store (L-108)
109. Andre's Shop (L-109)
110. Triangle Barbershop (L-110)
111. Anderson's Men's Wear (L-111)
112. Huber Jewelry Store (L-112)
113. Ed Salloum's Women's Wear (L-113
114. Bomar's Shoe Store (L-114) (Later) Smart Shoes (L-114)
115. H&J Sports (L-115)
116. Gulf Typewriter & Equipment(L-116)
117. Hurd's Style Shop (L-117) (Later) Scottie Discount Store (L-117)
118. Ashton's Food Store (L-118) (Later) Standard Furniture Company (L-118)
119. Greyhound Bus Station and Snack Bar (L-119)

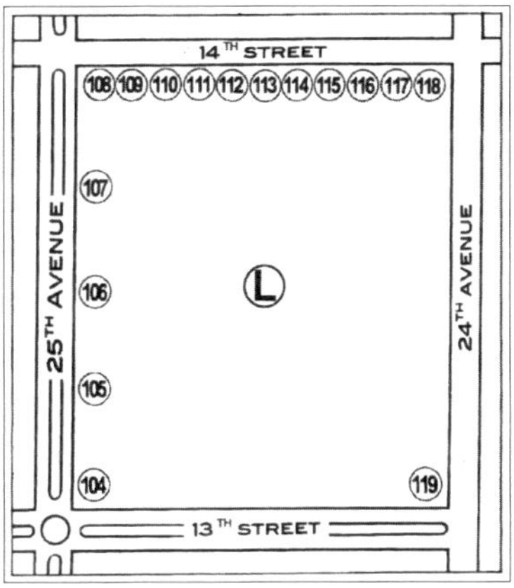

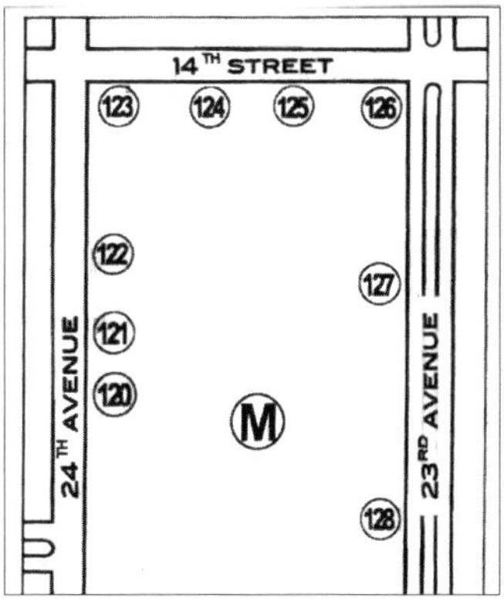

Block M

120. The Gulfport Carnegie Library (M-120)
121. The County Courthouse (M-121)
122. The Confederate Monument (M-122)
123. Standard Oil Service Station (M-123)
124. The Abstract Building (M-124)
125. Holder's Café (M-125)
126. Markham Hotel (M-126)
127. Markham Hotel Swimming Pool (M-127)
128. Women's Club of Gulfport (M-128)

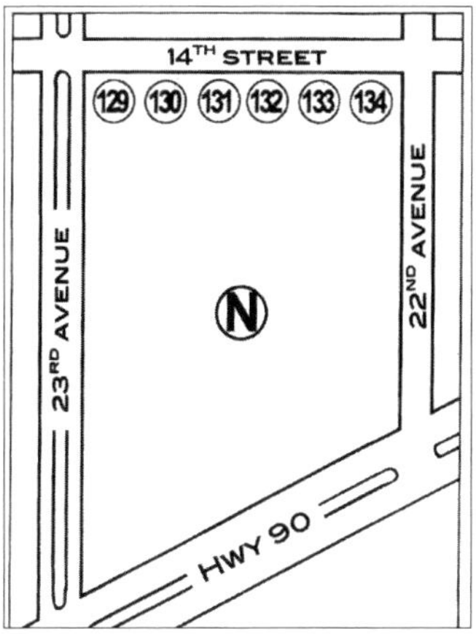

Block N

129. The *Daily Herald* (N-129)
130. Maxie Broadus Furniture Store (N-130)
131. Pecoul's TV (N-131)
   (Also) Pete the Top Man (N-131)
132. The Stone Ice Cream Company (N-132)
133. Owen Palmer Attorney (N-133)
134. Gulf Service Station (N-134)

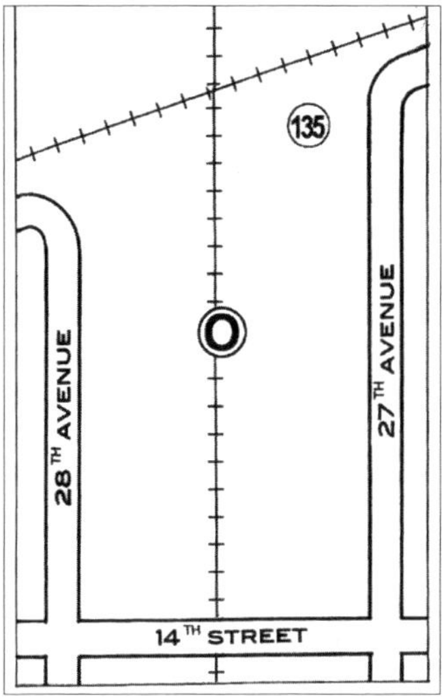

Block O

135. L&N Train Depot (O-135)

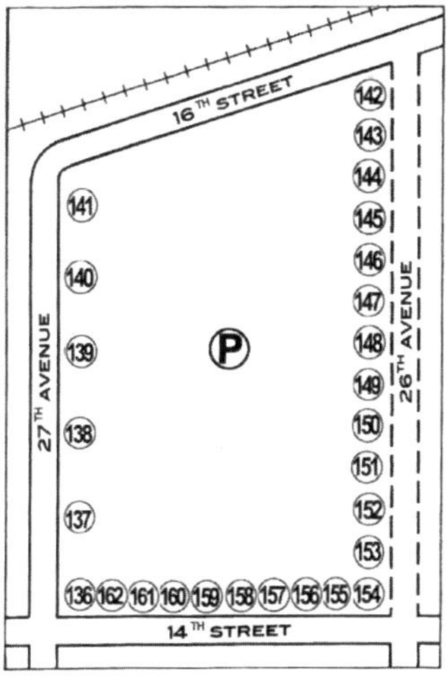

Block P

136. Crescent Jewelry (P-136)
(Later) The Purple Lantern (P-136)
137. Joe's Pool Hall (P-137)
138. Leroy McWhite's Fruit Store (P-138)
(Later) Union Café (P-138)
(Later) The Legion Theatre (P-138)
(Later) The Gulf Theatre (P-138)
139. Gulf Savings and Loan (P-139)
(Later) Totsy's Pool Hall (P-139)
(Upstairs) Union Hotel (P-139)
(Later) Legion Hotel (P-139)
(Later) Gulfport Bowling Center (P-139)
140. Gillis Furniture Company (P-140)
(Later) Wharton Furniture Company (P-140)
141. Rayner Hotel (P-141)
(Later) Frazier Hotel (P-141)
(Later) Nelson Hotel (P-141)
142. Lander's Café (P-142)
(Later) Bill's Place (P-142)
143. Simpson and Company (P-143)
144. Broach Finance (P-144)
(Later) Grand Prize Stamp Redemption Center (P-144)
145. Coast Printing Company (P-145)
(Later) Grand Prize Stamp Redemption Center (P-145)
146. The Shoe Hospital (P-146)
(Later) Barnett Cleaners (Shared Space) (P-146)
147. Barnett Cleaners (P-147)
148. The Royal Theatre (P-148)
(Later) The Don Theatre (P-148)
149. Sew 'n' Save Fabric (P-149)
(Later) Fulton Photography Studio (P-149)
150. Glass Women's Wear (P-150)
(Later) Kean's Children's Wear (P-150)
(Later) Gulfport Business Machines (P-150)
151. Palace Pool Hall (P-151)
152. Atkinson Brokerage (P-152)
153. Roy Anderson Real Estate and Insurance (P-153)
(Later) Lenwood Sawyer Realty and Insurance (P-153)
(Shared Space) Luther Maple Attorney (P-153)
154. Central Barber Shop (P-154)
155. Royal Jewelry Store (P-155)
156. Larson's Men's Wear (P-156)
157. Central Barber Shop (P-157)
(Later) Ernie's Hamburgers (P-157)
(Later) Ernie's Corral (P-157)
158. Gulfport Hat Cleaning & Shoe Shine Shop (P-158)
159. Gus's Bar (P-159)
160. Dixie Amusement Company (P-160)
(Later) Palace Restaurant (P-160)
161. The Dog House Jr. (P-161)
162. Dixie Lunch Room (P-162)

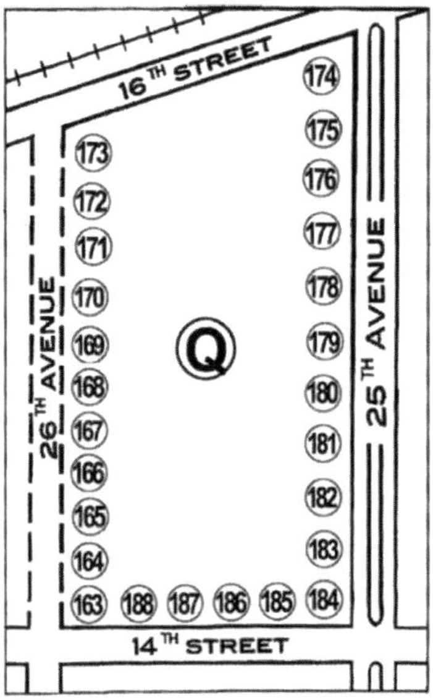

Block Q

163. H&H Hotel (Q-163)
164. Sally's Beauty Shop (Q-164)
 (Later) Vacant Store Front (Q-164)
165. H&H Hotel Bar (Q-165)
 (Later) Matt's Bar (Q-165)
 (Later) Blue Mirror Gifts (Q-165)
 (Later) Chuck's Bar (Q-165)
166. United Gas Company Office (Q-166)
 (Later) King's Dollar Store (Q-166)
 (Later) ADS (American Discount Store) (Q-166)
167. Anthony's Grill (Q-167)
168. Social Security Office (Q-168)
 (Later) Mill End Fabric (Q-168)
169. Smith Alteration Shop (Q-169)
170. United Stores (Q-170)
 (Later) Dixie Amusement Company (Q-170)
 (Later) Pete the Top Man (Q-170)
 (Later) Brumfield's Women's Bargain Annex (Q-170)
171. Yellow Cab Company (Q-171)
 (Also) U-Haul (Q-171)
 (Also) Avis Car Rental Company (Q-171)
172. Our Barber Shop (Q-172)
173. Turan's Corner House Café (Q-173)
 (Later) Palace Grill (Q-173)
 (Later) Rebel Grill (Q-173)
174. The Goodyear Store (Q-174)
175. This storefront was mostly empty (Q-175)
176. House of Music (Q-176)
 (Later) Holmes Barber Shop (Q-176)
177. Gulfport Printing Company (Q-177)
178. Gillis Furniture Store (Q-178)
 (Later) Brumfield's Bargain Annex (Q-178)
179. André Appliances (Q-179)
180. Gulfport Coffee Store (Q-180)
181. Fentiss Printing Company (Q-181)
182. Western Auto (Q-182)
183. Cabibi Shoe Service (Q-183)
184. First National Bank (Q-184)
 (Later) Hancock Bank (Q-184)
185. Elmer's Men's Wear (Q-185)
186. Rosenblum's Women's Wear (Q-186)
187. H&H Hotel Café (Q-187)
188. A.E. Morlan Jewelry Store and Watch Repair (Q-188)
 (Later) C.L. Bullock Jewelry (Q-188)

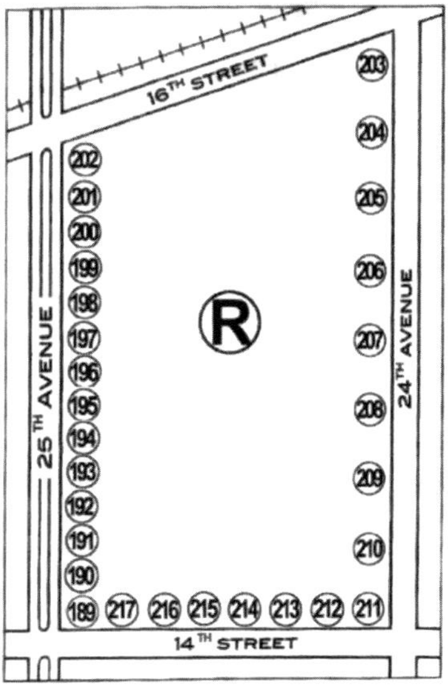

Block R

189. The Ideal Shop (R-189)
190. Cottage Grill (R-190)
191. Gulf Paint & Glass Company (R-191)
192. Standard Furniture Company (R-192)
193. Ward's Fisk Tire and Appliances (R-193)
   (Later) The Firestone Store (R-193)
   (Later) The Dome Theatre (R-193)
194. Western Union Office (R-194)
195. The tenant in this space is unknown (R-195)
196. Home Furniture (R-196)
197. B. Havard Insurance (R-197)
198. Stewart-Sneed-Hewes Insurance Office (R-198)
199. Sherwin-Williams Paint (R-199)
200. B.F. Goodrich Company (R-200)
201. Gulfport Battery Company (R-201)
202. Hancock Bank Parking Lot (R-202)
203. The tenant in this office space is unknown (R-203)
204. Office of Dr. E.T. Riemann Jr. (R-204)
205. The tenant in this office space is unknown (R-205)
206. Southern Bell Telephone Office (R-206)
207. Group of four to five offices with unknown occupants (R-207)
208. Dixie Press Printing Company (R-208)
209. Southern Bell Telephone & Telegraph Exchange Building (R-209)
210. Lang Funeral Home (R-210)
   (Later) Ellis Salloum's Men's Wear (R-210)
211. Northrop's (R-211)
212. Town House Restaurant (R-212)
   (Later) Austin's Style Shop (R-212)
213. Fisher Office Building (R-213)
214. Fasold's Jewelry (R-214)
215. Cardinal Flower Shop (R-215)
216. Elite Shop (R-216)
217. Koury's Men's Wear (R-217)

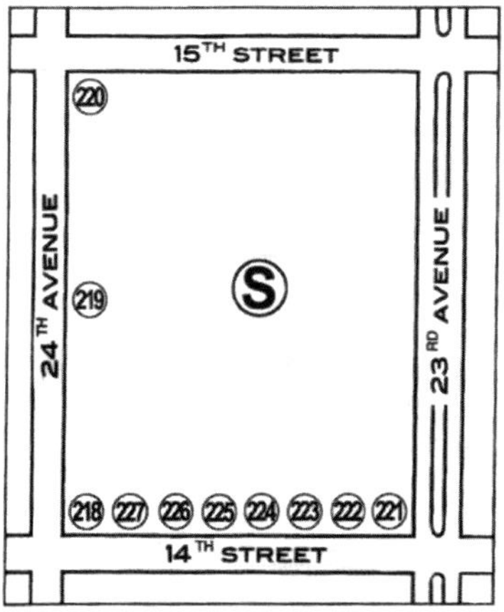

Block S

218. The Hatten Building (S-218)
219. McDaniel Refrigeration Sales & Service (S-219)
220. First United Methodist Church (S-220)
221. H.G. Hill Food Store (S-221)
   (Later) Winn-Dixie Hill Food Store (S-221)
222. Mississippi State Employment Office (S-222)
223. Coast Federal Savings and Loan (S-223)
224. The occupant of this store front is unknown (S-224)
225. Sneed Insurance Company (S-225)
226. Trailways Bus Depot (S-226)
227. Oberlies Radio and Television (S-227)

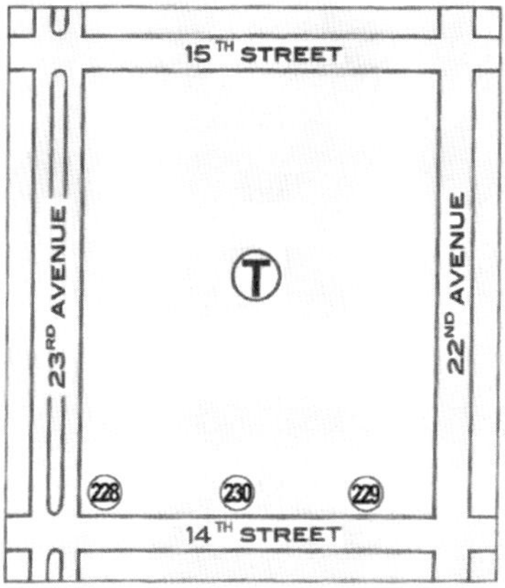

Block T

228. Shorty Platt's Gulf Service Station (T-228)
229. Sporting Goods and Tackle Shop (T-229)
   (Later) Dairy Queen (T-229)
230. Coast Inn (T-230)

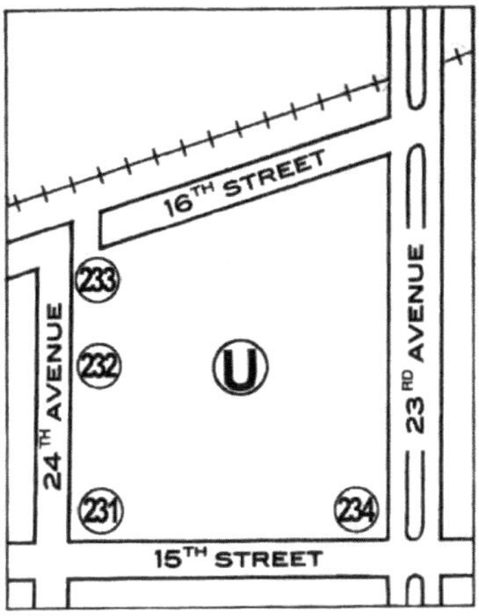

Block U

231. Gulfport City Hall (U-231)
232. Gulfport Fire Department (U-232)
233. Gulfport Police Station and City Jail (U-233)
234. Gulfport Recreation Center (U-234)

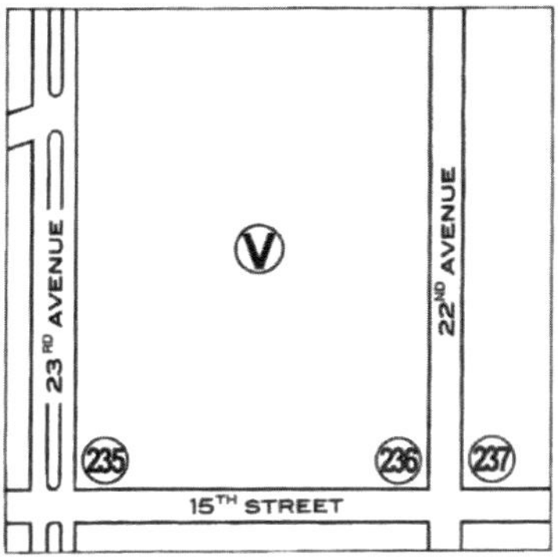

Block V

235. United Gas Company Office Building (V-235)
236. Shannon Motors (V-236)
237. Jay-Jay Chevrolet (V-237)

HOME AND BUSINESS PROFILES

Now that we have gone back in time and strolled through the streets of Gulfport, I think it would be fitting to visit some of the stores and learn a little about them and the owners who made them successful. Unfortunately, details were not available on all of the stores, so for those few that we don't know, we will just pop our heads in and say hi and then move on to the next store on the street. Along the way we will meet Dan Stone of Stone Ice Cream Company; Clarence Welch, the Pop Corn King; Mack McKnight of Quality Bakery; John Lewis Lyle of Lyle's Variety Store; Otis Broussard of Broussard's Music; Mansour Salloum of M. Salloum's; Josiah Coger Clower of Clower's Furniture; Karl Joseph Fasold of Fasold's Jewelry; Vassar Anderson of Anderson's Men's Wear and the Anderson Theatre; Jim Day of Tripplet and Day Drugs; and many more merchants who created the city of Gulfport.

ATTORNEYS, DOCTORS, MORTICIANS AND INSURANCE SALES

Attorneys

Owen Palmer, Attorney (N-133)
Owen Palmer's law office was one of several small businesses on the south side of the block near Stone Ice Cream Company. Owen Palmer was a well-known lawyer in Gulfport during the '50s. As Stone expanded through the years, Dan Stone bought up the adjacent buildings until he and the *Daily Herald* building on the corner took up half of the block.

Luther Maple, Attorney (P-153)
Attorney Luther Maple shared space on 26th Avenue with Anderson/Sawyer Realty and Insurance. Maple later became a city judge.

Doctors

Dr. Lee B. Daron & Dr. Starr, Optometrists (J-63)
Dr. Lee Daron and Dr. Starr, Optometrists, had a small office next to J.C. Penney. The most memorable thing about the office was Dr. Daron's large myna bird he kept in a cage in the waiting room. It was the first time many in Gulfport had ever heard a talking bird. Dr. Daron owned the *Lysistrata* excursion boat that traveled to Ship Island.

Ear, Nose and Throat Clinic (Upstairs over Barber's Hardware) (J-71)
In the 1950s, tonsils were considered useless, as well as the source of several health issues. So, to help avoid future problems, it was a common practice to have the tonsils removed. Many children on the coast had their tonsils removed by Dr. Rouse or Dr. Sheffield in this clinic above Barber's Hardware Store. The only upside to the tonsillectomy were the perfunctory bowls of ice cream that were the prescription after surgery.

Dr. E.T. Riemann Jr. (R-204)
Dr. E.T. Riemann practiced medicine in Gulfport for forty years. He was a very accomplished student, having graduated from Gulfport High School at the age of fifteen, the University of Mississippi at the age of eighteen and

the University of Tennessee Medical School at twenty-one. After serving as a captain in the Army Medical Corps, Dr. Riemann returned to Gulfport to start his medical practice. In 1953, Dr. Riemann served as the secretary/treasurer of the Memorial Hospital Medical and Dental Staff, and in 1960–61, he served as chief of staff. He retired from his medical practice in 1988. Dr. Riemann was from a well-known and respected family. His father, Ernest Riemann, founded Riemann's Funeral Home in Gulfport.

FUNERAL HOMES

LANG FUNERAL HOME (R-210)

John H. Lang started Lang Funeral Home in Pass Christian in 1884. It was the first funeral home between Mobile and New Orleans. His son, Arthur Wallace Lang, continued the family business, followed by his grandson Arthur Wallace "Buzzy" Lang II and, later, his great-grandson Arthur Wallace "Bubba" Lang III. Buzzy Lang also served Gulfport for one term as mayor.

RIEMANN FUNERAL HOMES

Riemann Funeral Homes is a fourth-generation family-owned funeral business. It began in 1920, when Ernest Theodore Riemann Sr. and his wife, Ruth Danielson, moved to Gulfport from Michigan. After visiting a friend on the Mississippi Gulf Coast, they fell in love with the area and decided to move their existing funeral business from the cold North to the sunny South. They were able to purchase a half interest in Wilder Funeral Home in Gulfport, and after a year, they purchased the remainder of the business, creating the first Riemann Funeral Home in Gulfport. Over the years, the Riemanns gained the trust and friendship of the city. As the coast grew, Riemann Funeral Homes grew, adding four additional locations to serve the coast families.

INSURANCE COMPANIES

COAST CO-OP FARM STORE & FARM BUREAU INSURANCE (B-5)

This was originally the location of the Hamilton Brothers Plumbing Company. The Coast Co-op Farm Store & Farm Bureau Insurance took over the space and was mostly remembered here in the '50s. Coast Co-op was a farm supply store offering feed, seed and tools for the local farmers. The location was almost directly across the street from the old A&P grocery store.

LIFE OF GEORGIA INSURANCE (J-52)

After World War II, the Life of Georgia Insurance company, which was founded in Atlanta, spread to other southern states. The company sold policies to the working class, with weekly premiums based on how much the customers could afford. The five founders of the company had all experienced economic hardship in their lives and started the company to help other working people with their insurance needs.

ROY ANDERSON REAL ESTATE AND INSURANCE (P-153)
(Later) LENWOOD SAWYER REALTY AND INSURANCE

Located on 26th Avenue, this was originally the office of the Roy Anderson Real Estate & Insurance businesses. It later became Lenwood Sawyer Realty and Insurance. Len Sawyer married Roy Anderson's daughter, Anne, and after Anderson's death, the name changed to Sawyer. The office was later forced to move because of urban renewal.

B. HAVARD INSURANCE (R-197)

This is the office of Bert Havard, an independent insurance agent. As an independent agent, Havard did not represent any one company and therefore was able to give quick quotes from multiple insurance carriers. More quotes meant more savings for the client. Being an independent agent meant that Bert worked for the client and not a company. Therefore, he could remain your personal agent even if you decided to switch insurance companies. In the 1960s, Bert Havard retired from the insurance business and joined the Bank of Wiggins as a vice-president.

STEWART-SNEED-HEWES INSURANCE OFFICE (R-198)

Next to B. Havard Insurance on 25th Avenue was another successful insurance company, Stewart-Sneed-Hewes. Stewart-Sneed-Hewes was started by three prominent Gulf Coast natives but is now a division of Bancorp South Insurance Agency in Gulfport and represents the Traveler Insurance Company.

BUSES, TRAINS AND AUTOMOBILES

Transportation

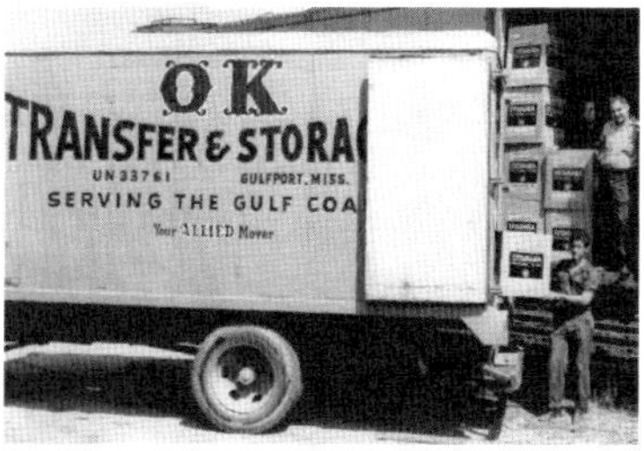

W.H. Fayard started O.K. Transfer Company in 1900. *O.K. Transfer, Clayton Rand Papers, Manuscripts Division, Special Collections Department, Mississippi State University Libraries.*

O.K. Transfer and Storage Company (H-33)
(Later) Fayard Moving and Transportation Corporation
W.H. Fayard started O.K. Transfer Company in 1900. When Mr. Fayard died in 1939, his wife, Frances, inherited the company, and the business continued to grow. Her son, Edward, joined her and together they continued to expand the company. After her death, the family changed the name to Fayard Moving and Transportation Corporation.

Pete's Electric Service (H-44)
(Later) Johnson's Auto Repair
Pete's Electric Service has been family owned and operated in Gulfport since 1935. The company specializes in automotive electrical repair and maintenance. The company's services include diagnostics, brake service, air conditioning, alignments, restorations and painting. The company occupied this space in the early '50s and is still in business at 2407 19th Street. In the later '50s, Johnson's Auto Repair moved into this store space.

Greyhound Bus Station and Snack Bar (L-119)
In the 1940s, the Greyhound Bus Station was located in the Hatten Building on the corner of 24th Avenue and 14th Street. In the 1950s, Greyhound constructed a new building on the corner of 24th Avenue and 13th Street behind Sears and the Sears parking lot. The new station had one of the city's best snack bars. Even people who were not there for the bus service would come in to enjoy the hamburgers, milkshakes and other delicious items.

L&N Train Depot (O-135)
The L&N Train Depot was built in 1904 as the first permanent station of the Gulfport & Ship Island Railroad. The brick building featured an old-fashioned ticket window, black-and-white tiles on the floor and a pressed tin

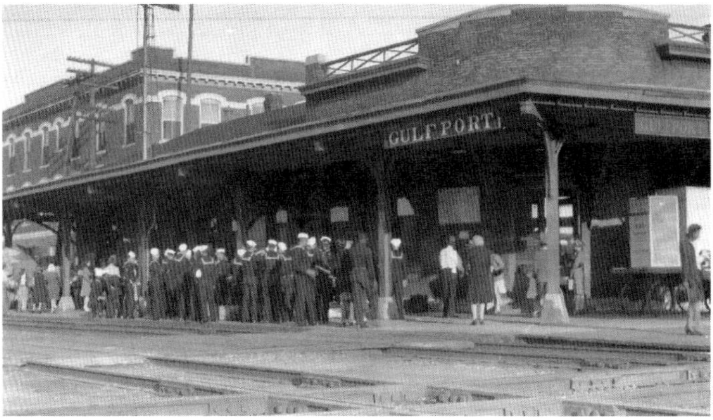

The L&N Train Depot was built in 1904 as the first permanent station of the Gulfport & Ship Island Railroad. *Paul Jermyn Collection.*

ceiling. In the early 1900s, the railroad carried a large amount of timber from south Mississippi to the port of Gulfport, ultimately turning the port into the world's largest timber shipping port at that time. The popular Humming Bird passenger train ran from New Orleans to Mobile and north to Cincinnati, Ohio. The Humming Bird was one of the named trains of the L&N railroad. Other trains were the Dixie Flyer and the Pan American. The Humming Bird began operations in 1947 and was discontinued in 1969.

YELLOW CAB COMPANY (P-171)
(Also) U-HAUL (P-171)
(Also) AVIS CAR RENTAL COMPANY (P-171)

Earl Owen owned the Yellow Cab Company. He also ran the U-Haul and Avis Car Rental Company in this same location. When we were seniors, we didn't have stretch limos for our proms and formal occasions like the kids do today, but Mr. Owen would rent the graduates a new car to take their date to the prom. The rental rate was an amazing five dollars per day and ten cents per mile. The Yellow Cab slogan was "A thinking fellow calls a Yellow," even though the cabs were actually painted an orange color.

TRAILWAYS BUS DEPOT (S-226)

The Trailways Bus Depot was in the Hatten Building. In the 1940s, this was the Greyhound Bus Station, but after building a new terminal on the corner of 24th Avenue and 13th Street, Greyhound moved to that location. Trailways, which was originally located on the east side of 26th Avenue near the railroad tracks, occupied the old Greyhound depot in the Hatten Building during the '50s, '60s and '70s.

AUTO DEALERSHIPS

NUNNALLY FORD (C-6)
(Later) BRAUN FORD (C-6)
(Later) BUBBA OUSTALET FORD (C-6)
(Later) BUTCH OUSTALET FORD (C-6)
Nunnally Ford was an automobile dealership located next to the railroad tracks cutting across 13th Street, heading toward the port of Gulfport. The dealership eventually changed hands at this location, first becoming Braun Ford and later Bubba Oustalet Ford. Butch Oustalet took over when his father, Bubba, retired, changing the name to Butch Oustalet Ford.

SHANNON MOTORS (V-236)
Shannon Motors, the Lincoln/Mercury dealership, was on the corner of 23rd Avenue and 15th Street. Ritchey Motors occupied this space before Shannon Motors.

JAY-JAY CHEVROLET (V-237)
Jason "Jay-Jay" Harry obtained the Chevrolet agency and opened a dealership on 25th Avenue in Gulfport. He later moved to his permanent location on 23rd Avenue and 15th Street. In 1938, he also obtained the Buick dealership.

Harry was born in Handsboro on February 22, 1896. He was a student at Gulf Coast Military Academy, a school his grandfather J.F. Harry was instrumental in forming. After graduation, he joined the army to fight in World War II. When he returned to the coast after the war, he worked at the First National Bank of Gulfport. When the bank closed, Jay-Jay Harry obtained the Chevrolet dealership.

Jay-Jay Harry was from a prominent family. His father, Dr. J.J. Harry, was the son of Dr. J.F. Harry, who had moved from Jasper County to Ocean Springs after graduating from medical school at Tulane in New Orleans. During the yellow fever epidemic of 1878, he moved to Handsboro, where Jay-Jay was born. Dr. J.F. Harry was instrumental in forming not only the Gulf Coast Military Academy but also Gulf Park College.

In 1983, Harmon Turan, a twelve-year employee at Jay-Jay Chevrolet, teamed up with Gerry Lane of Bay St. Louis to purchase the dealership. The company became Turan-Lane Chevrolet. Prior to working at Jay-Jay Chevrolet, Turan had worked for ten years in the auto industry at Keyes-Dorman Motor Company. In 1958, he moved to Dumas Miller Motor

Company, located in New Orleans. In 1991, Rick Foley, Turan's son, bought a part interest in the company that then became known as Turan-Foley Chevrolet-Buick. The following year, the company purchased the old Keyes-Dorman Building, formerly Watkins Cadillac on Highway 49, next to St. John the Evangelist Catholic Church in Gulfport.

Service Stations and Auto Repair

Billups Service Station (A-3)

Above the Billups Service Station building, there was a large sign with the words "Fill-Up with Billups" and a drawing of the company's signature handshake. The famous slogan became a well-known and easily recognized company symbol throughout the Southeast during the 1950s and 1960s.

Rowell Billups along with his brothers, W.L. "Buddie" Billups and Guy Billups, founded the Billups Company in 1927 as a single gas station, one of the nation's first convenience stores. This was a new concept at the time and quickly took off. The Billups franchise quickly spread from Virginia to Texas. Billups was the first successful oil company from the South and became the number-one independent oil company in the United States.

In the mid-'50s, Billups had a unique marketing promotion. The company gave away books of three-dimensional circus cutouts with each tank of gas. The book of colorful items included animals, tents and other circus paraphernalia that could be punched out like paper dolls. By folding the pieces as instructed and placing Tab A into Tab B, the whole circus could be put together. It was great fun and somewhat challenging.

Buddie continued to operate Billups for several years after Rowell's death in 1960, eventually selling the company to the Signal Oil Company in 1966.

Master Brake and Tire Company (H-37)

Master Brake is situated directly at the end of 14th Street on 28th Avenue and had one of the largest and most iconic signs in the city of Gulfport. A large automobile was the central feature, with neon lights attached around the tires like spokes. The lights flashed in sequence, giving the illusion that the tires were rotating.

On top of the sign just above the car was probably the largest directional sign in the city. A large neon arrow that read "On Beach" pointed the way south to Angelo's Place in large neon letters. It could be seen all over downtown.

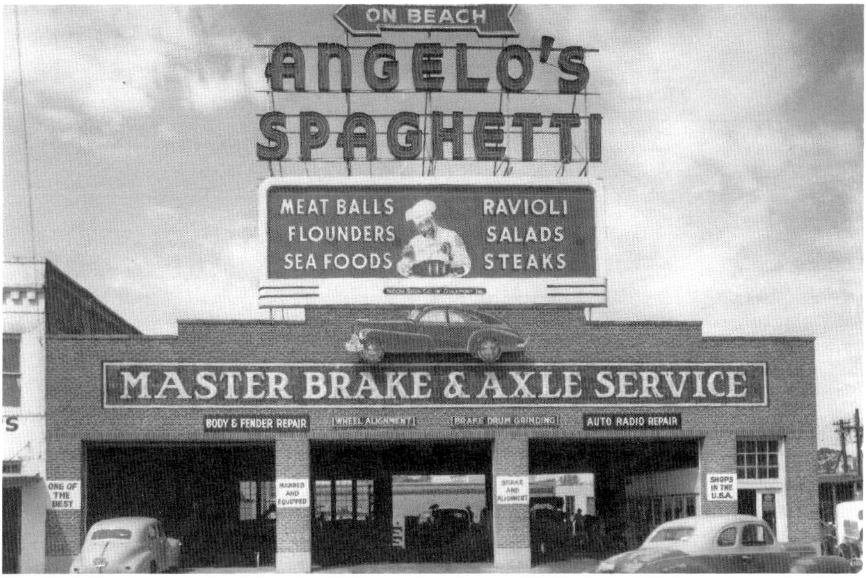

Master Brake and Tire Company had the largest and most recognizable sign in the city of Gulfport. *Paul Jermyn Collection.*

AUTO-LEC STORE (K-95)

Auto-Lec was a national chain similar to Western Auto. Both stores had service bays that opened from the alley behind the stores for tire installation and other auto services. Both Western Auto and Auto-Lec sold small appliances, radios, TVs, parts, auto accessories and even bikes. The Auto-Lec store in Gulfport was originally located on 13th Street next to Gryder's Shoes but later moved to 25th Avenue (K-99).

STANDARD OIL SERVICE STATION (M-123)

This familiar Standard Oil Station was on the corner of 24th Avenue and 14th Street, one of the few gas stations in the downtown area.

PETE THE TOP MAN (N-131)

Pete the Top Man specialized in automobile upholstery and ragtops for convertibles. The owners, Pete and Joseph Casano, originally shared space with Pecoul's TV next to the Stone Ice Cream Company on 14th Street but later expanded to a shop on 26th Avenue (N-167).

In the early to mid-'60s, Pete moved from downtown to a shop on the Pass Road. When Pete left this location, Brumfield's Women's Bargain Annex took over the space until the bargain annex closed.

The Goodyear Store (Q-174)

The Goodyear Tire Store was located on 25th Avenue near the railroad tracks. The store offered a whole array of products along with the standard Goodyear tires. The store sold batteries, brake parts and other supplies for auto maintenance.

Western Auto (Q-182)

Western Auto is a retail store that specializes in auto parts and accessories. Mr. George Pepperdine, who later started Pepperdine University, started Western Auto in 1909 as a catalogue store. The company grew to about 1,200 company-owned stores nationwide, mostly in metropolitan areas. It initiated the first franchise concept in the United States by opening about 4,000 privately owned associate stores. These franchise stores were located in the smaller towns and cities. The Gulfport Western Auto was one of these franchise businesses.

Western Auto was also known for certain private label brands that were very popular during the '50s. Western Auto made Western Flyer bicycles, TrueTone televisions and radios, Wizard tools, Citation appliances and other products.

In the early '50s, many of us had never seen a television. Thanks to Western Auto, however, many of us saw TV for the first time. Western Auto would place a few sets in the front window of the store for passersby to watch. Some of those who crowded there to experience the flickering black-and-white moving pictures stood for long periods of time transfixed by the new form of entertainment.

Ward's Fisk Tire and Appliances (R-193)

In the early '50s, this was the location of Ward's Fisk Tire and Appliances store. Almost everyone who lived during the '50s will remember the Fisk Tire advertisements. The iconic ad featured a small child in his pajamas holding a candlestick and yawning as if he were sleepy and ready for bed. The slogan said, "Time to retire…Buy a Fisk."

Ward's was also an appliance store that sold refrigerators, stoves and other household necessities.

The Firestone Store (R-193)

In the mid-'50s, Ward's became the Firestone Store. The store featured automotive products along with Firestone tires.

B.F. Goodrich Company (R-200)
The B.F. Goodrich tire store was located on 25th Avenue. Benjamin Franklin Goodrich was a medical doctor who got interested in the rubber industry. The Goodrich Company began by producing rubberized hoses and belts. In 1896, it produced the first pneumatic tires for automobiles. The Gulfport store sold tires and other automobile accessories.

Gulfport Battery Company (R-201)
Next to the Goodrich tire store on 25th Avenue was the Gulfport Battery Company. Gulfport Battery specialized in selling batteries of all types, specifically car batteries.

BOOKSTORES, DRUGSTORES AND GIFT SHOPS

Bookstores

Southern Bible Store J-54
The Southern Bible Store specialized in various editions of the Bible, biblical translations and other religious items. There were devotional Bibles, children's Bibles, large/giant print Bibles for the visually impaired, study Bibles and more.

Jordan's Newsstand (J-65)
Jordan's was a small newsstand on the west side of 26th Avenue, tucked in between Zollman's Music and the Charcoal Grill. Jordan's was a typical newsstand. The small space was filled with paperback books, magazines and the latest editions of the nation's major newspapers. For the businessmen in Gulfport, daily copies of the *Wall Street Journal*, the *New York Times* and other pertinent publications were only available at Jordan's.

Marshall's Books and Gifts (K-85)
In 1952, Aubrey Marshall bought out Barber and Thatcher Books at this location. Before Barber and Thatcher Books, this was the original location of Burt Signoff's Shoe Hospital, which moved over to 26th Avenue in the late '40s. Marshall's carried books by local authors as well as bestsellers. The bookstore also carried novelty and gift items such as the Magic 8

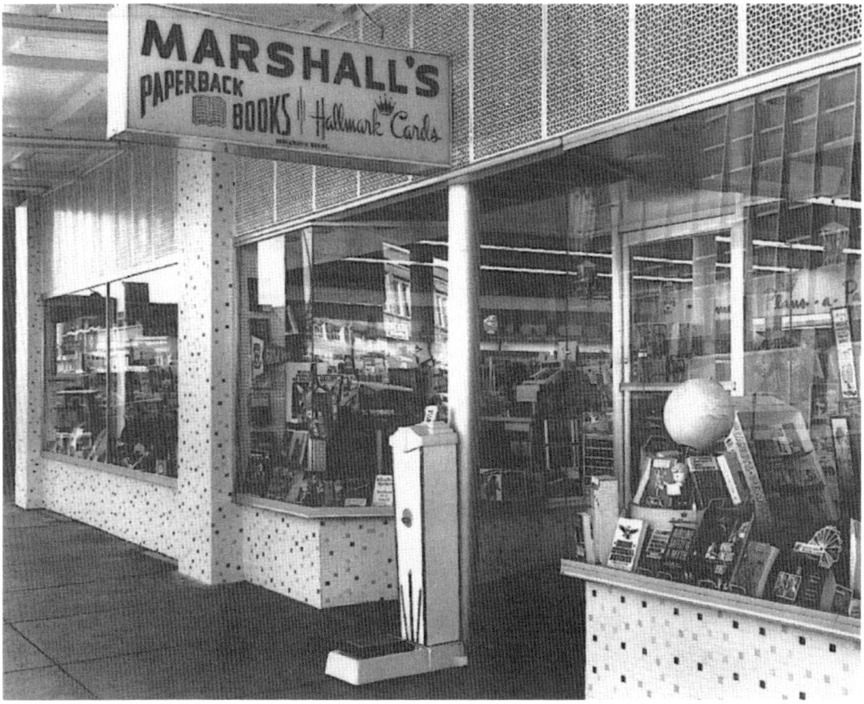

Aubrey Marshall carried books by local authors as well as the national bestsellers. The bookstore also carried novelty gift items. *From Aubrey Marshall.*

Ball. When Cooper's Jewelry closed next door, Marshall's Books and Gifts expanded into that space. In about 1990, Marshall's Books and Gifts moved from this original store over to 13th Street in the former Shamis Ladies Fashion location.

DRUGSTORES

ALBRIGHT & WOOD DRUGS (E-18)

Roy Albright founded Albright & Wood Drugs store in 1954. The store carried the usual drugstore items, but customers mostly gathered around the soda fountain.

By the 1950s, drugstore soda fountains had become standard features, and Albright & Wood had one of the better ones in Gulfport. Its specialty dessert was a cranberry chiffon pie that has never been equaled.

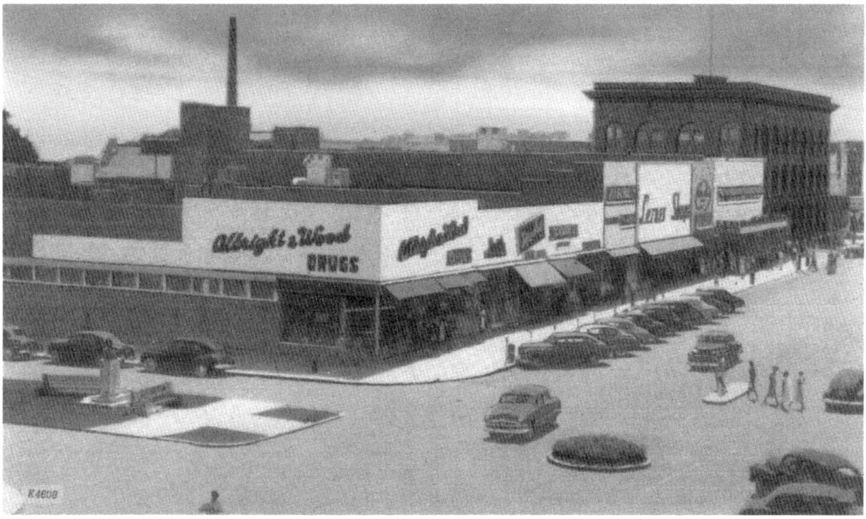

Roy Albright founded Albright & Wood Drugs in 1954. *Paul Jermyn Collection.*

BRUMFIELD DRUGS (J-67)

Brumfield Drugs was next to the Charcoal Grill on 26th Avenue. Like the other downtown drugstores, Brumfield's filled prescriptions and sold health and beauty items.

WALGREEN DRUGS (K-77)

(Later) GRANT DRUGS

In the '40s and early '50s, Walgreen Drugs was in a narrow storefront between the Darling Shop and Woolworth. According to the company, Walgreens is the second-largest pharmacy chain in the country. In 1958, the Rexall Drug Company was the largest in the United States. Grant Drugs took over this space in the late 1950s.

Few people realize that it was the Walgreen Drug Company that made the malted milkshake popular.

JONES BROTHERS' DRUG STORE (K-82)

Jones Brothers' Drug Store was on this corner of 26th Avenue and 14th Street. It was by far the most iconic drugstore in the '50s, probably because of its proximity to the four downtown theaters: the Paramount, the Legion, the Gulf and the Don. The drugstore had a convenient telephone that was available to the public right at the entrance to the store. Almost every kid in Gulfport would use the phone to call their parents when the movie they were watching was over. While waiting for a ride home, they enjoyed the snack bar in the store, which had one of the best ham sandwiches in the city.

There was always a pleasant smell when entering the front door because the perfume counter at the entrance featured Emeraude, Coty and other popular fragrances of the day.

The pharmacists worked upstairs in the mezzanine overlooking the main floor. The medical prescriptions were sent up to them by way of wire baskets suspended on wires.

DAY DRUG STORE (K-91)
(Later) THE TOGGERY

In the early '50s, Day Drug Store was located on the corner of 14th Street and 25th Avenue next to the Stratakos Candy Company.

The Day Drug Store was typical of the early drugstores in Gulfport. Most of them began as apothecaries. Unlike many of today's druggists, they were not just pill counters; they used mortars and pestles to actually mix medicines right in the store. The druggists often developed their own compounds that were effective in curing several illnesses. Since cocaine and opium were legal, these drugs were often included in the formulas.

Soda fountains were later introduced to aid upset stomach. Soft drinks like Coca-Cola were developed as a medicine to replace bicarbonates. With the popularity of soft drinks and the addition of ice cream, the high volume of customers forced the druggist to the back of the store.

Patent medicines like Lydia Pinkham Vegetable Compound ("A Positive Cure for Painful Complaints and Weaknesses so Common to Our Best Female Population") and a local product, Hadacol ("What Put the Pep into Grandma?"), contained so much alcohol that the government eventually banned their sale without a liquor license. You might recall the popular recording in the '50s as a promotion for the product. "Hadacol Boogie" was first recorded by Bill Nettles and later made popular by Jerry Lee Lewis.

GLENN'S DRUG STORE (L-108)

In the early '50s, Glenn's Drug Store occupied this corner location at 2429 14th Street. When Mr. Glenn, the owner and pharmacist, died, his wife ran the store for a few more years. Some remember Mrs. Glenn in the store. She seemed to always wear a black dress that contrasted nicely with her gray hair. She wore her hair in a bun reminiscent of Aunt Bea on *The*

Andy Griffith Show. When the store got to be too much for her, she sold it to Tripplet-Day in the mid-'50s.

TRIPPLET-DAY DRUG STORE (L-108)

Tripplet-Day Drug Store opened in 1955 and has had a popular soda fountain and grill since that time. Jim Day, the co-owner, has been the pharmacist since the store opened. Old friends and classmates gather regularly for breakfast or lunch to reminisce or to just enjoy the great food. Going to Tripplet-Day is like going back in time. The tables are the same, the ambiance is the same and the service is excellent. The award-winning beignets rival those in New Orleans.

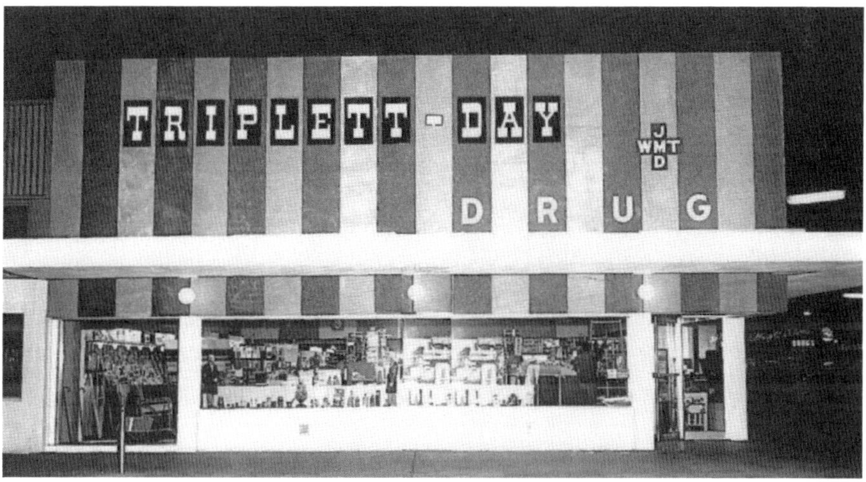

Tripplet-Day Drug Store opened in 1955 and continues to have a popular soda fountain and grill. *From Jim Day.*

GIFT SHOPS

THE PURPLE LANTERN (E-20)

Shortly after graduating from college in the mid-1950s, Mary Jo Sternberg opened her Purple Lantern store here in Gulfport. Mary Jo leased this building in a somewhat questionable part of town. She began by painting the exterior purple, and while that might have seemed a bit extreme, the unusual color actually blended in with the somewhat seedy surroundings.

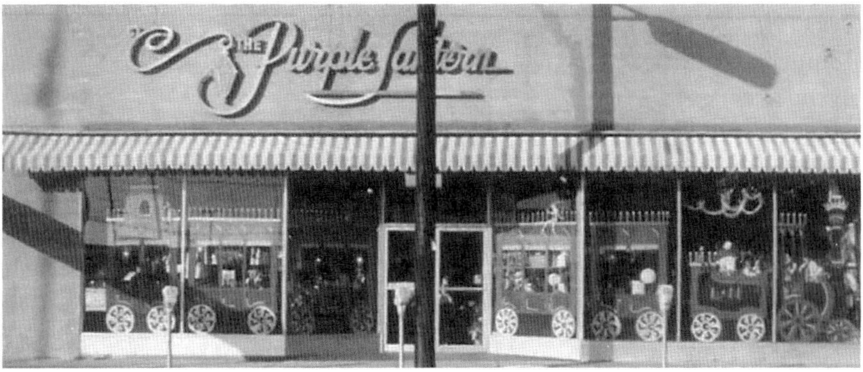

Mary Jo Sternberg's Purple Lantern store opened in the mid-1950s and carried exotic items from around the world. *From Nels Anderson.*

After establishing the Purple Lantern as a place to find exotic items from around the world, her business outgrew the space. In the late '50s, she took over the Campbell Appliance Company space on 25th Avenue. As her business continued to grow, she expanded into the space occupied by the Be-Wise Food Store (P-136).

E.J. YOUNGHANS NOVELTY SHOP (J-70)
(Later) BARBER'S HARDWARE

Edward J. Younghans owned a novelty shop in this location at the turn of the century. Although his store was no longer open during the '50s, it is worth acknowledging. Younghans was one of the coast's leading enterprises during its day. The store carried souvenirs, stationery, fine china, foreign and domestic novelties and Kodak cameras and film. From his first day in business, picture postcards were his biggest selling items, and he found it increasingly difficult to keep the cards in stock. This was during the golden age of postcards, when the whole country was caught up in the fad. Since the post office delivered mail twice a day at that time, postcards were like e-mail is today. They were a fast, inexpensive way to communicate.

Younghans became one of the most prolific photographers of the postcard genre, providing a historic record of the Mississippi Gulf Coast in the early 1900s. He is credited with taking the only existing photographs of many of our buildings that have long been demolished.

Barber's Hardware occupied this space during the '50s.

TOOMER'S GIFT SHOP (K-93)
Toomer's Gift Shop was next to the Mississippi Power Company on 25th Avenue. The store carried a variety of floral arrangements, novelties and gift items for birthdays, weddings and anniversaries. The shop was owned and operated by Lois Toomer, whose husband was a Mississippi Power Company employee for many years.

4-H MARKET (K-96)
The 4-H Market, located on 25th Avenue next to the Mississippi Power Company offices, sold handmade items and home accessories.

CHURCHES AND CIVIC ORGANIZATIONS

FIRST PRESBYTERIAN CHURCH OF GULFPORT (F-24)
This was the last of four buildings built for the First Presbyterian Church of Gulfport since its founding. Reverend Dr. Richard L. Summers became the sixth pastor in July 1954, serving as the head of the church until 1986. Hurricane Katrina destroyed the church in 2005, and as a result, the congregation decided against rebuilding at this location. A new church was built on O'Neal Road in Gulfport.

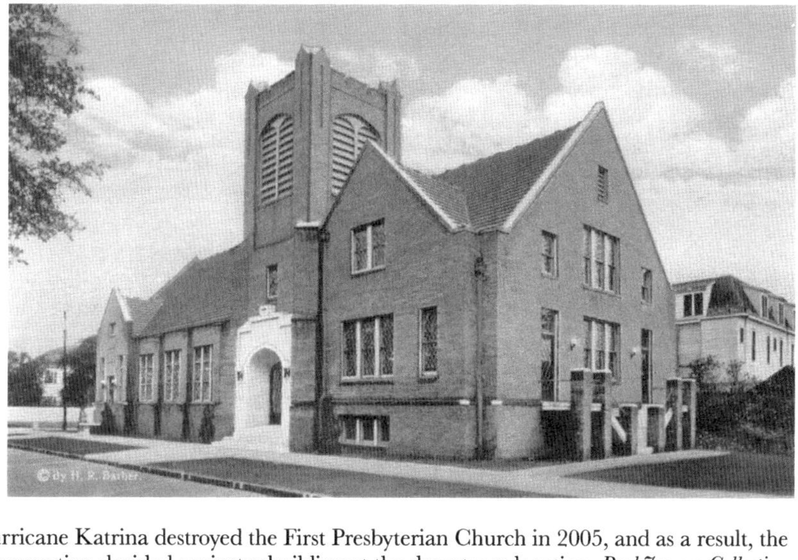

Hurricane Katrina destroyed the First Presbyterian Church in 2005, and as a result, the congregation decided against rebuilding at the downtown location. *Paul Jermyn Collection.*

WOMEN'S CLUB OF GULFPORT (M-128)

The Women's Club of Gulfport was founded in 1915. Nineteen women formed the organization to promote the group's interests in social, educational, domestic and philanthropic endeavors. The meetings were held in the afternoons followed by a formal tea. In 1929, the group purchased the lot facing the beach on the south side of the Markham Hotel, as well as an existing house that was on the Markham property. The house was moved to their new lot, where they shared the facility with the Gulfport Garden Club until Hurricane Camille destroyed the house in 1969.

FIRST UNITED METHODIST CHURCH (S-220)

The First United Methodist Church was one of the oldest churches along the Mississippi Gulf Coast. The exterior is of Beaux-Arts design, with Greek and Roman columns accented with decorative floral patterns and trim. Originally, the church was called 25th Avenue Methodist and was opened in a one-room schoolhouse on 25th Avenue. By 1900, the church had erected a larger building, but after a fire destroyed the building, the church moved to this present location.

The church is best known for the beautiful stained-glass dome ceiling in the sanctuary that depicts the story of Genesis. The church was able to acquire the dome for half of its cost of $3,000. The dome had been created for a wealthy oilman for his own church in Texas, but after he lost

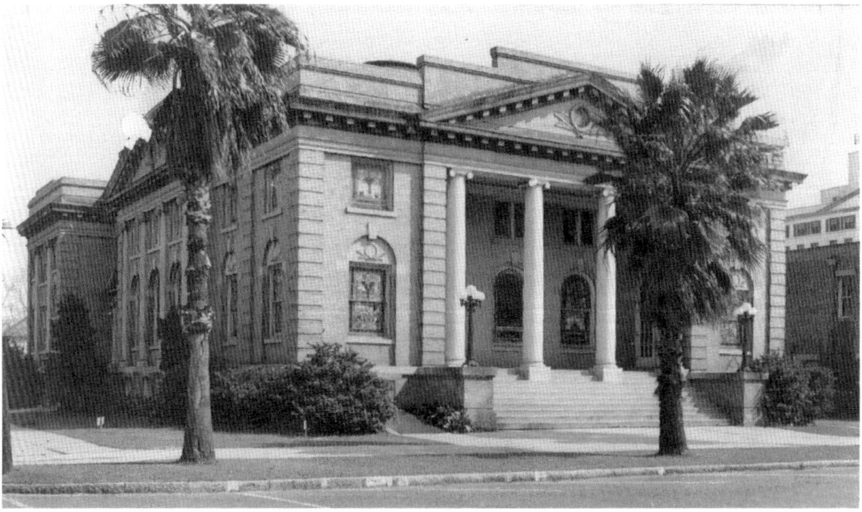

First United Methodist Church is best known for the beautiful stained-glass dome ceiling in the sanctuary that depicts the story of Genesis. *Paul Jermyn Collection.*

his fortune before the dome was completed, it sat in a warehouse in New Orleans, unclaimed. The man had paid an initial down payment of $1,500, with the balance to be paid upon completion. When he was unable to pay, First United Methodist Church paid the remaining $1,500 and acquired the dome for its new building.

St. John the Evangelist Catholic Church

St. John Parish began in 1900. Prior to that, Gulfport was a mission church of Mississippi City. Reverend Monsignor J.M. Prendergast was the first pastor. The original St. John the Evangelist Church was a wooden building on the corner of 24th Avenue and 17th Street. Parish records show that Edwin A. Deseamus was the first person baptized in the church and that Mr. Henry Swann and Miss Cora Green were the first couple married there.

As one of his first acts as pastor, Reverend Prendergast petitioned Mother M. de Sales, superior of the Sisters of Mercy in Vicksburg, to send sisters to Gulfport to start a convent and school. Mother de Sales agreed with the pastor's request, and on April 6, 1900, Mother Benedict along with sisters

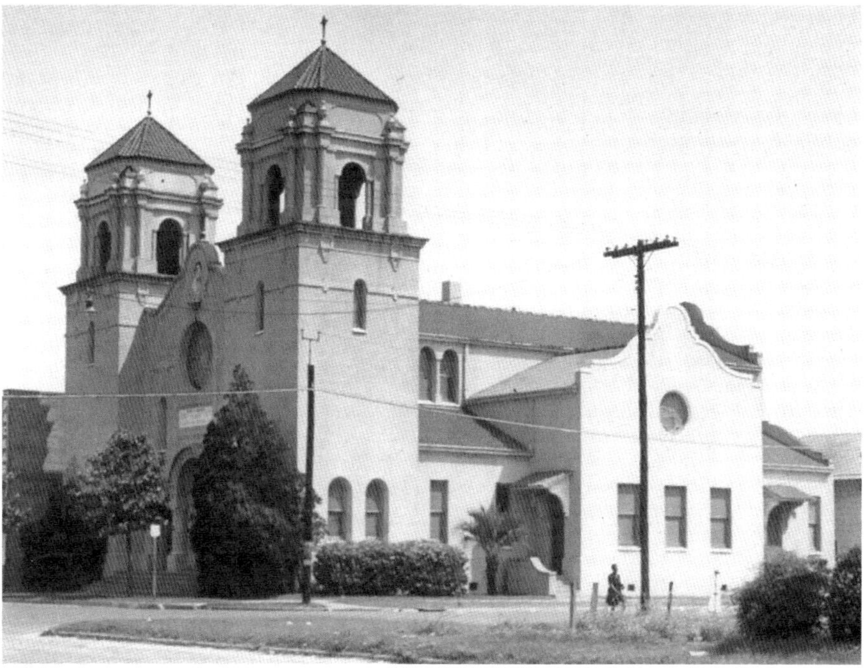

St. John the Evangelist parish began in 1900 as a mission church of Mississippi City. Monsignor J.M. Prendergast was the first pastor. *Paul Jermyn Collection.*

Mary Ambrose, Mary Cecelia and Mary Gonzaga arrived in Gulfport. The school, named St. Francis de Sales, opened on September 10, 1900, with a class of thirty students.

As the parish grew, a new church was constructed on the corner of 25th Avenue and 17th Street. The Spanish Mission–style building with two bell towers was dedicated on July 20, 1924, and is the church that most people in Gulfport remember. A fire destroyed the original convent in 1941. A new brick convent, renamed St. John's, was built next to the church.

One of the longest-serving and most beloved pastors was Right Reverend Monsignor Hubert A. Spengler. He was appointed pastor of St. John's on October 2, 1914, and was elevated to the rank of monsignor on January 28, 1945. Monsignor Spengler served as pastor for thirty-one years until his death on December 9, 1953. During his tenure, he oversaw the construction of a new church, a school, a convent and a rectory.

By 1955, the original school building had become inadequate for the size of the classes. The old building was also much in need of repair. Under the direction of Monsignor Thomas E. Williams, the pastor at that time, a new modern high school was built on thirteen acres of land on Pass Road near Hewes Avenue.

On August 17, 1969, the coast was struck by Hurricane Camille. This Category 5 hurricane damaged St. John's church beyond repair. On March 12, 1972, a new modern St. John the Evangelist Church was dedicated.

CLOTHING AND ACCESSORIES

MEN'S WEAR

SCHWOBILT'S MEN'S WEAR (Q-85)
(Later) ELMER'S MEN'S WEAR

Simon Schwob started Schwobilt's Men's Wear in Columbus, Georgia, in 1902. The store featured men's suits, slacks and sport coats. In Gulfport, the company's logo and familiar slogan, "Schwobilt Suits the South," was posted in the window next to a mannequin wearing a sport coat. Schwobilt's Men's Wear occupied this space in the early 1950s. Elmer's Men's Wear took over the location in the later part of the decade.

Rex Hats (E-16)

Rex Hats operated here in the early 1950s, when men's hats were still in fashion. Many of the old photos of the period show men in stylish fedoras. It was the last decade that men's hats were generally considered an essential part of men's wardrobes. In the fall and winter, felt hats were mostly displayed. The most popular colors were black, gray and brown. Although blue and green were also available, gray was the color of choice.

In the spring and summer, the store featured straw hats, which were a necessity on the coast. Straw hats were similar in style to the felt hats, except for the bands, which were wider and featured bold colors. The front brims of the straw hats were also slightly larger than the back to help shade the eyes from the sun. With the trend away from hats, Rex closed in the early 1950s, and in the later '50s, the American Plan Corporation, an insurance company, took over this location.

Elmer's Men's Wear (E-15) (E-19)

Locally owned Elmer's Men's Wear was originally located on 14th Street next to the Hancock Bank. It later moved to its final location on 13th Street next to Albright & Wood Drugs. Mr. Elmer, whose real name was El Muir, was a member of one of the several successful families in Gulfport who emigrated from Lebanon.

Elmer offered the latest in men's fashions and was the first merchant in Gulfport to recognize the trend in preppy clothes for young men. Elmer's opened the Oxford Shop on 25th Avenue to specialize in clothes for high school and college students. Later, M. Salloum's followed with its version of Elmer's Oxford Shop called the Toggery.

Robertson's Men's Wear (J-58)

Robertson's Men's Wear was a small, independent shop that remained in business through much of the '50s. It was one of several stores that carried a traditional line of men's clothing.

Deluxe Shoeshine and Hat Cleaning (K-83)

Deluxe Shoeshine and Hat Cleaning was a sidewalk shoeshine shop tucked between Jones Brothers' and Sale Studio on 14th Street. In addition to great "rag snapping" shoe shines, the shop also offered hat care. At that time, almost every man wore a hat of some kind. Wool hats particularly needed an occasional brushing to revitalize the nap. The service included cleaning, blocking and stiffening.

Shoe Hospital (K-85)

This was the original location of Bert Signoff's Shoe Hospital. The shoe shop moved over to 26th Avenue in the late '40s. After the Shoe Hospital moved, Barber and Thatcher Books opened in the space.

The Shoe Hospital shared a space on 26th Avenue with Barnett Cleaners (P-146) from the mid-'40s to the late '60s, when urban renewal took away the stores on that street. The Shoe Hospital had moved into this space from its original store on 13th Street between 25th and 26th Avenues, the space that Marshall's Book and Card Shop later occupied. Signoff's Shoe Hospital moved to its final location in a standalone building on 25th Avenue.

The M. Salloum Toggery (K-91)

When the Day Drug Store closed in the late '50s, the M. Salloum Toggery opened at this location. The Toggery was a "traditional" clothing store that catered to high school and college customers. It featured such trendy clothes as Gant Oxford cloth shirts and madras shorts. The store was competition for the successful Elmer's Oxford Shop, which opened on 25th Avenue next to Albright & Wood Drugs.

Anderson's Men's Wear (L-111)

Anderson's Men's Wear was the best high-end men's clothing store in Gulfport. Suits, coats and slacks were tailored to fit each customer perfectly. Vassar Anderson, owner of the Anderson Theatre on 25th Avenue, was also the owner of Anderson's Men's Wear. The store featured quality shoes like Florsheim and Allen Edmonds.

Gulfport Hat Cleaning & Shoe Shine Shop (P-158)

The Gulfport Hat and Shoe Shine Shop was a small hole-in-the-wall store. Kids didn't drop in to have their shoes shined, but they would always stop by to check out the latest comic books, which were kept in a rotating rack on the sidewalk. The rack was just outside the front of the store. It was a great marketing tool to get people to stop by. Even the businessmen would check out the comics as they had their shoes buffed. Some shoeshine shops of the time offered other services, such as tailoring. This store offered hat cleaning, blocking and care.

Larson's Men's Wear (P-156)

Larson's Men's Wear, next to Royal Jewelry Store on 14th Street, was a small, independently owned clothing store for men. The store offered a complete

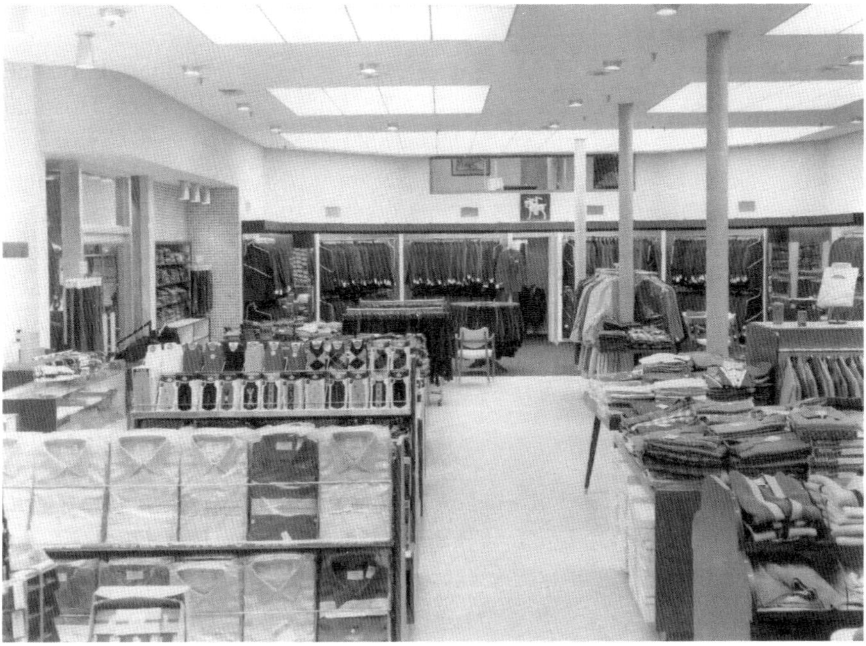

The Toggery was a "traditional" clothing store that catered to high school and college students. *The Toggery, Clayton Rand Papers, Manuscripts Division, Special Collections Department, Mississippi State University Libraries.*

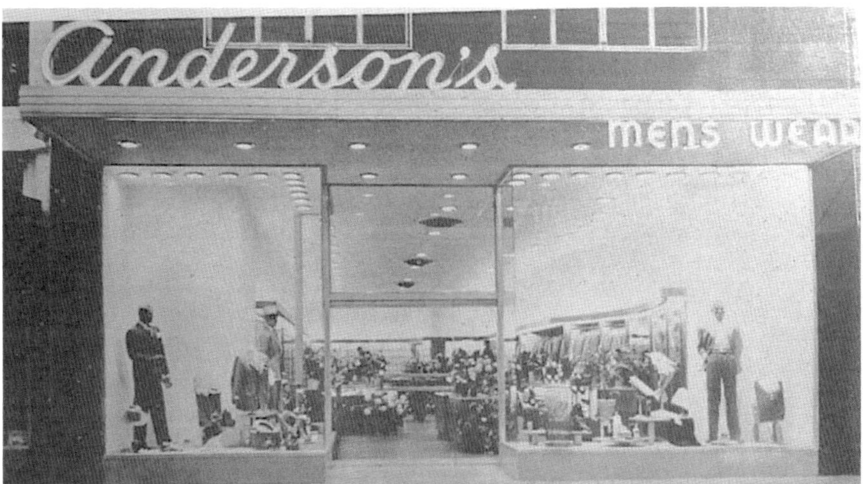

Anderson's Men's Wear was the best high-end men's clothing store in Gulfport. Vassar Anderson also owned the Anderson Theatre on 25th Avenue. *From Jim Day.*

line of suits, sport coats, slacks and shirts. Like all the stores on 26th Avenue, Larson's closed as a result of the urban renewal project that bought out all of the stores in that block.

CABIBI AND SON SHOE SERVICE (Q-183)

Back at a time when most people only had two pairs of shoes, even the least expensive pair was repaired. It was not uncommon to have more than one heel or sole replaced during the life of a pair of shoes. Cabibi and Son Shoe Service was the oldest continuing shoe repair shop in downtown Gulfport. John Cabibi started the business on 14th Street before moving to this permanent location on 25th Avenue.

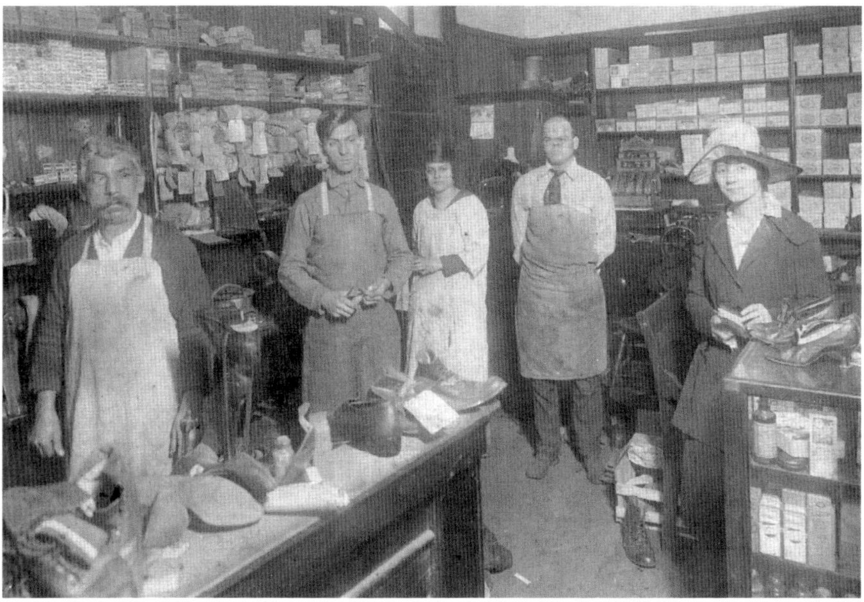

Cabibi and Son Shoe Service was the oldest continuing shoe repair shop in downtown Gulfport. *Paul Jermyn Collection.*

ELLIS SALLOUM'S MEN'S WEAR (R-207)

Ellis Salloum opened an upscale men's wear store in the old Lang building when Lang Funeral Home moved to a new location on the west side of town.

KOURY'S MEN'S WEAR (R-217)

Mr. Foaud C. Koury owned and operated this well-established men's and boy's store in downtown Gulfport. Mr. Koury married Isabelle Salloum, one of the four children of Mansour Salloum, founder of the M. Salloum store on the corner of 26th Avenue and 14th Street. After her husband died, Isabelle Koury continued to run the store.

MOSES DEPARTMENT STORE

Moses Department Store is one of the iconic clothing stores in Gulfport that is still in operation today after almost a century. Moses Department Store was and continues to be the place in Gulfport to buy Levi jeans. This family-owned business began around 1900 when Mr. Anneas Saadi Moses would drive into the rural areas of the coast selling his goods. Moses's first store opened on 12th Street but was later moved to 25th Avenue in the vicinity of 22nd Street. The current building, located at 1612 25th Avenue, was constructed in 1925. At first, Moses was a true department store, carrying just about everything, even though the space was small. In the late '60s, Moses began to specialize, and the name was changed to Moses' Mens Wear. Today, the fine tradition continues, with Anneas Moses's grandsons running the business.

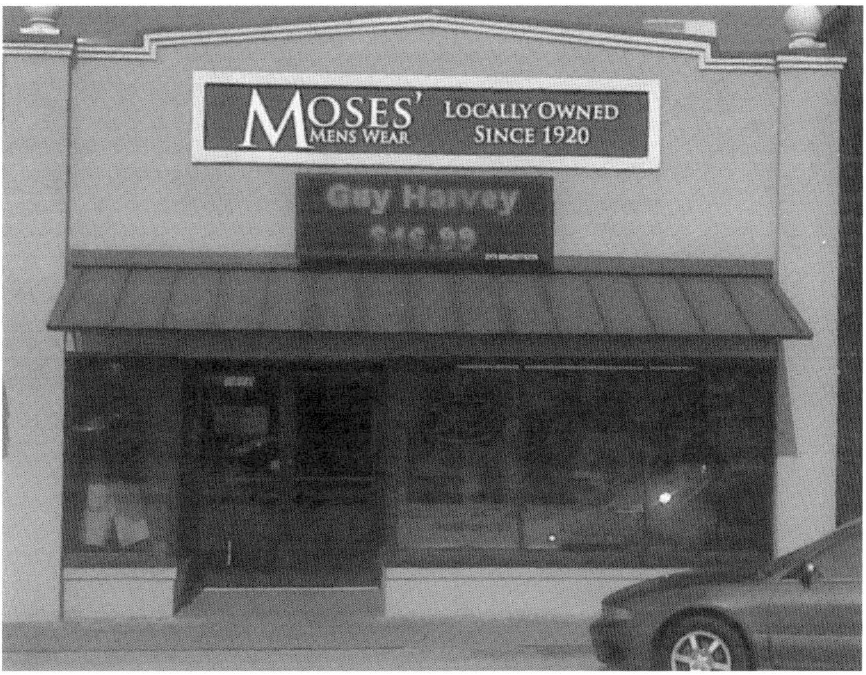

Moses Department Store is a family-owned business that began around 1900 and is still in operation in Gulfport today. *From Anneas J R Moses.*

Barbershops

Gremillion's Barber Shop (H-40)

Gremillion's Barber Shop, located next to the Lane Hotel, was one of several good barbershops in Gulfport during that period. Gremillion's was conveniently located next to Mack's Barber Supply Company.

Mack's Barber Supply Company (H-41)

Mack's Barber Supply Company provided everything for the hair and beauty profession. Products included barber jackets and apparel, barber poles, clippers and accessories, combs and brushes, hair dryers, lather machines and soap, liquids, creams and talc, massagers, mirrors, neck dusters, shop posters and so much more. Mack's was very up to date on the latest products and equipment when they came out. I suggest it for locals and the not-so-local.

Jay's Barbershop (J-57)

Next to the El Mecca Hotel is Jay's Barber Shop, another of Gulfport's several fine barbershops. It seems that every man in town had a particular shop and barber he preferred, and surprisingly, with so many barbershops in town, customers still had to wait to be served. None of the shops made appointments the way they do today.

Jack's Barber Shop (J-73)

Jack's Barber Shop, located next to Helwick Radio and Television on 13th Street, was one of several popular barbershops in downtown Gulfport. It was open through the early '50s.

Triangle Barbershop (L-110)

Triangle Barber Shop was located here on 14th Street. It seems that in the 1950s, there was a good barbershop in every block. Triangle was no exception. Triangle was a great place to meet friends and catch up on the latest news.

Central Barber Shop (P-154)

Central Barber Shop was located on the corner of 26th Avenue and 14th Street. Central was one of several barbershops that served the downtown area.

OUR BARBER SHOP (Q-172)
Our Barber Shop was a small two-man barbershop on 26th Avenue. It was folksier than the other shops in town. It was Gulfport's answer to Floyd's Barbershop on television's *Andy Griffith Show*. There were always some interesting people sharing interesting conversation while waiting for their turns in the barber chair. The owner told me that he named the shop Our Barber Shop so that when anyone was asked where he went to get a haircut, he could say, "'Our' Barber Shop."

HOLMES BARBER SHOP (Q-176)
Holmes Barber Shop took over the space when the House of Music closed. Gerald Holmes, the owner, was the barber of choice for students and teenagers. He gave the best flattop haircut in Gulfport. Flattops were the rage in the '50s, and not every barber could get the hair to stand up properly. Only Holmes had the magic touch—at least that's what his teenage customers thought.

WOMEN'S WEAR STORES

LERNER SHOP (E-12)
The Lerner Shop was one of Gulfport's favorite women's stores, featuring apparel and accessories perfect for work or casual wear. Many recall the wonderful fragrance that greeted customers as they entered the store. Samuel A. Lerner and Harold M. Lane founded the store in New York in 1918. As an aside, Samuel Lerner was the uncle of famed lyricist Alan Jay Lerner, who wrote such popular musicals as *My Fair Lady*, *Camelot* and *Gigi*.

SINGER SEWING MACHINE COMPANY (E-14)
The Singer Sewing Machine Company liberated the average housewife from the arduous task of hand-sewing. At a time when store-bought clothes were a luxury, many of our mothers and wives depended on their Singer sewing machines. The Singer Company made the machines available to the vast majority of families by offering credit to its customers and a rent-to-own financing plan that allowed people to rent a sewing machine, with the rental payments applied to the machine when the purchase was finally made.

In the late '50s, an adapter from the Singer Company converted the old pedal-type Singers into electric sewing machines. To the people of the '50s, this was an example of modern technology.

The Town & Country Shop (J-47)

The Town & Country Shop, located on the west side of 27th Avenue, was a women's specialty store. Most will remember the personal service and a wide variety of clothes, featuring distinctive weekend casuals, career suiting, coats and unique accessories for every occasion.

Stacey's Women's Wear (J-49)

Stacey's Women's Wear was located on the east side of 27th Avenue between 13th and 14th Streets. Stacey's featured stylish women's clothing at reasonable prices.

Reed's Dress Shop (J-69)

Reed's Dress Shop was a local women's store that carried a general line of dresses, coats and accessories. Reed's was successful in downtown Gulfport until the late '50s. When it closed, Brumfield Drugs expanded into this space.

The Darling Shop (K-76)

The Darling Shop took over this space, which was once occupied by the Splendid Café. The Darling Shop featured stylish clothing popular with younger women.

Shamis Ltd. (K-99)

Shamis Ltd., a women's fashion store, took over this space next to Gryder's Shoes when Auto-Lec moved to 25th Avenue. Helen Nasef Shamis was well respected in the world of fashion. Her store had the reputation for having some of the more stylish clothes of any of the ladies' stores in Gulfport. Shamis stayed in this location until the store closed in about 1990.

Ed Salloum's Women's Wear (L-113)

Edward Salloum opened a high-end women's store in this location. He was following in the footsteps of his father, George Salloum, and several cousins who were in the clothing business. Unfortunately, Ed died, and his brother Ellis chose to close his own dress shop in Baton Rouge, Louisiana, to take over his brother's store in Gulfport. Ellis later brought in his younger brother Kaleel, and together they built a thriving retail business that lasted for fifty-nine years.

Hurd's Style Shop (L-117)

Hurd's Style Shop sold women and men's clothing. Owner Murray "Ray" Hurd also owned a larger clothing store in New Orleans. Both stores sold basic women's clothing for everyday wear that was comparable in style and price to ones found at the Ideal Shop or Penny's. The men's clothes were to the left when entering the store, and the women's clothes were on the right.

In 1969, after Hurd's closed, Scottie Stores moved into the space from the old Rosenblum's location in the H&H Hotel on 14th Street.

Sew 'n' Save Fabric (P-149)

In the early to late 1950s, the Sew 'n' Save Fabric store occupied this space on 26th Avenue. This was a time when women actually sewed or mended clothes for themselves and their families. Many coast homes had some type of sewing machine, and Home Ec (Home Economics) was a popular course in high school. Sew 'n' Save offered a wide variety of fabrics, including batiks, flannels and quilting cottons. In addition to fabrics, the store also sold yarns, needles, hooks, patterns and more for knitting and crochet. Sew 'n' Save also carried everything needed for the finishing touches, such as whimsical embellishments, piping cord, bias tape and labels for any sewing needs.

Smith Alteration Shop (Q-166)

The Smith Alteration Shop was owned and operated by a mother and daughter. They provided alterations for men's and women's clothing. Although it was open for general business, the two women also provided alteration services for other clothing stores in Gulfport—such as Elmer's Men's Wear, M. Salloum's and others—when those stores' own alterations people were overloaded.

Brumfield's Women's Bargain Annex (Q-178)

There were several businesses at this location throughout the '50s. The first was United Stores in the early '50s. Then Dixie Amusement Company was here before it moved over on 14th Street. Then Pete the Top Man expanded here from its original location next to the Stone Ice Cream Company on 14th Street near the *Daily Herald* building.

When Pete moved from downtown to the Pass Road in the early to mid-'60s, Brumfield's Women's Bargain Annex took over the space until the store closed. The annex had done well over the years with its large selection and low prices.

Rosenblum's Women's Wear (Q-186)

Rosenblum's Women's Wear was an old, respected store in Gulfport throughout the '50s. It was located in the east corner of the H&H

Hotel building on 14th Street. Scottie Stores moved into this space when Rosenblum's closed. In 1969, Hancock Bank, which was located across the alley, took over the bottom two store spaces in the H&H Hotel building, forcing Scottie Stores to move. Scottie relocated to the old Hurd's Style Shop space next to the Standard Furniture Company.

THE IDEAL SHOP (R-189)

The store on the corner of 14th Street and 25th Avenue was the Ideal Shop. This was a favorite women's store for many in Gulfport. The store carried brands that were not found in other dress shops on the coast. One of the most requested was Mr. Fine blouses.

NORTHROP'S (J-60; R-211)

(Later) M. SALLOUM DEPARTMENT STORE

Northrop's was an upscale women's wear store in Gulfport. The founder, Dr. A.K. Northrop, came to the Gulf Coast in 1866 and opened a dental practice in Biloxi. He later moved to Pass Christian, where he continued to practice until 1875, when he gave up his practice. He opened the first Northrop's store the following year as a general merchandise store in Pass Christian. His son George E. Northrop later joined him, and in 1899, George opened the first Northrop's store in Gulfport on the corner of 14th Street and 26th Avenue

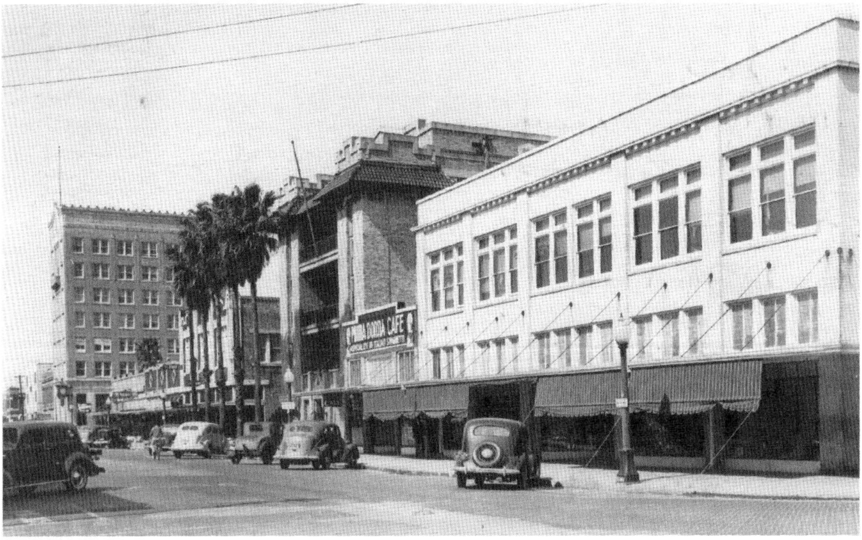

Northrop's is shown here on the right with stripped shades. *Shaw Design Group Collection.*

(J-60). In 1922, Elmer Northrop joined his brother, George, in the Gulfport store, and they moved the business to its new and permanent location on the corner of 14th Street and 24th Avenue (R-211). After Northrop's moved, M. Salloum took over this prime location, considered by some to be the cornerstone of the business district.

In 1944, Northrop's was sold to Mr. Joseph S. Perusse and his wife, Marie, who turned Northrop's into an upscale women's wear store. Marie placed H.E. "Pepper" Martin in the position of general manager, a position he held for years.

AUSTIN'S STYLE SHOP (R-212)

In 1949, when Austin H. Moritz and his brother, John R. Moritz, came to the coast from Nebraska, Austin went to work at the Rosenblum store in Biloxi. He became manager and served for two and a half years at the store. John opened Tots and Teens a year before Austin started at Rosenblum's. In March 1949, the brothers remodeled the Tots and Teens store and opened it as Austin's Style Shop in Biloxi. Austin's featured ladies', infants', boys' and girls' apparel. The Moritz brothers opened this store in Gulfport about ten years later.

CARDINAL FLOWER SHOP (R-215)

Cardinal Flower Shop was next to Fasold's Jewelry on 14th Street. There were always beautiful floral arrangements on display in the windows and inside the store. Cardinal was family owned and operated and provided for the floral needs of Gulfport since 1952; it was a popular florist throughout the '50s.

ELITE SHOP (R-216)

The Elite Shop was located on 14th Street next to Cardinal Flower Shop. Like several other women's wear stores in Gulfport, it offered a good selection of stylish and fashionable clothing for women.

CHILDREN'S WEAR

YOUNG AGES CHILDREN WEAR (L-107)

Young Ages Children Wear was located on 25th Avenue next to the old Anderson Theatre building. This store was all about the kids. The store featured children's active wear, jackets and coats, pajamas, sweaters, underwear, suits and dress wear, sets and outfits of all kinds.

Jewelry Stores

Keith Jewelry Store (E-17)
(Later) Busch Jewelry Store (E-17)
Keith Jewelry was the original jeweler at this location, but many will more likely remember Busch Jewelry, which took over this space. Busch was a chain store that promoted free financing and guaranteed savings of 40 to 70 percent on most of its items. This appealed to the people of the coast, as wages were low for many of the people in Gulfport.

A.E. Morlan Jewelry and Watch Repair (J-50)
This is the original location of A.E. Morlan Jewelry and Watch Repair. Mr. Morlan also operated an optometrist service at this store. In 1908, Mr. Karl Fasold moved to Gulfport and began fitting glasses for A.E. Morlan. Fasold had arrived at Ellis Island from Bavaria, Germany, in 1902. From there he moved to Chicago to attend Northern Illinois College of Optometry before taking the job at Morlan Jewelry.

In 1913, A.E. Morlan Jewelry moved to a new location on 14th Street (Q-188). When Morlan moved, Karl Fasold and another employee, a Mr. Harlass (first name unknown), formed a partnership and continued to operate their own jewelry store at this location. Later, Karl Fasold left his partner and opened the first Fasold's Jewelry on 14th Street.

Lyon Jewelry Store (J-55)
Lyon Jewelry Store was a small, independent jewelry store owned by John and Helen Vorhaben. Lyon offered a full range of products with easy financing. The shop was in the Bouslog Building, which also housed the El Mecca Hotel. This was the first location for Fasold's jewelry store after he left his job with A.E. Morlan.

The Vorhabens took over the space from the elder Karl Fasold, who had moved his jewelry store to a small shop in the left-hand corner of the Anderson Theatre building.

Karl's Jewelry (K-80)
Bradley Jewelry was located inside the left-hand corner of the Paramount Theatre. Karl Joseph Robert Fasold, son of Joseph K. Fasold, bought out Bradley Jewelry and opened his first jewelry store in Bradley's theater location. Karl had worked at his father's store on 14th Street after returning home from the navy and before opening his own company. His

store featured jewelry for high school and college students and younger adults.

In 2000, Karl moved his jewelry store from his first location in the Paramount Theatre building to 26th Avenue in the space that would later become Jordan's Newsstand (J-65).

Cooper's Jewelry (K-86)
(Later) Marshall's Books
Cooper's Jewelry was a small jewelry store on 14th Street during the early '50s. When it closed, Marshall's Books expanded into the space.

R.O. Besse Jewelers (K-103)
R.O. Besse Jewelers was a small, independently owned jewelry store located inside the Splendid Hotel building facing 26th Avenue. Mr. Besse was a well-known and respected member of the Gulfport business community. He carried a moderately priced line of jewelry that was a notch above the quality found in most chain stores.

Huber Jewelry Store (L-112)
Huber Jewelry Store was located between Anderson's Men's Wear and Ed Salloum's Women's Wear. Mr. Huber had worked for a short time with Joseph K. Fasold in the 14th Street store before starting his own jewelry business.

Royal Jewelry Store (P-155)
Royal Jewelry Store was located on 26th Avenue next to Central Barber Shop. Royal is a national chain of family-owned jewelry stores known for excellent craftsmanship and trend-setting designs. The company earned a reputation for honesty and passion for the jewelry business. The store offered an extensive line of jewelry and accessories.

C.L. Bullock Jewelry (Q-188)
Mr. C.L. Bullock took over this space on 14th Street from A.E. Morlan Jewelry Store and opened C.L. Bullock Jewelry. Mr. Bullock became very active in the business community. He was a popular man with the people and was a respected jeweler who was known as much for his watch repairs as for his jewelry sales. He later went on to become Gulfport's mayor. He unfortunately died in office after serving only two years (from 1973 to 1975). After a special election, funeral home director Arthur Wallace "Buzzy" Lang was chosen to fill Bullock's unexpired term.

FASOLD'S JEWELRY (R-214)

Joseph Karl Fasold, owner of Fasold's Jewelry, learned the jewelry trade working at the Kurz Chain Factory in Weissenhorn, Bavaria. In addition to jewelry and watch repair, he also learned hand engraving. His uncle, Karl Fasold, had arrived in Gulfport in about 1908. Karl went to work for A.E. Morlan before opening his own jewelry store with a partner in the space on 27th Avenue that would later be occupied by Broussard's Music. Karl later moved his store to a space in the Anderson Theatre building on 25th Avenue. As his business grew, he sent for his nephew, Joseph.

Joseph K. Fasold arrived in New Orleans in November 1921 and worked for his uncle for six years. He returned briefly to his native Germany to marry his sweetheart, Anna Maria Pfaeffinger. The couple returned to Gulfport and started their family. They had two sons: Karl Joseph Robert Fasold, who also became a jeweler, and Joseph Franz Fasold, who became an optometrist. Karl worked for his father before opening his own jewelry store in the Paramount Theatre building.

Franz opened Fasold's Optometry in the Agar Realty space next to M. Salloum's on 14th Street. Uncle Karl Fasold died suddenly, leaving his estate and business to his nephew, Joseph. His first act as the new owner was to move his uncle's store to this location at 2412 14th Street. When Joseph K. Fasold died suddenly in July 1964, his son Karl took over and ran both his store in the Paramount Theatre and his father's store on 14th Street. He continued to run his father's store for nine years before closing it in 1973. The father and son never competed, even though they each had their own separate store—Karl pointed out that Joseph Fasold handled the "Carriage Trade" with silver, china, crystal and upscale jewelry.

Joseph Fasold's Jewelry always featured a memorable display in its front store window. It included animated mechanical devices featuring simple, repetitive motions performed by doll-like figures in settings that were toy-like, cartoonish or Art Deco in design. The Baranger Studios of Pasadena, California, produced them as a form of advertising for jewelers. They were never sold, but rather were rented to jewelers under a contract that had the displays rotating monthly. The jeweler would return the old one and receive a new one to display. Fasold's would keep the displays for three or four weeks and then ship them on to a jewelry store in Hattiesburg.

Gulfport window shoppers looked forward to the latest display. The images ranged widely, with most of them centered on the general idea of buying diamonds or watches. The tiny figures of men and women were like players on a dramatic stage. An example was a Wells Fargo stagecoach, complete

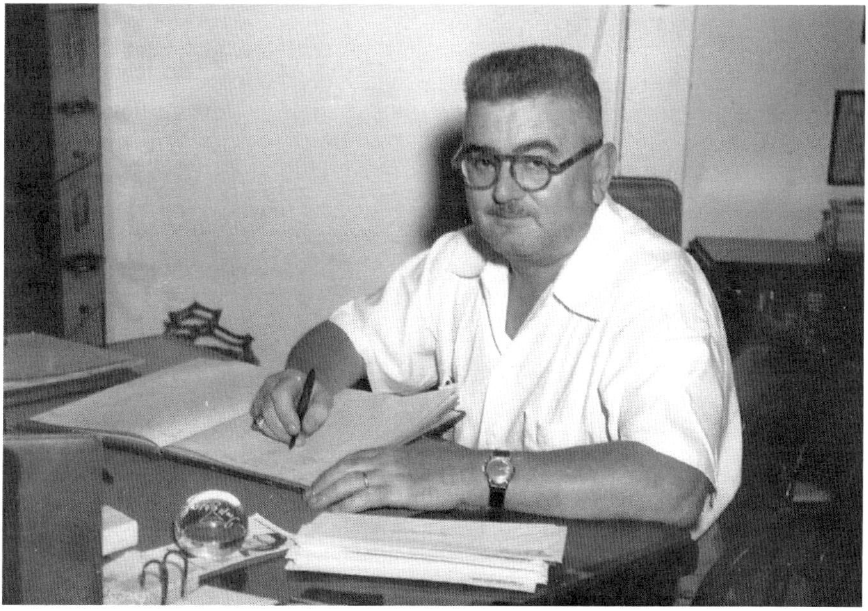

Joseph Karl Fasold, owner of Fasold's Jewelry, learned the jewelry trade working at the Kurz Chain Factory in Weissenhorn, Bavaria. *From Karl Fasold.*

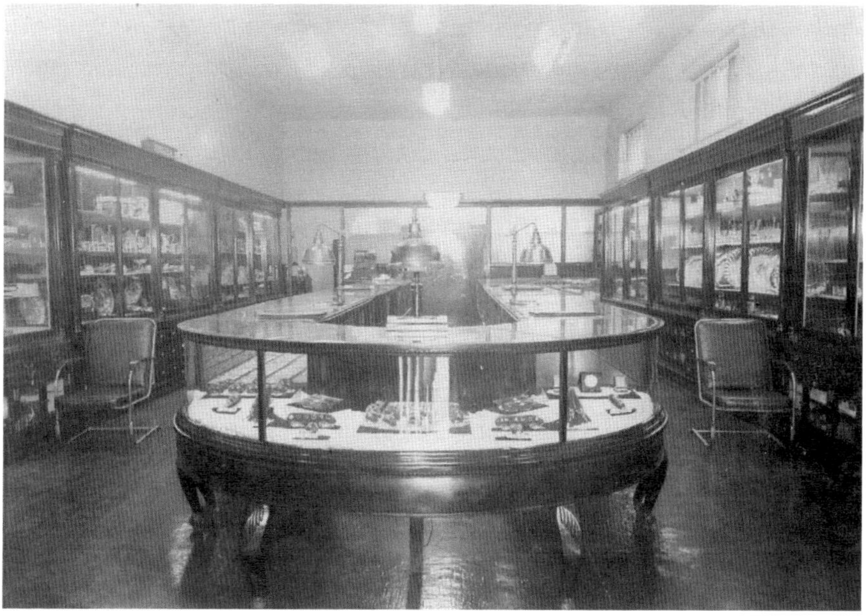

This is the showroom of Fasold's Jewelry on 14th Street. *From Karl Fasold.*

with stagecoach driver and a young couple inside, rocking along in a fanciful setting. The wheels of the coach were turning, and the horses were galloping along. An engraved placard noted, "You will always be on the right road with one of our beautiful diamonds." The placards on the displays always suggested that a diamond could assist in a favorable courtship outcome.

Shoe Stores

Butler's Shoes (D-11)

Butler's Shoes is next to McCrory's. It is a chain of shoe stores that carries many of the popular brands and style of shoes. Butler Shoes started around 1940 with the merger of two shoe store chains. Brothers Ben and Lou Pollack joined the Butler chain from Florida. The name of the stores was originally Butler Pollacks before becoming Butler's Shoes. Many Gulfport families relied on Butler's for their shoe needs.

Kinney Shoes (D-13)

Kinney Shoes sold a wide variety of men and women's shoes, affordably priced for average Americans. George Romanta Kinney founded the G.R. Kinney Company in 1894, and according to reports, it had at one time been the largest family-owned chain shoe retailer in the country. The chain continued to be popular because of its reasonably priced shoes. In 1963, F.W. Woolworth purchased the company, renaming it the Kinney Shoe Corporation. Although the Gulfport store closed, Kinney Shoes has continued to remain a fully owned subsidiary of Woolworth in other parts of the country.

Gryder's Shoes (K-97)

Gryder's Shoes was a local shoe store that carried quality brands such as Capezio and Bernardo. The store opened in the late '50s in the former Gulf National Bank building on the corner of 13th Street and 25th Avenue after the bank moved to Highway 90 and 25th Avenue.

COOKIES, CANDY AND STONE ICE CREAM

Bakeries

Harp's Bakery (E-19)
Mr. O.D. Harp and his wife, Wauneta, started Harp's Bakery on 25th Avenue in the late '40s. They later expanded to a store on 27th Avenue near the old L&N train station. In 1956, they opened next to the Purple Lantern on 25th Avenue. It remained there until the late '50s, when Harp Bakery made a final move to the Pass Road, where O.D. Harp retired.

Elmer's Men's Wear took over the space. This became the side door of the Elmer's store, with the main entrance on 13th Street.

Sunlite Bakery (J-53)
The Electrick Maid from Biloxi opened in Gulfport as the Sunlite Bakery and operated here on 27th Avenue from the early 1930s until it closed in the 1970s. Sunlite took over the space that had previously been occupied here by Harp's Bakery. Harp's moved from this location to a new store on 25th Avenue next to the Purple Lantern.

The Sunlite Bakery offered the same homestyle breads, cakes and other traditional baked goods that had made it popular in Biloxi since the turn of the century. Like other downtown stores, the Sunlite Bakery also offered a delivery service.

Wedding Bakery
(Later) Quality Bakery (J-74)
James Alfred "Mack" McKnight Sr. opened the Quality Bakery in August 1949. It has been a local family-run business since that time, known for its delicious goods and friendly service. Mack McKnight was born in Ariton, Alabama, and attended the Delgado Community College in New Orleans, where he studied pastry arts in the Culinary Arts Department. While in New Orleans, he met and married his wife, Rose. He started in the baking business at the Wedding Bakery with Edgar Ellis Wedding and a Mr. Hamilton (first name unknown). Wedding had started a bread company in Montgomery, Alabama, before moving the business to Gulfport. It was said that he offered the first sliced bread in Gulfport. Wedding sold only a limited variety of cakes, specializing more in bread, which he delivered to grocery stores all along the coast.

Sometime in 1949, the three men broke up and went their separate ways. That is when Mack McKnight opened the original Quality Bakery on 13th Street in Gulfport. When Mack McKnight died, the business was passed to his son, Al McKnight, and Al's wife, Cecelia. The two continued to run the bakery for more than twenty years. When Al died, his son, Patrick McKnight, and his wife, Alesia LeBatard (LeeLee), took over the bakery in about 1987 and have continued to run it to this day.

In 1969, Hurricane Camille destroyed the original bakery building on 13th Street shortly after Al and Cecelia took over the building on 25th Avenue that had been Phil's Bakery. Mr. Phil DeNicola had retired and left his building vacant. Quality Bakery has continued to operate at that location since 1970. Patrick and LeeLee's daughter, Danielle White, joined the company in 2013 and will run the bakery when her parents retire, becoming the fourth generation of the McKnight family to own and operate the Quality Bakery.

The bakery is open from Tuesday to Friday from 6:00 a.m. to 4:00 p.m. and Saturdays from 6:00 a.m. to 9:30 a.m. It offers a variety of delicious donuts and pastries, but by far its biggest sellers are its brownies and petit fours. It is also known for its specialty cookies and cakes, along with its beautiful wedding cakes.

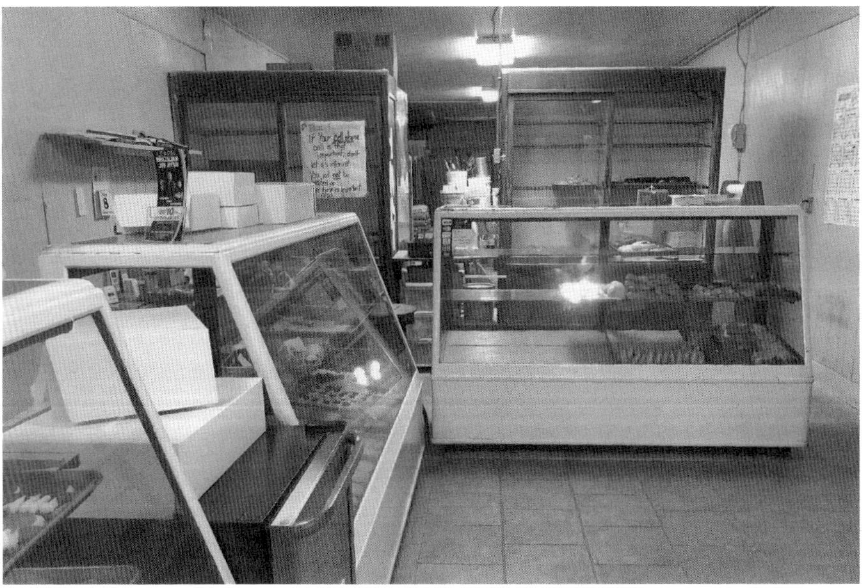

Mack McKnight opened the original Quality Bakery on 13th Street in Gulfport in 1949. This is the current interior of Quality Bakery, located in the old Phil's Bakery on 25th Avenue. *From Danielle White.*

Over the years, Quality Bakery has become more than just a place to buy donuts. Generations of families along the Gulf Coast have come through these doors. They have become more than customers—they are part of the bakery's extended family. Danielle reflects on the warm memories of the wonderful friends they have made over the years and looks forward to the new memories they will make in the future. A lot of the old bakeries have come and gone in Gulfport, but the Quality Bakery has continued for almost seventy years. She says that her young daughter doesn't realize it yet, but she gets to be a little part of Gulfport history. That is indeed special.

COLONIAL BAKERY

The Colonial Bakery was the most recognizable business on Pass Road in Gulfport, not just because of its beautiful setting but also because of the wonderful aroma of freshly baked bread that filled the air all around the neighborhood.

When the bakery first opened in 1946, the founder, Patrick Murphy, envisioned a building with spacious grounds and picnic areas. Murphy immediately set out to create beautifully landscaped paths that wound throughout the property, bordered by beautiful rose bushes and colorful flowers, kept meticulously manicured year-round by a crew of gardeners. One of the most notable groundskeepers was Otto Moody, who filled the property with not only tall pines and spreading oaks but also beds of more than two thousand gorgeous roses and azaleas. According to the *Daily Herald*, some of the roses measured "seven inches across the face." The grounds were so impressive that they became known as "Colonial Park."

Otto Moody's most outstanding creation was a large lake surrounded by colorful azaleas, visible to all traffic traveling on Pass Road. The ducks that were always skimming across the water to greet the young children, eager to offer the birds scraps of bread and crackers, were one of the favorite elements of the lake. Nestled near the magnificent rose beds, Moody built two small cabins for use by the bakery's employees. According to the *Daily Herald*, each cabin could accommodate four persons, with an icebox, a gas stove, a sink, built-in cabinets, a dining table and chairs, a bath and a screened porch.

During the Christmas season, children and adults alike looked forward to Mr. Moody's fabulous holiday decorations. The bushes and trees were adorned with multicolored lights that reflected in the silver and gold tinsel hanging from the limbs, while Rudolph and nine life-size reindeer and a sleigh stretched in front of the building in a memorable sixty-foot display.

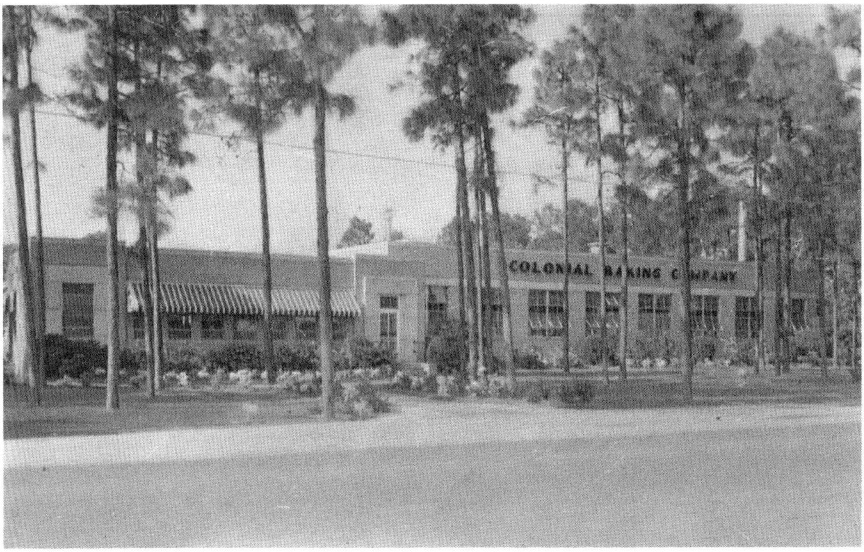

When the Colonial Bakery first opened in 1946, the founder, Patrick Murphy, envisioned a building with spacious grounds and picnic areas. *Paul Jermyn Collection.*

For more than thirty-five years, the Colonial Bakery was the most popular location for field trips and tours by groups like the Boy Scouts, Girl Scouts and almost every elementary school class in the city. Guides walked the children through the baking process, showing them exactly how bread was made. At the end of the tour, everyone received a miniature loaf of Colonial Bread.

Government regulations finally forced the Colonial Bakery to close in the early '90s. Asbestos linings in the old bakery ovens made them a health hazard, and the immense cost of purchasing new ovens was prohibitive. With that, the once popular Colonial Bakery closed its doors forever.

PHIL'S BAKERY

Phil's Bakery was located almost directly across the street from St. John the Evangelist Catholic Church at 1623 25th Avenue. Phil DeNicola, owner of the bakery, personally ensured that his goods were up to his high standards. Phil's was a favorite stop for the parishioners of St. John's, who would make a mad dash after Sunday mass to purchase hot, fresh loaves of French bread or assorted delicious pastries. The quality of Phil's baked goods was without question. The butter cookies and sugar cookies were always in demand, not to mention the delicious chocolate éclairs.

CANDY COMPANY

STRATAKOS CANDY COMPANY (K-90)
The Stratakos Candy Company was founded in 1909 by Louis Stratakos and was in business for almost thirty-five years. One of the featured items was Yeast Foam Malted Milk, which came in the form of milk balls. Yeast Foam Malted Milk was a highly nutritious food made from barley milk, wheat, whole milk and yeast. The foam was particularly popular as an aid to digestion.

ICE CREAM PARLOR

THE STONE ICE CREAM COMPANY (N-132)
Daniel McGee Stone opened the Stone Ice Cream Company at 2215 14th Street as an ice cream parlor toward the end of 1937. Stone's was strictly an ice cream store, not a soda shop or a hamburger stand, although the store did sell sodas for a very short time when Stone's first opened. Coca-Cola was the only fountain drink sold, with Barq's Root Beer, Dr. Pepper, Grapette, 7 Up and Orange Crush available in bottles. Stone was Gulfport's answer to the classic '50s malt shop. Dropping in at Stone was like being in a scene from the television show *Happy Days*. One would almost expect to see the Fonz or Richie Cunningham playing the jukebox or one of the pinball machines.

Hours were from 8:00 a.m. to 10:00 p.m. (11:00 p.m. in the summer), seven days a week, only closing on Christmas Day. The store was always crowded, especially on Sunday afternoons, the busiest day of the week, and on July 4, the busiest day of the year. No one had off on that day. The Fourth of July was the culmination of the big Gulfport Deep Sea Fishing Rodeo at Jones Park. The annual event drew large crowds, which meant there were longer lines of people in Stone waiting to be served.

Dan Stone attended Mississippi State University in dairy science but did not stay to graduate. He left Mississippi State to work for Roscoe Stewart in Port Arthur, Texas, at Stewart's ice cream plant/dairy. After gaining experience in the ice cream business working at Stewart's, Dan returned to Mississippi to work at an ice cream store in Gulfport. He was later transferred to the company's second store in Bay St. Louis as manager.

While in Bay St. Louis, Dan began dating Ruth Emma Lloyd. Ruth was working as a schoolteacher in Bay St. Louis after attending Mississippi

Woman's College (now William Carey College). It is likely the two had known each other before, having grown up in the same area of the coast. The Stone family lived in Landon, while the Lloyd family lived in nearby Lyman. Although Dan was four years older than Ruth, they had attended the same school and probably had seen each other on the campus.

Shortly after Dan and Ruth were married, Dan was transferred back to the Gulfport store. While in Gulfport, their first child, Danna Louise, was born. Dan's next move was to Hattiesburg, where he went to work at the Hattiesburg Creamery. While living in Hattiesburg, their second daughter, Mayme Vera, was born. Mayme was named after Roscoe Stewart's wife, who had no children of her own. Dan and Ruth had remained close friends with the Stewarts. Young Mayme was still crawling when the family moved back to Gulfport from Hattiesburg, where Dan started the Stone Ice Cream Company. Upon returning to the coast, the Stones lived for a short time with Dan's parents, William and Eulalie McGee Stone, in Landon. Sometime before Danna started school at East Ward Elementary, the Stones moved into their own apartment in Gulfport. The apartment was situated across the alley from the ice cream "plant," the name the family affectionately called Stone ice cream store.

From the start, it was a family business. Dan's wife, Ruth, worked side by side with him until after the birth of their third daughter, Barbara Jill. After having two wonderful girls, Dan really wanted a boy. When Jill was born, Dan jokingly said he wanted a Jack but got a Jill.

After Jill was born, Ruth only worked when needed on special occasions, like the Fourth of July. Dan's brother, Carroll E. Stone, joined Dan as a junior partner after serving in World War II. Dan and Ruth's three daughters all worked in the store. There was a family joke that you had to grow tall enough to reach the bottom of the three- or five-gallon containers before you could work at the store. Jill said that she was the shortest, so it took her longer to start work. Many of the girls' cousins also worked at "the plant" as they were growing up.

It wasn't long after opening the Stone Ice Cream Company that Dan began delivering his frozen treats to local merchants all along the coast and to the north on Highway 49 almost to Hattiesburg. The Stone Ice Cream Company eventually delivered to a regular customer list of forty to fifty merchants. Carroll mostly handled the deliveries, although Dan helped when necessary.

Having a refrigerated truck was very important to the business. Carroll related a story of how the truck was hijacked once while he was inside a

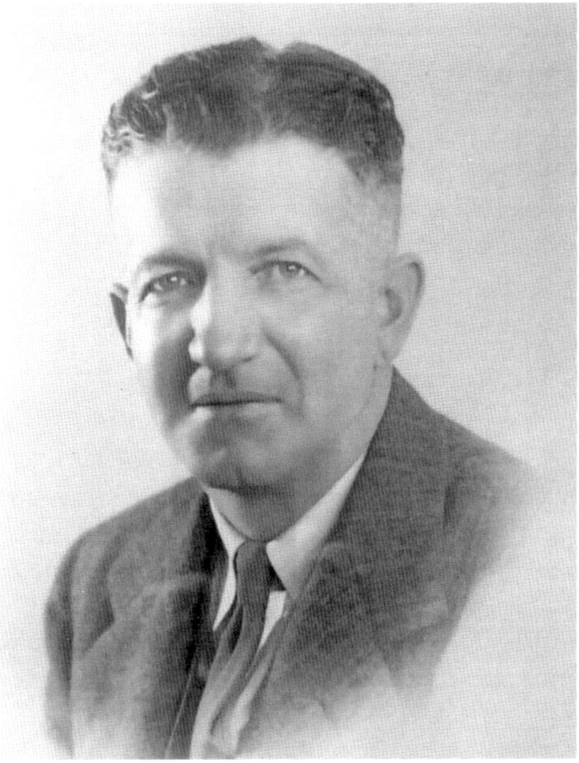

Right: Daniel McGee Stone opened the Stone Ice Cream Company at 2215 14th Street as an ice cream parlor toward the end of 1937. *From the Stone sisters.*

Below: Dan Stone, owner, and his brother, Carroll Stone, a part owner, standing by their refrigerated truck. *From the Stone sisters.*

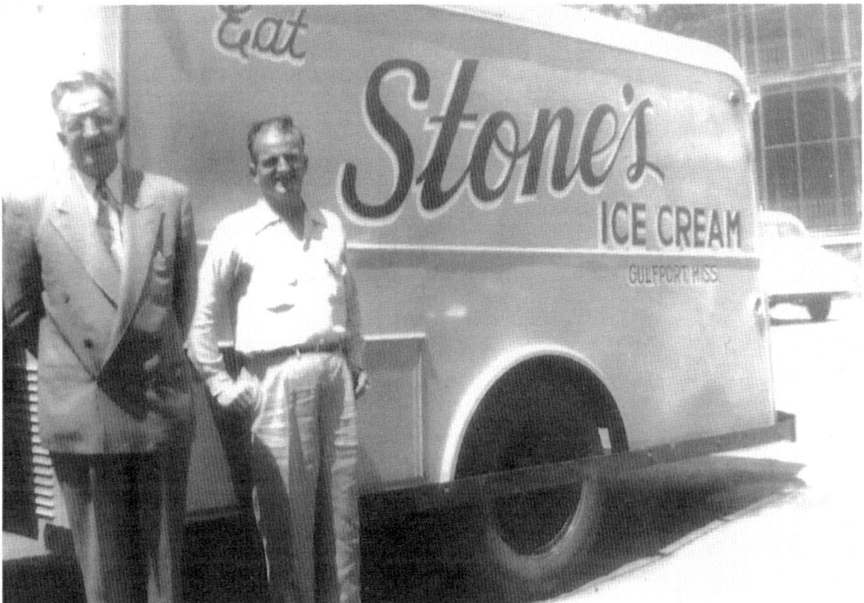

store. The police were called, and Dan was picked up to aid in the chase. It was not difficult to follow the truck once it was located. The chase lasted about thirty minutes, at which time the policeman drew his gun and was going to try and shoot out one of the tires. Dan pleaded with the officer not to shoot for fear of hitting one of the truck's refrigeration coils. That would be the end of Dan's refrigerated truck. Dan said he would rather continue the pursuit until the criminal ran out of gas. After a short time, the man pulled over, jumped out and ran. He was captured, and Carroll was able to continue his deliveries for the day and many days after.

Stone became the favorite hangout for students, families and businessmen throughout its long history. On Sunday afternoons, families would go to church and then drive around after lunch, ending up at Stone's for an afternoon treat. After the movies, students on dates would walk or drive to Stone's for an end to the evening. After lunch, businessmen and students would stop by Stone before returning to the office or school. It was the thing to do. Dan Stone was always there, wearing his characteristic hat and tie, even when he was making the ice cream.

As the company grew, Dan bought up the smaller stores that were next to the plant until the Stone Ice Cream Company and the *Daily Herald* took up half the city block. It was in the perfect location, close to town, churches, the high school and the beach. Stone's had no real competitors other than the national brands like Borden's or Brown's Velvet in New Orleans. There were no other ice cream manufacturers in Gulfport.

The daughters tell the following story that sums up the way all of Gulfport felt about the Stone Ice Cream Company. In the '50s, Dairy Queen first came to Gulfport. The much-touted soft ice cream "with the curl on top" opened directly across the street from Stone's. One day, Gulfport High School was holding a homecoming parade. The parade started at the nearby school and proceeded down 14th Street right past Stone's and the newly opened Dairy Queen. The radio club at school had sold advertisements as a way to make money. As the parade wound its way through the streets of Gulfport, a loudspeaker promoted the businesses that had paid for an ad. People had gathered on both sides of the street. Dan and the family were outside watching the parade passing by. They were waving, and people on the floats were waving. It was a good time. As the parade passed in front of Stone and the Dairy Queen, a voice came over the speaker announcing the new store: "A new business in Gulfport is Dairy Queen, home of soft ice cream and very good. It is right across the street from the all time favorite…the Stone

Ice Cream Company!" They were all surprised at their new designation as "the all time favorite." After such a glowing promotion, Dan laughed and wondered if Dairy Queen should pay for its commercial or whether he should. Regardless of the new competition, the people of Gulfport preferred Stone ice cream.

Many of us can still remember that wonderful place. It was a large store, brightly painted in green and white. The entire front of the building was wall-to-wall glass. Entering the store, Dan's office was in a corner on the left wall. The jukebox and two pinball machines were on the right wall, although the pinball machines were eventually eliminated. There was a tall counter that stood in front of the freezers. Five-gallon cans were stored under the counter. The servers working behind the counter would scoop ice cream from these containers to use for the cones, sundaes, banana splits and more. Five to seven people worked behind the counter, with family members helping during busy times. A soda fountain with a water dispenser was next to the freezers. A well of water by the dispenser held the scoops when not in use and was also used for rinsing the scoops when changing flavors. On top of the counter were various glass jars with bags of peanuts, packets of crackers with peanut butter filling, penny candies and more. There was also a glass case with sliding doors sitting on one end of the counter to keep other non-frozen snack foods. On the wall behind the freezer were containers for the various toppings, the milkshake blenders, the cones, malt, straws, wooden spoons, containers for making malts and milkshakes and various other supplies.

There were no stools at the serving counter, even when the store expanded. Instead, there were twelve square tables, each with four chairs. The tables were covered in black Formica, a design characteristic of the '50s. The tables could be pulled together to accommodate larger groups when necessary. There were no printed menus, just a chalkboard behind the counter listing the day's specials. The board was easy to change when flavors changed. The jukebox was always playing the popular music of the day—the Platters, Little Richard, Elvis and Chuck Berry—although there was no room on the floor for dancing.

Manufacturing ice cream was a daytime project starting at 8:00 a.m. and ending at about 6:00 p.m., but never on Sunday. In the beginning, only Dan made the ice cream until the business got too large. Then his brother, Carroll, would help, along with other employees. There were usually five to seven workers plus Dan and Carroll in the back making the ice cream. Dan always made ice cream while wearing a hat and tie.

Making the ice cream was hard work. At first, Dan only had a five-gallon single-batch freezer. He would have to make several successive batches of a particular flavor, such as vanilla or chocolate, and then wash out the freezer to change flavors. In later years, he installed a freezer that produced flavors continuously instead of in small batches.

Pints, quarts, half gallons and two sizes of cups were also filled from the freezer. The cups were filled manually, covered with paper lids and then placed in brown paper bags. The bags held a dozen of the larger cups that sold for ten cents each, as well as two dozen of the small cups that sold for five cents each. The bags were sealed with wide brown paper tape with glue on the back that had to be moistened to stick. The tape was rubbed over a water dispenser that resembled a Scotch tape holder to wet it enough to seal the bags.

There was a walk-in freezer room in which the ice cream was stored as it was made. A cooling tower on the roof of the building kept the freezer room at a very cold temperature, way below thirty-two degrees, so the ice cream froze quickly. When the truck drivers needed to fill an order, they went into the freezer and loaded the number of bags of the different sizes of cups or other items they needed into the refrigerated truck.

There was a brine tank used to make the novelty items. To make popsicles, the flavored syrup was poured into molds. The molds had covers into which the sticks were inserted. Then the molds were put into one end of the brine tank. As additional molds were inserted behind them, they pushed the other molds forward. By the time the molds got to the opposite end of the tank, they were frozen solid. The molds were then immersed in hot water to loosen the popsicles, which were then put into individual bags. These were the double type of popsicles with two sticks. They could be broken down the middle into two popsicles.

Dreamsicles and cheerios were made in the brine tank the same way as the popsicles. Those molds were not double, however. Vanilla ice cream was put into the cheerios molds. Once frozen, they were removed from the molds and dipped into liquid milk chocolate. The chocolate set very quickly on the cold ice cream. They were then bagged and put into the freezer.

Stone offered a wide variety of ice cream products, everything always deliciously made from fresh ingredients:

- ice cream by the scoop (five cents): Of course, Stone sold the basic ice cream by the scoop, which was served in cones and wax-coated cups. Small wooden paddle-type spoons were provided with the cups. Many of us ignored the paddle and would fold the cardboard lids in half, making a scoop to eat our ice cream from the cups. Both cone- and cup-shaped cones were used. A two-scope cone could be of two different flavors of the customer's choice. For a time, double cones were available with the two scoops side by side, but usually customers preferred the two scoops stacked on top of each other. Thus, the side-by-side cones were eventually eliminated. Dan was such a professional that he learned to hold six cones in one hand while filling each of them with ice cream. No one else ever mastered that.

- ICE CREAM FLAVORS included: Vanilla, Chocolate, Strawberry, Pecan Crunch, Orange Pineapple, Grape Pineapple, Peach (in season), Chocolate Chip, Fudge Ripple, Strawberry Swirl, Lemon Custard, Black Walnut, Banana, Chocolate Marshmallow, Caramel, Cherry Coconut, Peppermint (at Christmastime), Orange Sherbet, Lime Sherbet, Pineapple Sherbet and occasionally Lemon Sherbet. Stone did not have what could be called a signature flavor. Every customer had his or her own personal favorite. Some of the most requested were Orange Pineapple, Grape Pineapple, Pecan Crunch and Peach. Peach was probably the most popular because it was made fresh each summer, and people drove from all over for it. Dan would only allow the best peaches to go into this seasonal favorite. Although peach was everyone else's favorite, the Stone girls never cared for it because they remember the agony of sitting at home peeling bushels and bushels of peaches. Neither Jill nor Mayme eat peach ice cream to this day.
- COKE FLOATS AND ROOT BEER FLOATS: Floats were made by pouring either Coca-Cola or Barq's Root Beer over two scoops of vanilla ice cream.
- BANANA SPLITS: Stone's standard banana split consisted of one scoop each of vanilla, chocolate and strawberry on a fresh banana, split down the middle, with a different topping on each scoop. Chocolate, strawberry and marshmallow syrups with a maraschino cherry on top of the middle scoop were standard, although the customer could request his own choice of flavors and toppings. Yet no special toppings like whipped cream or nuts were ever needed. They didn't have to add anything—the banana splits were perfect the way they were.

- SUNDAES: Sundaes were made with three scoops of ice cream in a round cup. Syrup of a flavor chosen by the customer was poured over the top. The choices of syrup were hot fudge, hot caramel or butterscotch (which were interchangeable), crushed pineapple in syrup, canned strawberries in syrup and hot marshmallow. Stone would make sundaes to order. A favorite was hot fudge over vanilla ice cream. Many liked chocolate ice cream with marshmallow syrup. The toppings were kept in containers heated on the bottom to keep the syrup in a liquid state.
- MILKSHAKES AND MALTS: Milkshakes and malts came in basic flavors: vanilla, chocolate, strawberry and nectar.
- NEAPOLITAN: Neapolitan was a half-gallon brick of ice cream made up of three flavors: chocolate, vanilla and strawberry.
- DREAMSICLES: A dreamsicle is a vanilla ice cream bar on a stick covered by a sherbet-like shell of flavored ice, usually orange. Dreamsicles were never as popular as popsicles and cheerios.
- POPSICLES: Stone made popsicles in four basic flavors: lime, strawberry, orange and cherry.
- CHEERIOS: Some might not remember the name, although we all know the product. Cheerios are vanilla ice cream bars on a stick covered in a thin layer of milk chocolate. The name came about in 1931, when the product was invented to compete with the newly patented popsicle. Cheerio was the brand name just as Coca-Cola is a brand name. Over time, all vanilla ice cream on a stick covered with chocolate became known as a cheerio, just like today many people ask for a "coke" when referring to any soft drink. Also, over time, the cheerio name has become obsolete.
- POLAR BARS (ESKIMO PIES): Polar bars—or Eskimo pies, as some people call them—are basically a slab of vanilla ice cream covered in a thin layer of chocolate without the stick.
- FUDGSICLES: Fudgsicles are chocolate-flavored ice crystals on a stick.
- ICE CREAM SANDWICHES: An ice cream sandwich is a slab of vanilla ice cream between two chocolate wafers.
- BRICKS: Bricks were solid bars of ice cream. Stone made chocolate, vanilla and strawberry.
- WEDDING PUNCH: Dan Stone created a delicious punch that contained more than the usual amount of fruit. Alcohol was

> prohibited at the time and could no longer be used in punch, but Dan's wedding punch was the perfect substitute. It became known as Stone's Wedding Punch, as it was a much-requested drink for many weddings in Gulfport.

Daniel McGee Stone was a remarkable husband, father and businessman. He enjoyed his work in any capacity. He would make ice cream in the back of the plant, he would work the counter in the store and he would drive the trucks and make deliveries. His wife, Ruth, worked tirelessly by his side, often sleeping on the cement floor in the back of the plant to get much-needed rest. Dan respected his employees, and they respected him. He would assist them whenever they needed it, often mopping the floors and cleaning the ice cream cabinets before going home.

Dan and Ruth helped to celebrate special events in the community. When Gulfport High School won the Big 8 Conference in 1951, Dan told the coach that the players could come in one afternoon and have all the ice cream they could eat at no charge. One hungry player ate six quarts before leaving. Most of the others only ate two or three quarts.

Ice cream was a cure-all for the Stones. If the girls had a sore throat or had tonsils removed or upset stomach, lime sherbet was the cure. Ruth Stone used cones for teething babies to chew on, as they melted away and didn't break, and Dan sold popsicles to the hospitals for nausea.

The Stone Ice Cream Company remained at the original location on 14th Street until it was sold in 1964 to Bush Dairy Inc. of Laurel, Mississippi.

DEPARTMENT STORES, FURNITURE STORES AND FIVE-AND-DIMES

Department Stores

M. Salloum Store (J-60)

After Northrop's moved to its new location, M. Salloum took over this prime location, considered by some to be the cornerstone of the business district. Not only was it centrally located, but M. Salloum also became the largest independent clothing store in Gulfport.

Jake Mansour Salloum left his home in Beirut, Lebanon, to escape religious persecution. He settled in New Orleans, where he opened a wholesale dry goods business in the French Quarter. He closed that business in 1906 and moved to Gulfport along with his wife, Victoria. To start his new business, he went door to door selling dry goods to the local residents. Soon he was able to open a small store on 25th Avenue near 18th Street. His business continued to grow, and he moved to 25th Avenue and 22nd Street in what was the first brick building on 25th Avenue. In 1938, Mansour moved to the current building at what he then called "The Toggery," not to be confused with the M. Salloum's Toggery, which opened on the corner of 25th Avenue in the 1950s. Mansour shortened his name on the building to M. Salloum, and the name has been synonymous with good people and excellent service ever since.

Mansour had a policy of helping the citizens of Gulfport. Many acknowledge that they would not have survived the Depression without Salloum's willingness to let the people pay what they could, when they could. After the country pulled out of the Depression, Salloum was paid back, and the people of Gulfport never forgot his great generosity to so many in their time of need. The Salloum family have continued to be well-respected pillars of the Gulfport community.

J.C. PENNEY (J-61)

J.C. Penney, M. Salloum's (next door) and J.C. Clower in a row downtown were the three largest stores in Gulfport until the new Sears opened on the corner of 25th Avenue and 13th Street. Men's wear was on the first floor, with women's wear on the second. A staircase led to the mezzanine level, where the notions and sewing needs department was located. Women would stand for what seemed like hours going through the files of Vogue and Simplicity dress patterns, searching for the perfect dress to make for some special occasion.

The store's most unique feature was the pneumatic tube system that sent the sales receipts upstairs to the bookkeeper. Purchases at Penney's were wrapped in brown paper and then tied with string from a large cone-shaped roll kept on the counter. Bags were not commonly used at any of the Gulfport stores.

Until the mid-'60s, J.C. Penney stores were mostly located in downtown areas like in Gulfport, but as the trend toward suburban shopping malls began to grow, it began relocating to the malls. The Penney's store in Gulfport moved to Edgewater Mall in 1963 as one of the anchors.

SEARS (L-104)

In 1952, Sears opened across the street from the post office. The modern two-story building replaced a Pure Oil service station, a gift shop and a few other small businesses. The Sears building featured the only escalator between Mobile and New Orleans. The store carried a full line of merchandise from clothing to appliances and was a mainstay in the downtown business district until it moved to the Edgewater Mall in the early '60s.

The original Sears and Roebuck store in Gulfport was located a few stores north on 25th Avenue. The building was also two stories tall, with wooden stairs going up to the second floor. During the Christmas season, Sears would issue a special catalogue separate from its regular catalogue that became known as a "wishbook." Parents would spend hours with their children, looking through each page, dreaming of what Santa might bring. The catalogue was not only a source of ideas for toys but also a means of entertainment. The catalogue had a deeper connection for children living in rural areas who did not have an opportunity to see the toys in stores. For the children, it was like visiting Santa's workshop all in one book.

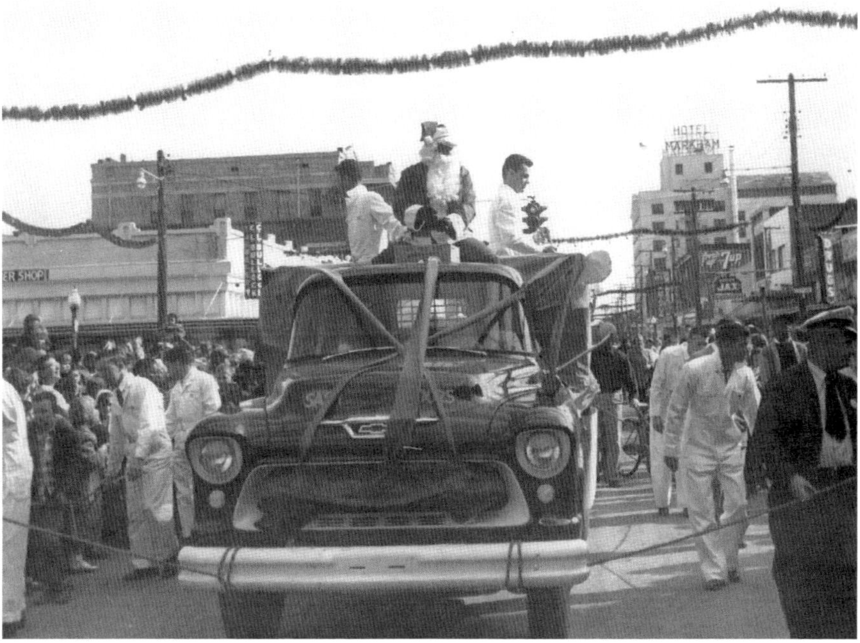

Santa arrived at Sears in Gulfport and was featured in the Christmas parades each year as he traveled down the main streets of the city on a bright-red fire engine. *Santa Claus, Clayton Rand Papers, Manuscripts Division, Special Collections Department, Mississippi State University Libraries.*

Sears took on a special role at Christmastime in Gulfport. It was the official location of Santa Claus. When Santa arrived in town, he was featured in a Christmas parade as he traveled down the main streets of the city on a bright-red fire engine. At the end of the parade, Santa settled in his special chair at the top of the wooden stairs at the old Sears and Roebuck store. There he greeted the children, gave out special comic books and took requests for presents until the Sears store closed on Christmas Eve. He was the only Santa in town. There were no "Santa's Helpers" on every corner and in every store the way there are today. To the children of Gulfport in the early '50s, the only "real" Santa was at Sears and Roebuck.

BRUMFIELD'S DEPARTMENT STORE (L-105)

The Brumfield's Department Store was located next to the new Sears store on 25th Avenue. Mr. Joe W. Brumfield settled in Pascagoula in 1919 and started Brumfield's Department Store there in 1921.

After first driving a taxi, he went to work at a men's clothing store, and by 1923, he owned the store. As the business expanded, he brought in his brother and sister to help. Under Joe's leadership, Brumfield's grew into a premier men's clothing store. The Pascagoula store became the headquarters for a chain of Brumfield stores that prospered from the '30s to the '50s in Biloxi, Moss Point, Fairhope and Bay Minette, Alabama, as well as at this store in Gulfport. Brumfield's employed hundreds at one time along the coast and would have continued to grow if Joe had not died at a very young age. The family sold the business in the late '60s.

HEWES BROTHERS DEPARTMENT STORE (L-105)

In the late '60s, Charles P. Hewes and Archibald C. Hewes, two brothers from an old and respected Gulfport family, opened the Hewes Brothers Department Store at 1310 25th Avenue. This was the former location of Brumfield's Department Store. Hewes Brothers featured an economical line of men's suits, shirts and sport coats. The business was open for forty-eight years until Hurricane Katrina destroyed the building in 2005. The brothers decided against reopening the business, and the Hewes Brothers Department Store was closed forever.

FURNITURE STORES

J.C. CLOWER FURNITURE STORE (J-62)

In 1894, Josiah Coger Clower moved from his home in Hillsboro, Mississippi, and opened his first furniture store on the coast in Biloxi. In 1911, Clower opened this furniture store in Gulfport and quickly became an honored addition to the city's merchants. J.C. Clower Furniture Store sold carpets, furniture, lamps, stoves and assorted furnishings for the home and patio. In the early '60s, the store moved to a smaller space on 27th Avenue (J-51). J.C. Penney expanded into this space after Clower moved. Three generations of the Clower family ran the store until it closed for good in 2002.

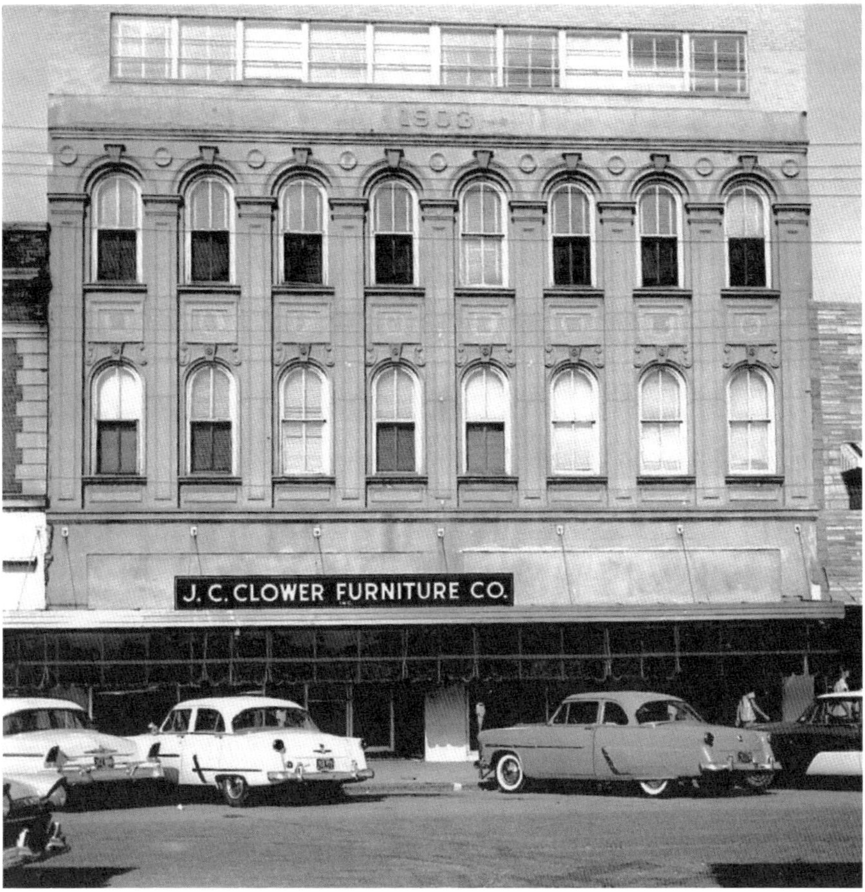

Josiah Coger Clower opened this furniture store in Gulfport and quickly became an honored addition to the city's merchants. *J.C. Clower Furniture Store, Clayton Rand Papers, Manuscripts Division, Special Collections Department, Mississippi State University Libraries.*

Maxie Broadus Furniture Store (N-130)

Maxie Broadus owned and operated this small furniture store next to the *Daily Herald* building until he later moved to a new location in north Gulfport on Highway 49. Broadus served as Harrison County sheriff in 1943, having beaten his opponent, Deputy Sheriff Arthur W. Lang, by only twenty-eight votes. Broadus carried a medium grade of furniture, reasonably priced for all families.

Gillis Furniture Company (P-140)

The Gillis Furniture Company was next to Totsy's before moving to a new location on 14th Street. The company had been around Gulfport for several years and had moved to several different locations around downtown. It carried modest furniture and never competed with the more upscale J.C. Clower Furniture Company.

When the Gillis Company moved to 14th Street in the '50s, the space next to Totsy's was taken over by the Wharton Furniture Company (Q-78). Frank and Allie Wharton owned and operated the store. They also owned the old Pierre Saucier home, Union Quarter and Wharton Hardware in Pass Christian.

Standard Furniture Company (R-192)

The Standard Furniture Company was one of the smaller furniture companies in Gulfport. In the later '50s, the store moved here on 25th Avenue.

Five-and-Dime Stores

McCrory's Five and Dime (D-9)

Walking in front of McCrory's Five and Dime, we shuffle through a flock of pigeons strutting around on the sidewalk. The birds always gathered en masse in front of the store, begging for handouts from the shoppers.

McCrory's was part of a national chain of five-and-dime stores based in York, Pennsylvania. The stores sold shoes, clothing, housewares, fabrics, penny candy, toys and cosmetics. McCrory's lunch counter was also a favorite with shoppers, featuring some of the best sandwiches, hamburgers and milkshakes in town. Many people came to the store just to enjoy the banana splits. The cost of a banana split varied based on a game the customer could play. Several different prices were written on pieces of paper and placed in balloons. Diners could choose a balloon to pop. The price that was on the paper inside the balloon was the price the customer was charged.

F.W. WOOLWORTH (K-78)
The building that housed the Dixie Theatre was one of the three storefronts that would later become part of Woolworth. Woolworth is a five-and-dime store. Merchandise was displayed on flat counters rather than on stacked metal shelves like most stores use today. Woolworth's counters were particularly nice, made of dark-brown wood and constructed with features like fine pieces of furniture. Merchandise was separated on the tables by glass inserts that could be adjusted to accommodate different sizes. The height of the tables was just perfect for kids to see the toys at eye level.

The Woolworth lunch counter was the most memorable feature of the store. The counter ran along the north wall with a row of red vinyl stools along the front. The lunch counter was crowded at lunch with businessmen and shoppers alike, much the same way food courts are in today's malls. The menu included favorites like triple-decker toasted bacon, lettuce and cheese sandwiches for fifty cents; triple-decker toasted chicken salad sandwiches for sixty-five cents; super jumbo banana splits with choice of strawberry,

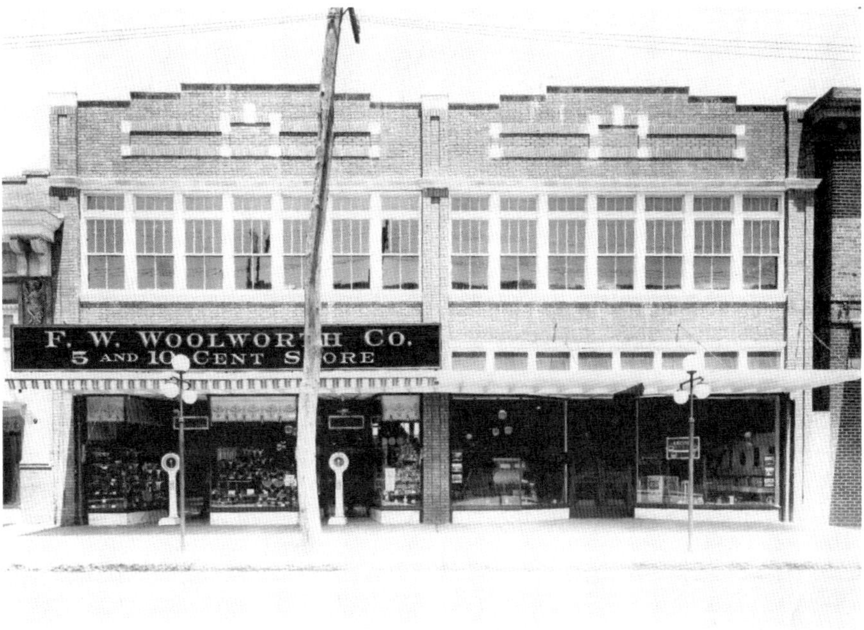

Three individual storefronts were connected to form the one large Woolworth store. This photo shows two of the storefronts. *Shaw Design Group Collection.*

pineapple, cherry, chocolate or hot fudge syrups topped with whipped topping and toasted nuts for thirty-nine cents; and so much more. We would often drop in for a delicious ice cream sundae after a movie at the Paramount Theatre next door.

SCOTTIE DISCOUNT STORE (L-117)

Scottie Discount Store in downtown Gulfport was located in the old Rosenblum's Women's Wear space in the east corner of the H&H Hotel building on 14th Street. The store was a discount variety store selling a wide range of items like health and beauty aids, greeting cards, magazines, housewares, records and tapes, fabrics, cigarettes, cameras, film and processing and fishing equipment.

In 1969, when Hancock Bank, which was across the alley, took over the bottom two store spaces in the H&H Hotel building, Scottie was forced to move. Scottie relocated to the old Hurd's Style Shop space shortly before Camille destroyed many of the downtown buildings. Scottie moved again to a smaller location on 14th Street next to the Standard Furniture Store.

LYLE'S VARIETY STORE

John Lewis Lyle was born and raised in Petal, Mississippi. The youngest of eight children, he was left to care for his mother when his older siblings grew up and left home. Needing money for the family, he rode his bicycle to nearby Hattiesburg looking for work when he was still a youngster in school. He applied for a job at the local Woolworth's store but was told there were no openings. Young Lyle was persistent and returned daily to Woolworth, asking for a job only to be turned down time and time again. The manager of Woolworth was impressed by John's apparent sincerity and desire for work, and he eventually hired him. Starting from the ground up, his honesty and hard work paid off, and it wasn't long before he was promoted. As he continued to show his dedication, the promotions continued until he was eventually transferred to Georgia to a managerial position. While serving as manager of the Woolworth's in Norfolk, Virginia, he met his wife. He was finally transferred to manage the Gulfport store in 1948.

In 1952, John Lyle, an entrepreneur at heart, left his secure job as manager of the Gulfport Woolworth store to open his own five-and-dime. Lyle's Variety Store, located on Pass Road, was popular and successful from the beginning. The day of the grand opening was quite festive. Even the governor of Mississippi attended.

John Lyle was very creative and looked for improved ways to do things. His new store incorporated many of these new ideas. Lyle's Variety Store was one of the first stores on the coast to offer a self-service experience for the customers, where shoppers could pick up what they wanted and take the items to the register for check out. At Woolworth, people had to wait for assistance from the sales clerks. John Lyle also neatly organized his store into separate departments and carried just about everything imaginable. The store even sold parakeets, canaries and myna birds that Mr. Lyle raised in his own backyard.

John had a knack for marketing. Many of his old customers will remember how at Christmas he had the salespeople dressed as Santa's helpers working the cash registers and restocking shelves. As a promotion, he even had circus animals at the store for the children to ride. His daughter recalls riding one of the elephants in the Christmas parade downtown.

From the beginning, there was a steady flow of customers through the store, as well as at the Jitney Jungle grocery store next door. One day, the Jitney Jungle store caught fire only feet away from Lyle's. Lyle's Variety Store was not damaged, but unfortunately the fire disrupted business enough to cause Lyle concern. In addition to the negative impact on his business caused by the fire, other similar stores were beginning to crop up in the area. To stay ahead of the competition, Lyle began adding fabrics, customized draperies and floor coverings. As that part of the business became more successful, John transformed Lyle's Variety Store into Lyle's Carpet Mart. The carpet business became as successful with Gulfport shoppers as the five-and-dime store had been.

Lyle's store continued to operate until 1987, when John was diagnosed with pancreatic cancer. He sold the business and died shortly after Christmas that year at the age of seventy-seven.

Throughout his career, John Lyle was a well-respected member of the community. He loved music and could play the piano by ear. He had a great faith in God and treated his customers the way he would want to be treated. Not being able to attend college was his greatest regret. He was proof that with hard work and determination, anyone can succeed.

FAMOUS HOUSES

Cahill Mansion

Unlike the Gutman House, the Cahill Mansion is not admired for its architecture or even its positive place in the community. The Cahill Mansion is more about "ghoulies and ghosties, and long-legged beasties, and things that go bump in the night." The Cahill Mansion was a true haunted house, and anyone who grew up in Gulfport during the '50s has probably heard the stories.

This large, three-story dormitory-like structure was located at 10 Kimball Drive on a bluff overlooking Bayou Bernard. The house was built in 1915 about a block and a half east of Courthouse Road on five and a half acres of overgrown trees and untended flowers. The backyard sloped down to the bayou and was covered with shrubs and blooming azaleas. In relationship to the city of Gulfport, it was considered "way out there" at the time, but in the '50s, the property was part of the upscale Bayou View subdivision.

The house had been built by Joseph T. Jones, one of Gulfport's founders, and given to his son and daughter-in-law, Grace Stewart, as a wedding present. Ownership changed several times between 1915 and 1941, with several different families occupying the home. In 1941, the United States Air Force leased the house for use as a noncommissioned officers' club. The sergeant who had been assigned to run the club began to bring in gambling equipment, which was set up in the large master bedroom. Not only did the club offer gambling to the airmen, but a steady flow of prostitutes was also provided. When the sergeant's superior officers discovered the illegal operation, the club was immediately shut down.

In the mid-'40s, shortly after the end of World War II, Dr. Richard Newell Cahill, a local chiropractor, purchased the house and lived there with his wife, Rebecca Cox; his daughter, Mae Jean; and his son, Richard, called "Richie." The house was really not much of a mansion but rather just a large, rambling house in need of repairs even when the Cahills moved in.

The house had three floors, which was unusually large for houses on the coast. The nine-foot-high front doorway opened into the living room. Next to the living room was a gigantic den with a fireplace. All the ceilings on the ground floor were at least ten feet high. The kitchen was off the living room, as was the dining room. A full bathroom was next to the kitchen. A staircase led up to a long sleeping porch in the rear that ran the whole length of the house on the second floor. Each of the three bedrooms upstairs opened onto the porch, which was eventually glassed in by a future owner. The enormous

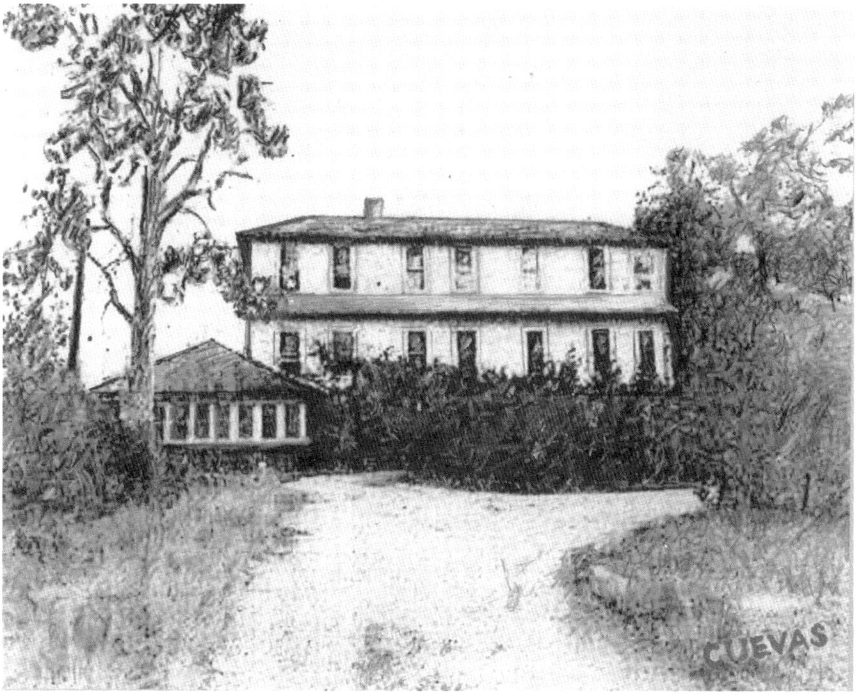

The Cahill Mansion was a true haunted house, and anyone who grew up in Gulfport during the '50s has probably heard the stories. *Author's collection.*

master bedroom was directly above the massive den. Although huge and cumbersome, the house still had a certain mysterious charm.

In the spring of 1953, a tragedy occurred that was at the root of the mansion's sinister hauntings. On March 14, young Richie Cahill and a ninth-grade classmate were together in the backyard. Richie, age fourteen, was playing on a tractor that was being used to pull stumps in the rear of the property. Like a typical teenager, Richie began showing off by doing wheelies with the tractor to impress his friend. The friend sensed the danger and warned Richie to be careful. The next day, on March 15, at about 2:00 p.m. in the afternoon, Richie was on the tractor again, but this time it flipped, rolling over and pinning Richie underneath. His mother rushed to his aid. He didn't seem to be injured at first, but when she later noticed him turning pale, she immediately called for an ambulance. Unfortunately, Richie died of internal bleeding on the way to the hospital. His funeral was held at the First United Methodist Church in downtown Gulfport, and his body was buried at Evergreen, the city cemetery. The Cahill family never really got over Richie's death, and four years later, they moved out of the house.

In September 1957, Dr. Kendall D. Gregory, a prominent internist in Gulfport, and his wife, Virginia, bought the Cahill place and moved in with their rather large family. The house was in such bad shape that the much-needed repairs were too costly and were never completed, leaving the house in a deteriorating condition.

Strange events began shortly after the Gregorys moved in. At first, footsteps were heard on the upstairs porch when no one was there. Later, when one of the sons was about five, he told his parents that the closet door in his bedroom was moving back and forth. Of course, they thought he was dreaming and didn't take him seriously. On another occasion, he told them that he woke up and there was someone leaning over him with their faces almost touching. Frightened, the boy jumped up and turned on the lights, but whatever it was had vanished.

One night, the boy's sister was sleeping in his room, and at about 2:00 a.m., she woke up to see a figure come out of the closet and stand next to her by the bed. The bed was against the wall, so there wasn't any room for anyone to stand there. The terrified girl watched as the apparition appeared to walk through her and then went away.

Dr. Kendall and Virginia were skeptical at first, of course, because everyone knows that there are no such things as ghosts. But after experiencing loud screams, heavy objects being dragged across the floor and some strange apparitions, the spirits in the Cahill Mansion could not be ignored.

In 1969, the Kendalls allowed paranormal researcher Suzy Smith to come to the house and investigate. In her book *Ghosts Around the House* (World Pub. Company, 1970), Smith reported some of the strange events that took place in the old house. In her chapter "The Doctor's Dilemma," she tells of a visitor who was interrupted while on the telephone by a young boy who stood next to her. When she scolded him for listening in on her conversation, the boy stared blankly at her, walked out of the room and disappeared. When the Kendalls showed the woman some old school pictures, she unknowingly identified the boy as Richie Cahill. She was so convinced that what she saw was real that she immediately submitted to a sworn statement.

When two other researchers asked Mrs. Kendall for permission to take pictures of the house, she confirmed an interesting fact. There are no photos of the interior of the Cahill Mansion, even of the families at Christmas, birthdays or other special occasions. Exposed film would not process properly. The researchers thanked her for the information and proceeded to carefully load film into their Nikon camera. After spending an afternoon shooting pictures, they opened it to take the film for processing and discovered that there was no film in the camera.

After the apparitions were becoming physical with grabbing, pushing and shoving, the owners closed the house and would no longer allow visitors for fear they might be hurt. They also announced that the old house would be demolished and a new house would be built on the property. The insurance on the big house had become prohibitive. Some of the researchers who had studied the paranormal activities with the use of a Ouija board had received messages from the alleged spirits warning that the house would be destroyed by fire before the spirits would allow it to be demolished.

One of the Kendall children reported that in the summer of 1971, the Cahill mansion was almost destroyed by two consecutive fires. Both fires were determined to be the work of the same arsonist, Bill Oliver. Oliver, as it turned out, was a close childhood friend of little Richie Cahill's and wanted to burn down the house to set Richie's soul free. Mrs. Kendall turned the house over to the fire department for practice drills. Once the Cahill Mansion was leveled, a new house was built, and the property was subdivided.

FLYING SAUCER HOUSE

The Gutman House, located on the north side of Bayou Circle in the Bayou View subdivision, was unique because of its otherworldly design. Called the "Star of David" house, it was also known as the "Flying Saucer" house because it looked like a spacecraft hovering among the pines along the south shore of Gulfport Lake. It was designed by Bruce Goff (1904–1982) and built for the Emil Gutman family in 1958.

Bruce Goff was one of the most inventive architects of the twentieth century. Considered to be a child prodigy, he started in architecture at the age of twelve. The majority of his projects were private residences, although he also designed both large- and small-scale commercial and civic buildings in fifteen different states. His organic designs defy classification.

Goff spent a considerable amount of time with the Gutmans, as he did with all his clients, to learn their likes and dislikes. Only after understanding his clients' individual personalities did he present them with his plans. According to a July 25, 1960 article by Marie Langlois, a feature writer for the Gulfport/Biloxi *Daily Herald*, Goff considered the Gutman home "the creation of a lifetime" and the best thing he had done.

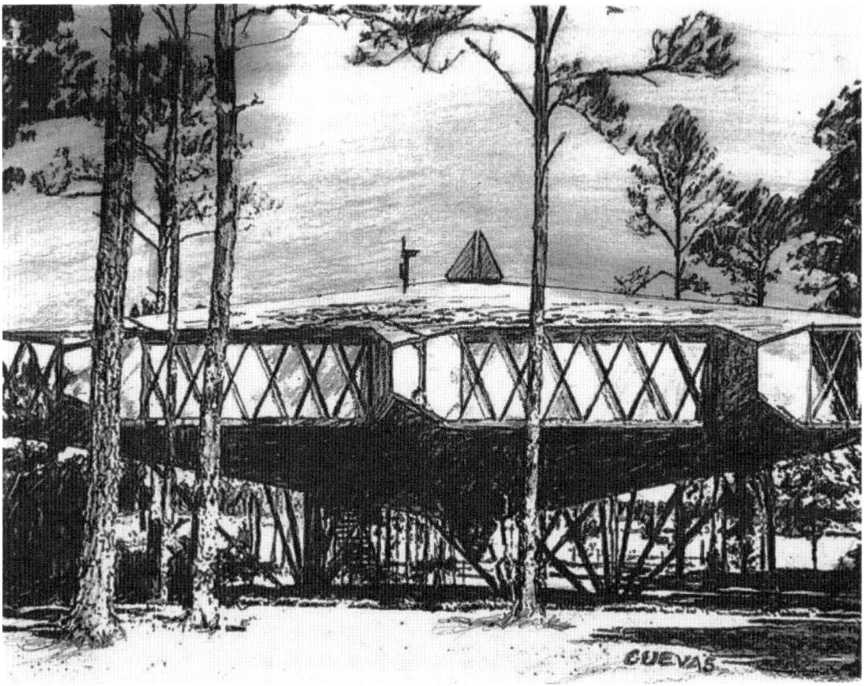

The "Star of David" house, also known as the "Flying Saucer" house, looked like a spacecraft hovering among the pines on Gulfport Lake. *Author's collection.*

While many believed that its basic design was the Star of David, it was not. In fact, the house was actually a perfect triangle, with three structural sides perched on metal poles fifteen feet above the concrete base. It was quite a sight, since no one had ever seen anything like it. At first, there was a continuous line of curiosity seekers that slowly passed the house daily.

When the "Flying Saucer House" was completed, the world was in the middle of an obsession with extraterrestrial visitors. By the late 1950s and early 1960s, sightings of alien aircraft were being reported almost daily all around the globe. The interest in unidentified spacecraft had grown out of the U.S. military's fear that the Soviet Union might have developed secret weapons in space, so it was understandable how the name "Flying Saucer House" became associated with the Gutman home. Other architects of the period had actually incorporated the flying saucer theme in their structures. The most notable is the revolving restaurant on top of the Space Needle that served as the unofficial symbol of the 1962 Seattle World's Fair.

Although it appeared small, the house had three thousand square feet of living space containing three full-sized bedrooms, two and a half baths, plenty of spacious closets and a large storage and utility room. The entire interior flowed together through the use of a specially chosen turquoise-colored wall-to-wall carpet throughout that complemented the pumpkin-colored accent of the cabinets. The unusual shape of the house was designed so that every room would have a sweeping view of the Gulfport Lake, and it was elevated fifteen feet above the ground for the family's privacy, as well as to guard against flooding from the lake.

The Gulf Coast was fortunate to have the only two Bruce Goff–designed houses in Mississippi. In addition to the Gutman House in Gulfport, there was also his creation known as the "Cat House" in Ocean Springs. Located at 1212 Iola Road in a quiet, unassuming neighborhood on Old Fort Bayou, it incorporates flowing whimsical concrete forms and even a moat. The house, built for the W.C. Gryder family, became eligible for listing in the U.S. National Register of Historic Places. From the front, the house gives the appearance of a crouching cat, leading to the popular name. The Cat House was built in 1960, two years after the Gutman House, and is the only one of the two houses still in existence. The Gutman House was destroyed by fire in 1986.

Merry Mansion

One of the true stately mansions in Gulfport is also probably the one locals remember most because of its distinctive architecture, as well as its prominent location on the west corner of Highway 90 and Lorraine-Cowan Road. Henry M. Piaggio started building the beautiful Italian villa in 1915 for his wife, Margaret Muldowned of Mount Vernon, Ohio. Unfortunately, Henry died before it was completed.

Henry Piaggio was born on March 17, 1874, in Genoa, Italy. His father, who was a wealthy businessman, owned a successful timber exporting business based in Pensacola, Florida. When he was about eighteen years old, Henry moved to Florida from Italy to learn all about his father's timber business from the ground up.

Henry moved to Gulfport from Pensacola in about 1903 to start his own timber export business. The port of Gulfport was experiencing a surge in growth handling timber from around the state, and Henry recognized the great potential. The abundance of longleaf pine—found almost exclusively in the southern portion of the United States in massive forests stretching from Virginia to Texas—had created a boom for the port of Gulfport. There

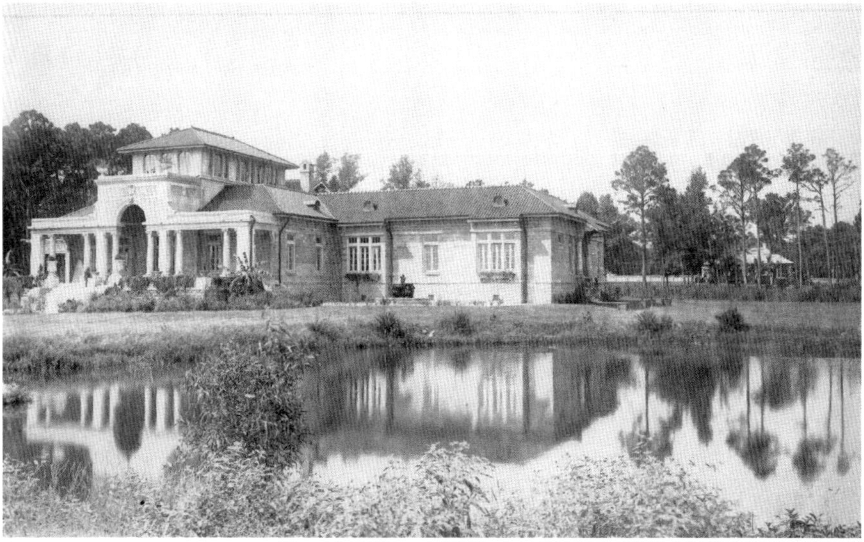

Henry M. Piaggio started building this beautiful Italian villa in 1915 for his wife, Margaret Muldowned, but he died before it was completed. *Paul Jermyn Collection.*

was a worldwide demand for heart pine lumber because of the durable nature of the wood.

His timber business prospered, but in 1916, Henry saw a new opportunity. During World War I, the United States suffered huge shipping losses, and there was a need to replenish the naval force. The Piaggio family in Italy had also been successful in the shipbuilding industry, so with his family's knowledge, Henry decided to start a shipbuilding operation. Although wooden sailing ships were no longer being used, Piaggio saw an opportunity to blend his timber business with the wooden sailing ships. The U.S. government had strict controls over all shipbuilding except for sailing ships. Without having to deal with government oversight, Henry formed the International Shipbuilding Company. He opened shipyards in Orange, Texas, and Pascagoula.

With the success of this new business venture, Henry felt a desire to build a magnificent home befitting someone of his position. He selected well-known architects Burton and Bendernagel from New Orleans. The style of the house was Renaissance Revival, featuring Ionic columns across the front accented with concrete urns full of colorful flowers. Seven marble steps led up to the portico. Tall, narrow windows accented the front. The interior was like a museum with marble floors throughout and mahogany paneling covering the walls. Murals of cherubs painted by artists whom Henry had brought over from Italy adorned the ceilings in the large, stately rooms. Long hallways ran on both sides of the house. It was truly a mansion in every sense of the word.

Although it was not evident from the front, the house was never completed. Construction on the mansion stopped when Piaggio was apparently fired as president of his shipbuilding enterprise a short time before his death. He had been accused of embezzlement from the firm. He died about a year later in 1921 at the young age of forty-seven, leaving his widow, Margaret, alone and without support. She was eventually forced to leave the mansion and move to a small cottage on the property in the back.

In 1924, Charles Glenn Collins of New Orleans acquired the home. According to the *Jackson County Times* in 1924, he planned to convert the building into the Gulf Coast Sanitarium, which was to be used by Louisiana and Mississippi physicians. This never happened, and the house stood vacant until World War II.

The club era of the Piaggio estate began during the war, when the U.S. government converted the stately mansion into a lavish officers' organization called the Embassy Club. The military used the house until after the war. In the early 1950s, it was converted to a private dinner club called the Merry Mansion.

The Merry Mansion became famous all over the country for its lush surroundings, great food and top-notch entertainment. Chef Joe Famiglio served such specialties as filet mignon, porterhouse steaks and fried milk-fed chickens. Regular dinner was served in the paneled dining rooms from 5:00 p.m. until 9:30 p.m. There was dancing nightly until 1:30 a.m. in the lounge to the vocal stylings of Miss Joy Gimel, the featured vocalist of the Bob Slade Orchestra. Other great orchestras also played. The club was the classiest the coast had ever seen. It was the *in* place to be. Much of the appeal was the gambling that the club offered. Slot machines were in the lounge for everyone to try their luck.

The Merry Mansion lasted through the early '50s. In 1955, the widow Piaggio died, and the property again lay vacant. After the club closed, a local liquor distributor used the building to store his stock.

August 17, 1969, marked the end of the Piaggio home, when Hurricane Camille devastated the coast and completely destroyed the Merry Mansion, leaving the stately villa in a pile of rubble. The mansion was never rebuilt.

FEDERAL, COUNTY AND CITY SERVICES

CITY BUS SERVICE (D-10)

The transit bus service in Gulfport during the '50s was excellent. The buses were large, with two doors for ease of boarding and exiting—one that opened in the front side near the driver and one toward the back. Next to the driver's seat was a gumball-shaped container for depositing the fares. The seats were bench style, with only minimal storage above. There were handrails running above the aisle on each side for riders to hold on to while standing. There were designated routes with designated stops along the bus routes. A concrete marker about five feet high and four inches square identified the stops. Riders who wanted to get off the bus at a particular stop would pull a cord that ran along the top of the windows on each side. If no one rang to get off and there was no one waiting at the stop to get on the bus, the driver would choose to keep going and pass the stop. The buses ran on schedule, with one bus about every thirty minutes. There was the Handsboro bus that ran along Pass Road and then buses from the west side of town and up Highway 49 to the Milk of Magnesia plant.

Riders wishing to go from one area to another would have to change buses. The transfer point for the city bus service was on the sidewalk in front of McCrory's. Often, there were as many as three or more buses lined up waiting to start their routes. A roll-type sign above the front of the bus notified riders as to the route. Sidewalk benches were provided for waiting passengers. To pass the time while waiting for their bus, riders would share morsels of food from the McCrory's lunch counter with the pigeons. The birds had become so tame that they would almost eat out of the shoppers' hands.

GULFPORT POST OFFICE (F-23)

The Gulfport Post Office is on the southeast corner of 25th Avenue and 13th Street. Originally known as the Federal Building, it is an impressive structure built in 1910 on a base of Georgia granite with walls of extraordinarily white limestone. In the early 1950s, mail delivery service did not extend to north Gulfport, where I lived, so my family and other residents outside the central district had to rent a mailbox in this post office. I would ride into town with my father to check the mail. I still remember the grand feeling I had as I climbed the stone steps to enter the building. The post office seemed so regal. I felt as though I were in a big city. The interior of the post office was equally impressive with its marble

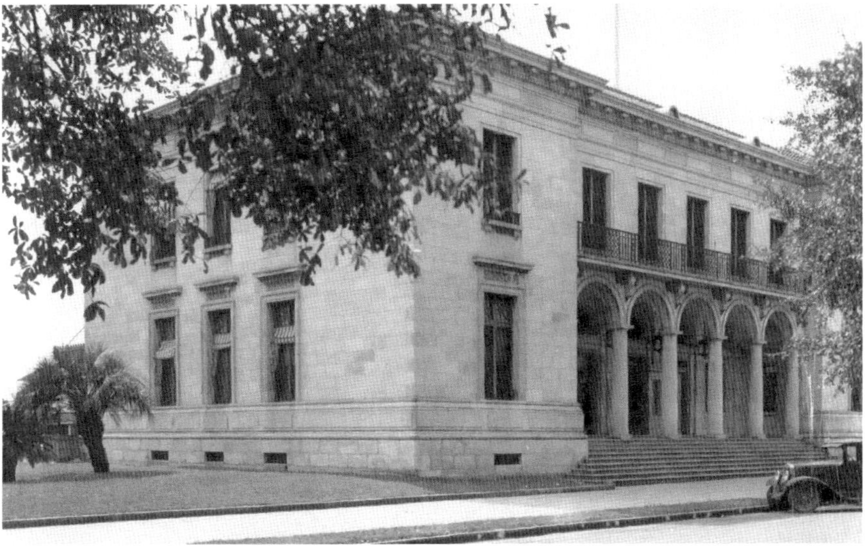

Originally known as the Federal Building, the Gulfport Post Office is an impressive structure built on a base of Georgia granite with walls of extraordinarily white limestone. *Paul Jermyn Collection.*

floors and stained wood walls. There were even brass spittoons, a reminder of days gone by, although I could hardly imagine that anyone would ever use them. To a child, the building seemed solid and reassuring, unlike the almost throwaway look of many post offices today.

GULFPORT CARNEGIE LIBRARY (M-120)

The Gulfport Carnegie Library was one of 2,800 free public libraries throughout the country financed by steel magnate and philanthropist Andrew Carnegie. This was not, however, the first library in Gulfport. Mayor George M. Foote had provided a room for a library in city hall. The books, which were mostly donated, quickly outgrew the space. The Library Association decided to take advantage of Carnegie's generosity and put in a request for a grant. The Carnegie Corporation approved the application, and Gulfport became the first library on the coast funded by Andrew Carnegie. The library opened on November 20, 1916.

Captain Jones had donated land on which to build a courthouse. After the courthouse was completed, it was decided that land left over would be a perfect location for the new Carnegie Library. So, with Jones's blessing, the county donated the land to the city for the library.

An article in the *Daily Herald* described the new building: "The library is a thoroughly modern concrete foundation and press brick front building of classic architecture. It is lighted by electricity, using the eye comfort system of lighting fixtures and heated by hot water. It is plastered throughout. Its ground floor will contain a very spacious lecture room, trustees, staff and clubroom, storeroom, heater room and toilet room. The first floor will be devoted entirely to the librarian's room, stack room, reading room and children's room, and this floor will be decorated in ornamental plaster and mill work." The building is magnificent.

The Carnegie Library holds fond memories for many who grew up in the '50s. Each year, elementary school students were assigned a summer reading list. Completing a summer reading list was a challenge for those children who would rather be out riding their bicycles or swimming at the Markham Hotel pool. But those students who persevered came to realize that there was something special about going through the stacks of books and discovering new topics in the reverent quietness of the library.

The Harrison County Courthouse (M-121)

The Harrison County Courthouse building was opened in 1903. Mississippi City was the original seat of Harrison County. The seat was moved to Gulfport in 1902.

The Confederate Monument (M-122)

The Confederate Monument standing in front of the Harrison County Courthouse was placed there through the efforts of the United Daughters of the Confederacy. There were some who preferred the monument to be located in front of the Federal Building on 13th Street because of the greater visibility. That location was abandoned in favor of the courthouse when it was discovered that a sewer line under 13th Street made the ground too soft to support the bronze statue's tremendous weight. The statue was dedicated on Thanksgiving Day 1911.

Social Security Office (Q-168)

The Social Security Office was located here on 26th Avenue. When the office eventually moved, the Mill End Fabric store opened here in 1960.

MISSISSIPPI STATE EMPLOYMENT OFFICE (S-222)

The Mississippi State Employment Office was located here on 14th Street. The agency provided a service to Mississippians who are unemployed. Through a network of job centers, it matched qualified employees with employers. The service also included administering the unemployment benefits program to assist workers who had lost their jobs by providing temporary compensation while they searched for a new job.

GULFPORT CITY HALL (U-231)

The Gulfport City Hall is a two-story building facing 15th Street. Four impressive Corinthian columns characterize the front. The solid, old-fashioned tongue-and-groove roof decking is more than one hundred years old. H.D. Moore was the mayor of Gulfport when the city hall was built in 1905.

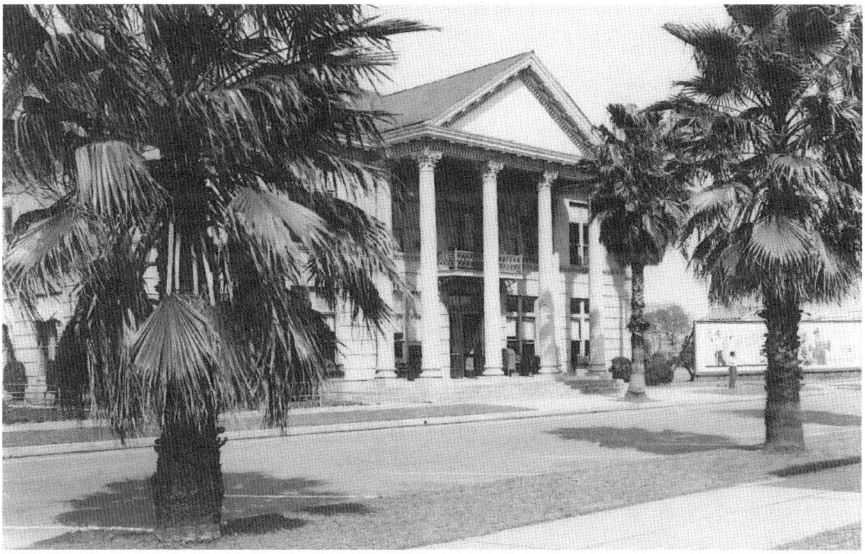

The solid, old-fashioned tongue-and-groove roof decking of the Gulfport City Hall is more than one hundred years old. *Paul Jermyn Collection.*

GULFPORT FIRE DEPARTMENT (U-232)

The Gulfport Fire Department was on the north end of 24th Avenue near the railroad tracks. There was an interior garage large enough for one fire engine. The building also housed the Gulfport Police Station and City Jail.

GULFPORT POLICE STATION AND CITY JAIL (U-233)

The Gulfport Police Station and the City Jail were in the same building with the fire department. Prisoners could often be heard yelling through the bars of the open windows, since the jail was not air-conditioned at that time.

UTILITIES

THE POWER PLANT (A-1)

The tour begins in front of a large imposing structure on the corner of Highway 90 and 30th Avenue. Although heavy traffic passed it regularly, many people probably never gave it much thought. The feature that was most prominent was the tall, round chimney that often belched out black smoke. This was the original power plant, built by Captain Jones and his Mississippi Coast Traction Company for the Great Southern Hotel. In

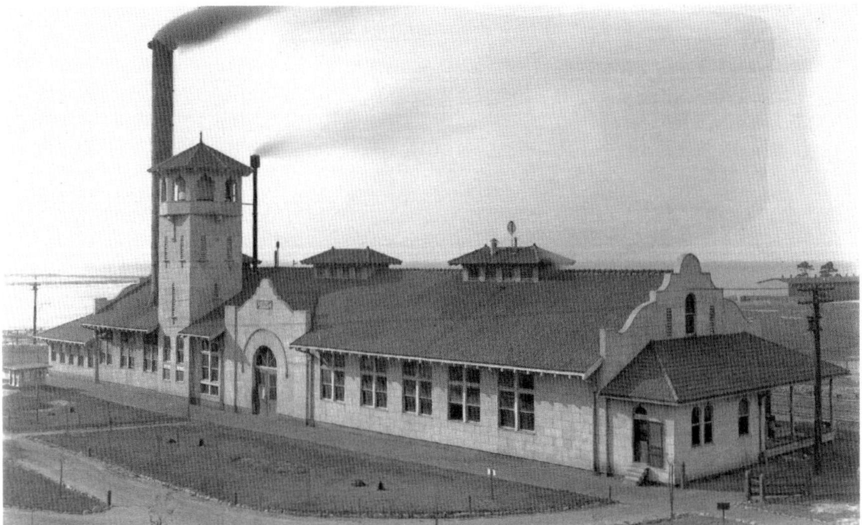

This was the original power plant built by Captain Jones and his Mississippi Coast Traction Company for the Great Southern Hotel. *Paul Jermyn Collection.*

addition, this plant also provided power to the trolley line that ran along the beach and in town. By the late '50s, the plant was no longer functional and was replaced.

MISSISSIPPI POWER COMPANY (K-92)

Mississippi Power Company was established in 1938. In 1949, it became a wholly owned subsidiary of the Southern Company based in Atlanta. The Southern Company also includes Georgia Power, Alabama Power and Gulf Power in Florida. In 1976, the Mississippi Power Company name was shortened to Mississippi Power.

This was the headquarters of Mississippi Power Company before the new corporate office building was constructed at the corner of 30th Avenue and Highway 90 on the site of Captain Jones's power plant for the Great Southern Hotel. Mississippi Power's appliance store and bill payment center was next to the Toggery. A staircase to the right of the store led upstairs to the Mississippi Power Company engineering center and offices.

UNITED GAS COMPANY OFFICE (Q-166)

This was a storefront in the H&H Hotel building. The United Gas Company office was originally operating in the H&H Hotel during much of the early to mid-'50s, at which time the gas company moved to a new office building across from the GRC on 22nd Avenue and 15th Street.

United Gas Corporation was a major oil company second only in size to Gulf Oil. It was started in 1930 and served the Mississippi Gulf Coast until 1968, when it was forced to merge with Penzoil. The gas distribution section became Entex Energy in 1970. The company was headquartered in Shreveport, Louisiana, and according to annual reports, in 1953 United Gas owned and operated more than nine thousand field and transmission lines serving 309 cities, towns and communities. ADS (American Discount Store) finally opened in this location.

The United Gas Company erected its new office building on the corner of 23rd Avenue and 15th Street. The gas company offices were moved into its new building in the late '50s (V-235).

WESTERN UNION OFFICE (R-194)

This was Gulfport's Western Union Office. For those too young to remember, Western Union was the closest thing we had to the Internet. We could transfer money from person to person, purchase money orders and make payments to our creditors just the way we do online today. We could also send and receive messages almost overnight.

Southern Bell Telephone Office (R-203)
The offices of the Southern Bell Telephone Company were located on 24th Avenue. A desk inside on the first floor was set up for making bill payments, connecting or disconnecting phone service or to conduct other telephone business. The switchboard operators and the actual mechanical connections were located down the block in the Southern Bell Telephone & Telegraph Exchange Building (R-206).

HOME IMPROVEMENT AND REAL ESTATE SALES

Appliance Stores

Campbell Appliance Company (E-20)
Campbell Appliance Company was a trusted appliance store in Gulfport. The store not only carried a line of household appliances but also offered in-home repair. It occupied this space for a short time before the Purple Lantern took over this location and the Be-Wise Food Store space next door.

André Appliances (Q-179)
André Appliances was located on 25th Avenue next to Brumfield's Bargain Annex. André carried a small range of appliances but was never able to compete with the larger stores like Sears.

McDaniel Refrigeration Sales & Service (S-219)
McDaniel Refrigeration Sales & Service next to the Hatten Building was a trusted company in Gulfport that sold and repaired washers, dryers, refrigerators and freezers. In addition, McDaniel sold and serviced window unit air conditioners.

Hardware and Paint Stores

Barber's Hardware (J-46)

Jerome Barber owned Barber's Hardware on the east corner of 27th Avenue and 13th Street. Only a growing town like Gulfport was in the '50s could support so many hardware stores, including the big stores like Sears, which was known for its excellent tools.

Smith-Todd Hardware (K-87)

Smith-Todd Hardware store, located here on 14th Street, was incorporated in 1932 and lasted for more than eighty-four years. The hardware store competed with Sears and other hardware stores but retained a reputation as the preferred in-town source for tools and garden items for home and business.

Gulf Paint & Glass Company (R-191)

Not only did Gulf Paint & Glass Company sell house paint, but it was also the store for artists' paints, brushes and supplies. Anyone who took art from Mrs. Effie Griddley at the GRC bought their oils and canvas from Gulf Paint & Glass.

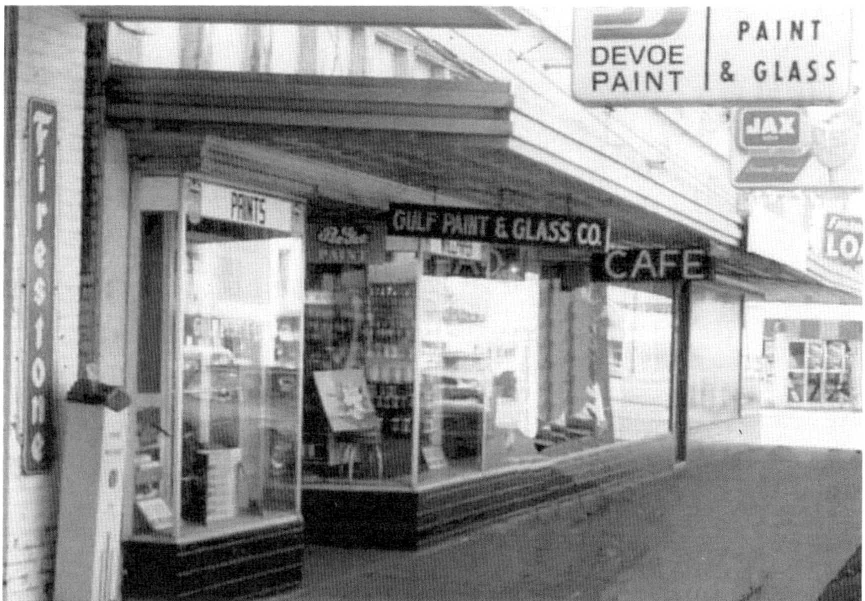

Gulf Paint & Glass Company not only sold house paint, but it was also the store for artists' paints, brushes and supplies. *Paul Jermyn Collection.*

Sherwin-Williams Paint (R-199)

The Sherwin-Williams paint store was on 25th Avenue. Henry Sherwin and Edward Williams started the company in 1866. Sherwin-Williams developed, manufactured and distributed various paints, coatings and related products. The paints were very popular on the coast, especially for their durability.

Real Estate Companies

Myrick Real Estate (J-48)

The Myrick Real Estate office was located next to the Town and Country Shop. Myrick was one of the real estate firms that was well respected during the boom years of Gulfport.

Agar Realty (J-59)

(Later) Fasold's Optometry

Agar Realty was an old and trusted real estate firm in Gulfport. Located on 14th Street, it was next to the M. Salloum Department Store. In the later '50s, Joseph Karl Fasold's youngest son, Joseph Franz Fasold, opened Fasold's Optometry in this space.

Kerr Real Estate (K-94)

The Kerr Real Estate office was next to Toomer's Gift Shop on 25th Avenue. Kerr had been in the real estate business on the coast for a number of years.

HOTELS, BANKS AND OFFICE BUILDINGS

Hotels

Lane Hotel (H-38)

The Lane Hotel on the corner of 13th Street and 28th Avenue was a familiar landmark in downtown Gulfport for much of the '50s. It was famous as much for its coffee shop as for the hotel itself.

LANE HOTEL COFFEE SHOP (H-39)
Many in the downtown area met in the Lane Hotel Coffee Shop for breakfast or midmorning breaks. The donuts were favorites, along with some of the best brewed coffee in the city.

EL MECCA HOTEL AND CAFÉ (J-56)
The El Mecca Hotel was a familiar but mostly ignored hotel in the Bouslog Building on the corner of 14th Street and 27th Avenue. The El Mecca might at one time have been a decent hotel, but most will remember the El Mecca as a cheap flophouse. It catered to transient workers and the homeless poor who needed an inexpensive place to live. The occupants shared bathroom facilities and bunked in small rooms that were more like office cubicles than regular hotel rooms. The El Mecca Café was inside the hotel, serving food mostly to the tenants of the hotel.

SPLENDID HOTEL (K-103)
The Splendid Hotel was one of several small, in-town hotels that served as home to transients and workers from the docks. The entrance faced 13th Street.

MARKHAM HOTEL (M-126)
The grand Markham Hotel, located on the corner of 23rd Avenue and 14th Street, was built in the 1920s at a cost of more than $1 million. This two-hundred-room resort hotel was named for the president of the Illinois Central Railroad, Charles H. Markham. There were several remarkable architectural features. Among them was its beautiful mahogany-paneled

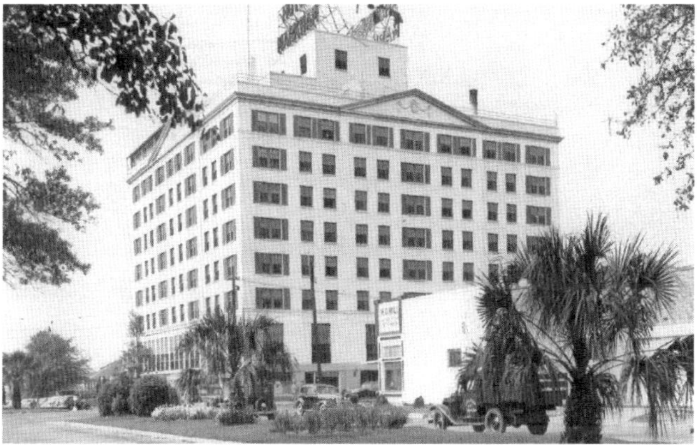

This two-hundred-room resort hotel built in the 1920s was named for the president of the Illinois Central Railroad, Charles H. Markham. *Paul Jermyn Collection.*

lobby that stretched up two floors. At the top of the grand staircase was the mezzanine. Off from the mezzanine was a ballroom. A coffee shop was on the first floor. On the top was a grand ballroom used for formal dances, parties and other fancy occasions. A screened-in sunporch was at the rear of the hotel overlooking the lighted swimming pool.

MARKHAM HOTEL SWIMMING POOL (M-127)

The Markham Hotel Swimming Pool was behind the Markham Hotel on 23rd Avenue. Work began on the aboveground pool in the summer of 1929. It was located on property that had been the site of the Gulfport Women's Club. The club was moved south to a new building on an adjacent lot. The pool was open to the public, ensuring that almost every kid in Gulfport swam in the Markham pool. Many of us took swimming lessons there or just hung out with our friends.

Entrance to the pool was through a turnstile. The pool featured multicolored tile and was partially covered by an awning-type structure with open bracing. There were sprinkler heads in the metal beams overhead that worked much like a misty rain when activated. The pool was more than thirty feet at its deepest to accommodate the high diving board at the far end. A regular diving board was also on the deep end for the kids and the

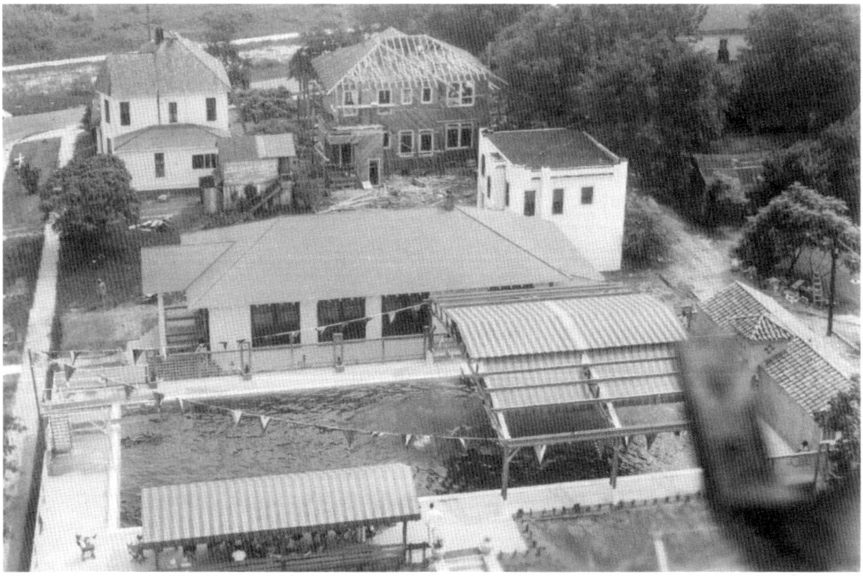

The Markham Hotel pool was open to the public. Almost every kid in Gulfport swam in the Markham pool, and many of us took swimming lessons there. *Paul Jermyn Collection.*

less adventurous. At the opposite end of the pool, near the bathhouse, was a large fountain with a ferocious lion's head that gushed a thick stream of water into a large semi-round concrete bowl.

UNION HOTEL (P-139)
(Later called) LEGION HOTEL
There was an open stairway entrance just to the left of the entrance to the Legion Theatre balcony (later the Gulf Theatre) that led upstairs to the small Union Hotel. The name of this flophouse was changed to the Legion Hotel after the American Legion built the Gulf Theatre there in the '50s. The hotel continued operations into the late '60s.

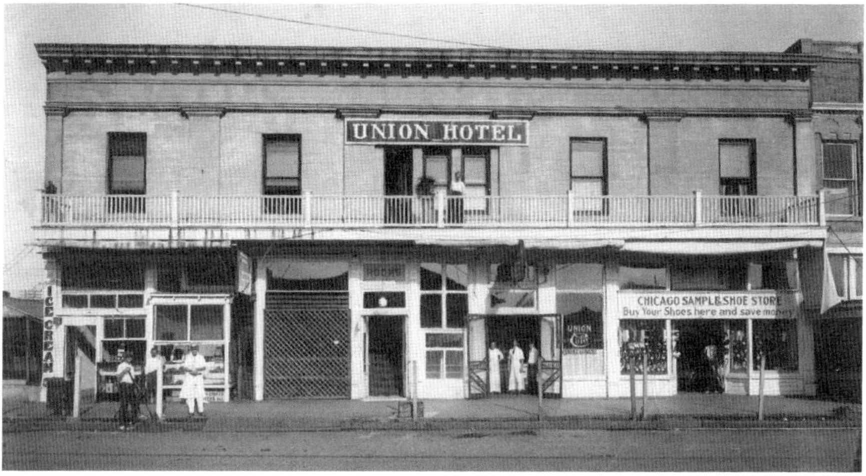

The Union Hotel was renamed the Legion Hotel after the American Legion opened the first Legion theater in the building. *Paul Jermyn Collection.*

RAYNER HOTEL (P-141)
(Later) FRAZIER HOTEL
(Later) NELSON HOTEL
The Rayner Hotel was located on the corner across from the L&N depot and was open until about 1949. It changed hands and became the Frazier Hotel until about 1953, when it was finally changed to the Nelson Hotel.

The Frazier Hotel advertised room and board for fifteen dollars per week in the early '50s. Frank and Allie Wharton, along with Allie's aunt, Margaret Nelson McGrath, operated the hotel until it closed. Margaret McGrath also owned and operated the Nelson Hotel in Pass Christian. She had inherited a number of hotels from her parents. There was also a café in the hotel through the '50s, as well as a barbershop, although the café was not open in the '60s except for a brief period. When the Nelson Hotel was forced to close during the urban renewal period, Allie Wharton was concerned about where the people who had lived there for years would find an affordable place to live.

H&H Hotel (Q-160)

The H&H Hotel was one of a few small hotels in Gulfport that functioned more like a boardinghouse than a hotel. Transients and dockworkers were the typical residents. The entrance to the H&H Hotel faced 26th Avenue. In the south end of the lobby, inside the hotel, Ernie Duvall operated his restaurant, Ernie's Corral.

There were several businesses that rented storefronts in the H&H Hotel building. In the south end of the lobby inside the hotel, Ernie Duvall operated his restaurant, Ernie's Corral. Chuck's Bar in the H&H Hotel building was originally opened as the H&H Hotel Bar and later became Matt's Bar. For a short period, Matt's Bar became a retail store, Blue Mirror Gifts, until finally becoming Chuck's Bar. Other businesses in the H&H Hotel included the United Gas Company offices, King's Dollar Store, Rosenblum's Women's Wear and ADS (American Discount Store). Anthony's Grill was another small café that occupied space in the H&H Hotel building. In 1969, Hancock Bank took over the bottom two spaces, forcing Scottie Stores to move.

Urban renewal ultimately took the hotel.

Banks and Finance Companies

First National Bank (J-69)

The First National Bank opened in 1902 after taking over the Bank of Gulfport. In 1926, the First National began construction of its seven-story building on the corner of 14th Street and 25th Avenue. In 1931, the bank took over the Commerce Bank and Trust, but because of the Great Depression, it closed the day after Thanksgiving that year, leaving Gulfport without a bank.

Gulf National Bank (K-97) (E-22)

The Gulf National Bank opened in the beautiful Kramer building on the corner of 25th Avenue and 13th Street. Five prominent citizens of Gulfport—Sam Alman, W. Huntley Caraway, Thomas S. Clower, Lawrence James and Webb Mize—formed the bank in the early 1940s. Mr. William C. Carter,

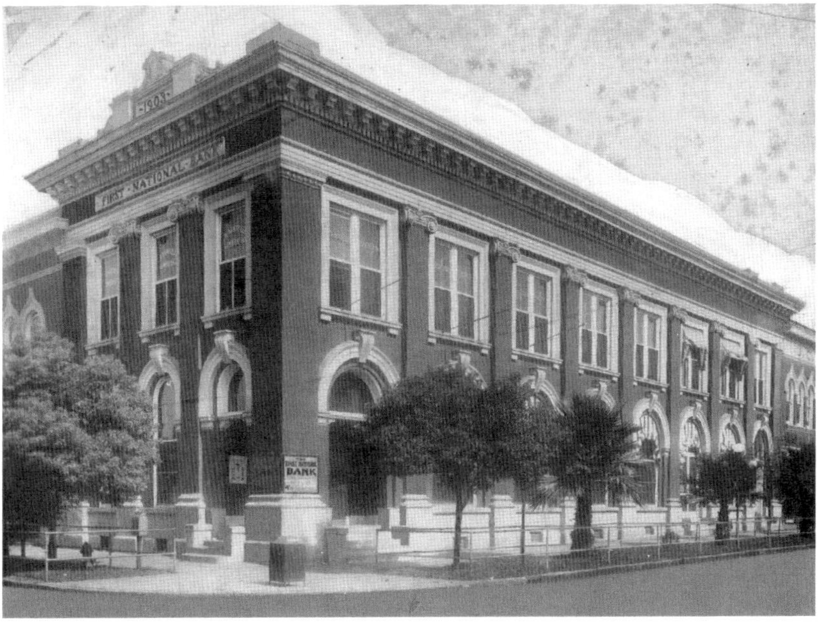

The First National Bank opened in 1902 after taking over the Bank of Gulfport. *Paul Jermyn Collection.*

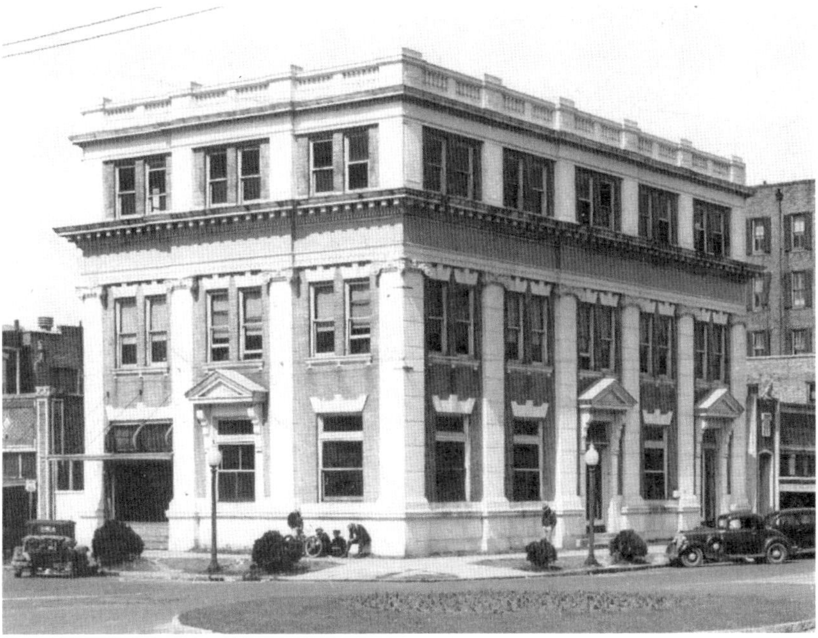

The Gulf National Bank opened in the beautiful Kramer building in the early 1940s. *Paul Jermyn Collection.*

who had banking experience in his home state of Florida, served as the first president. The bank started in a single room and later expanded into the remainder of the building. The bank's first vault was an antiquated fixture from the 1890s.

In 1955, the bank announced plans to build a new facility on the corner of Highway 90 and 25th Avenue (E-22). The new bank offered complete financial services and was the first bank in Gulfport to provide a drive-in window. In keeping ahead of its competition, Gulf National was the first bank in the city to computerize its operations. In 1988, the Peoples Bank of Biloxi acquired the Gulf National Bank.

When the bank moved to its new building, Gryder Shoes took over this location.

HOUSEHOLD FINANCE CORPORATION (K-101)

Household Finance Corporation was a national finance company that was located in the Splendid Hotel building for a number of years. Frank J. Mackey of Minneapolis, Minnesota, founded Household Finance Corporation in 1878. The company claimed to have been the first to introduce the installment plan, which allowed customers to repay their loan on a monthly basis rather than having to pay the total amount of the loan on the due date. In the late 1800s, the loan business was neither a bank nor a savings and loan company. Loans were due in full after three months. R.L. Read, an employee, suggested an "Extension Plan" that would extend the loan for an additional month at the same rate as the original loan. Some branch managers preferred an installment plan. By 1905, all of the branches were offering a plan. In 1896, one of the branches began to solicit new customers by mail, something else that had never been done before.

HANCOCK BANK (Q-184)

This is the home office and main branch of the Hancock Bank. It has consistently been rated as one of America's most trustworthy banks.

Gulfport's only bank in the beginning was the First National Bank of Gulfport. The bank unfortunately failed during the 1929 stock market crash, leaving the city without a bank. Gulfport residents were forced to look for other banks. Some of the people were already using the Hancock County Bank in Long Beach.

The Hancock County Bank was founded in 1899 in Bay St. Louis by nineteen of its citizens. In 1902, a branch was opened in Pass Christian, and later another branch was opened in Long Beach. Several of the city's

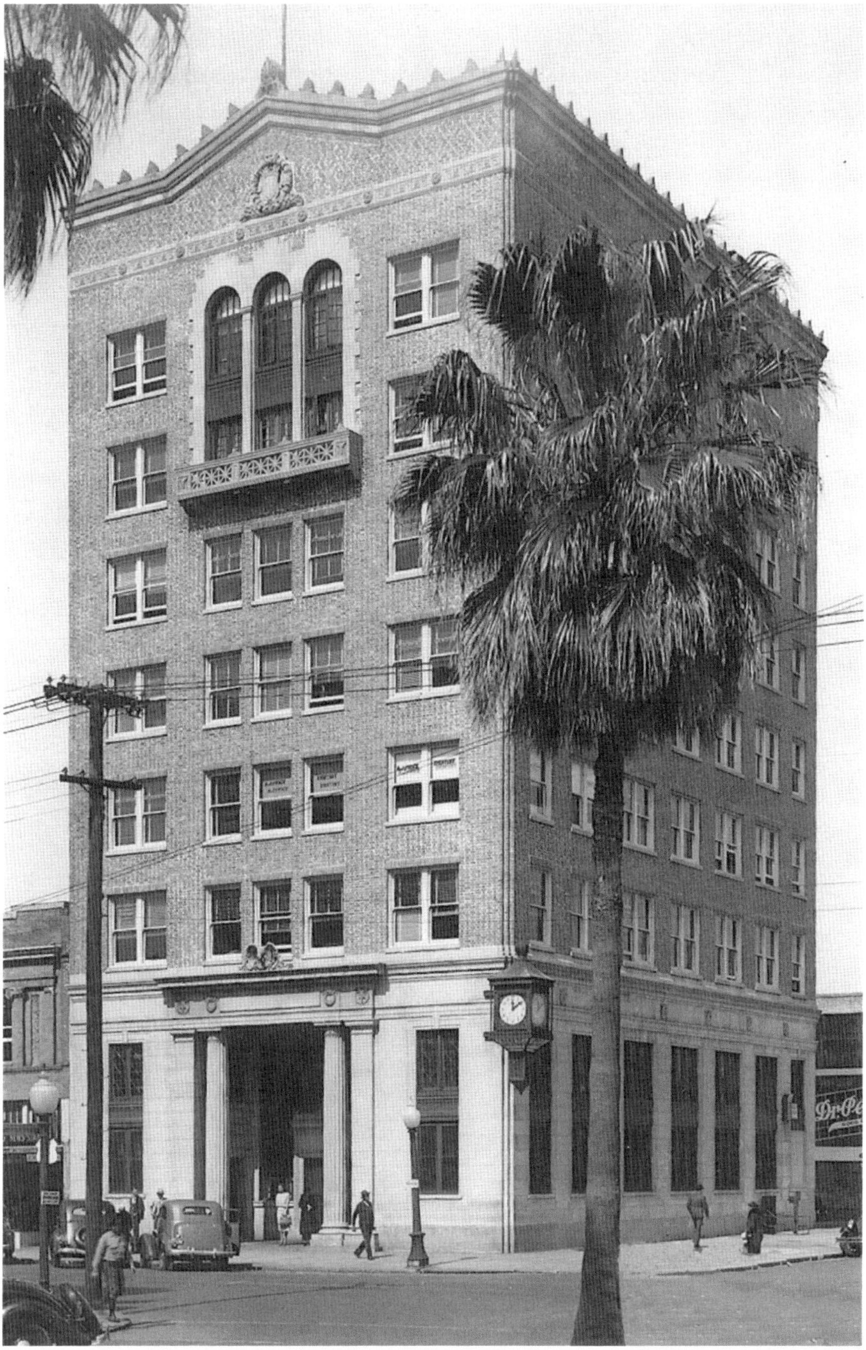

In 1933, the Hancock County Bank moved to this new permanent location, where it remains today. The name was changed to Hancock Bank. *Paul Jermyn Collection.*

businessmen approached the bank about opening a much-needed branch in Gulfport. Acknowledging the need and the opportunity, the bank opened a branch office on the corner of 13th Street and 26th Avenue in the building that formerly housed the then defunct First National Bank of Gulfport.

In 1933, the Hancock County Bank moved from the First National Bank building to this new permanent location on the corner of 14th Street and 25th Avenue, where it remains today. The Gulfport branch eventually became the home office, and the name was shortened to the Hancock Bank.

The iconic clock that hung on the corner of the bank building was refurbished and reinstalled in 1989 after being damaged in Hurricane Elena in 1985.

Coast Federal Savings and Loan (S-223)

The Coast Federal Savings and Loan office was next to the State Employment Office and provided basic bank functions.

Office Buildings

Gulf and Ship Island Railroad Building (D-8)
(Later) The American Legion Building
(Later) The Commerce Building

The Gulf and Ship Island Railroad Building was built in the early 1900s to house the offices of the Gulf and Ship Island Railroad. William H. Hardy, Gulfport's founder, had started the Gulf and Ship Island Railroad between Gulfport and Hattiesburg. After Hardy ran into financial difficulties, Captain Joseph T. Jones stepped in to complete the rail line.

In the early 1950s, the name was changed to the American Legion Building, and in the later 1950s, it became the Commerce Building. In 1962, the building underwent a complete renovation. The original façade was covered over, masking everything except the heavy timbers and the original stone walls, which are a solid two feet thick.

Hewes Office Building (Entrance) (K-89)

The Hewes Office Building in the heart of downtown Gulfport is one of the oldest buildings in the city. Several prominent physicians have had their offices there, as did other businesses. The defining features of the building were the open lobby and the cage-style elevator, which was clearly visible from the sidewalk. Since the elevator could be seen from the street, everyone in town was aware of it even if they had never ridden it. The elevator was manually operated by an attendant, as were most of the elevators of that period.

The birdcage construction resembled something that a child would make with an Erector set and dates back to the turn of the century. Many of the old buildings had ornate metal elevators, although this was the most prominent elevator of its kind in Gulfport.

THE ABSTRACT BUILDING (M-124)

The Abstract Building housed several law offices where lawyers put together abstracts of title for real estate transactions. Abstracts record all deeds, wills, mortgages and other documents that would affect ownership of each property. An abstract allows the owner to trace the various purchases and transfers related to the property to determine clear title.

FISHER OFFICE BUILDING (R-213)

The four-story Fisher Office Building was the location of a wide variety of businesses. The elevator in the building was a manual, self-operating style typical of the period. A large wheel, about twelve inches in diameter, controlled the elevator. By turning the wheel left or right, the operator could move the elevator up or down.

One of the popular tenants in the Fisher Building in the late '50s and early '60s was the Marinello Beauty Shop. Hattie Hobbs owned the shop. She moved to the west side of Gulfport after Hurricane Camille destroyed the Fisher Building in 1969.

THE HATTEN BUILDING (S-218)

The modernistic, three-story Hatten Building was built in 1941 and was named for Norman Harold Hatten. The Hatten Building was the depot for the Greyhound and Trailways buses at different times. The Oberlies Radio and Television Store was in the southwestern corner of the building, having moved from its location on 27th Avenue.

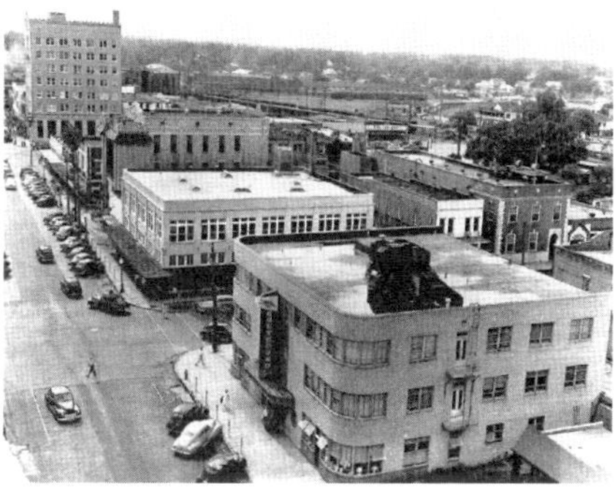

The modernistic, three-story Hatten Building seen here on the bottom right was built in 1941 and was named for Norman Harold Hatten. *Paul Jermyn Collection.*

MOVIE THEATERS, SPORTS AND OTHER FUN THINGS

MOVIE THEATERS

THE LEGION THEATRE (D-7)
(Later) THE SAND THEATRE (D-7)
The Gulfport movie theaters were like musical chairs during the '50s, moving from one location to another. The Legion Theatre, which was jointly owned by the Joe Graham Post 119 of the American Legion and Ed Ortte of Bay St. Louis, had moved to this location on 13th Street in 1951 from its original location across the street from the L&N train depot on 17th Avenue. The new Legion Theatre on 13th Street seated six hundred, including the balcony. The old Legion Theatre on 17th Avenue was renamed the Gulf Theatre after the Gulf moved from the old Anderson Theatre location on 25th Avenue.

The Legion was arguably one of the most popular movie theaters in Gulfport. A long entry hall led to the concession stand, lobby area and entrance to the theatre. Two small businesses, Charm Beauty Shop and Royal Jewelry store, were located on the west side of the entry hall, while movie posters lined the east side of the walls. In the late 1950s, acoustical panels were added over the plaster walls inside the theater to improve the sound quality. The panels were decorated with paintings of Mickey Mouse and other cartoon characters, as well as various boating scenes. In 1961, after a popular contest to choose a new name, the Legion Theatre was renamed the Sand Theatre.

DIXIE THEATRE (K-78)
(Later part of) F.W. WOOLWORTH
The Dixie Theater opened next to Walgreen Drugs around 1915 with great fanfare. It boasted being electrically cooled, an enticing feature at the time. It closed in 1920, when the owner, Edgar N. Hirsch, built the elegant Strand Theatre next door. The Strand would later become the Paramount Theatre.

STRAND THEATRE (K-79)
Edgar N. Hirsch built the new Strand Theatre to replace his Dixie Theatre next door. The Dixie Theatre became one of the three storefronts that made up the Woolworth Building. According to newspaper accounts, it was standing room only for the formal opening of the Strand, which took place

at 8:00 p.m. on Monday, November 1, 1920. Shaw and Woleben designed the 1,800-seat theater with state-of-the-art equipment, including the first concave Clifograph screen in the South. It was also the first sound movie theater on the Gulf Coast. The mayors from all of the coast cities attended the gala, including guests from New Orleans. Tickets were fifty cents for the opening movie, *Yes or No*, starring Norma Talmadge and Harry T. Morry. The Strand Orchestra provided live music, although the new pipe organ had not arrived in time for the opening. It was later installed and was used for the first time on New Year's Day 1921. The theater not only played the best movies of the day but also featured live performances on its large stage.

In 1921, the Saenger Amusement Company of New Orleans bought the Strand from Hirsch. Saenger also bought the Anderson Theatre on 25th Avenue at that same time from its owner, Vassar Anderson. The company continued to use the Strand name after the sale. In 1930, Saenger moved the projection equipment of the Strand over to the Anderson Theatre while it made extensive renovations to the Strand building. Movies continued playing at the Anderson until the newly renovated Strand, with "every new device in the theatrical world," opened as the Paramount Theatre on December 20, 1930.

PARAMOUNT THEATRE (K-79)

The Paramount continued to be the most elegant theater in Gulfport, although in 1960, the theater underwent a complete renovation that included respacing the seats to allow for greater legroom. This reduced the seating capacity to seven hundred. The box office was moved inside, and token-operated turnstiles were installed. The concession stand was moved from its location on the north side of the lobby to the center. The balcony

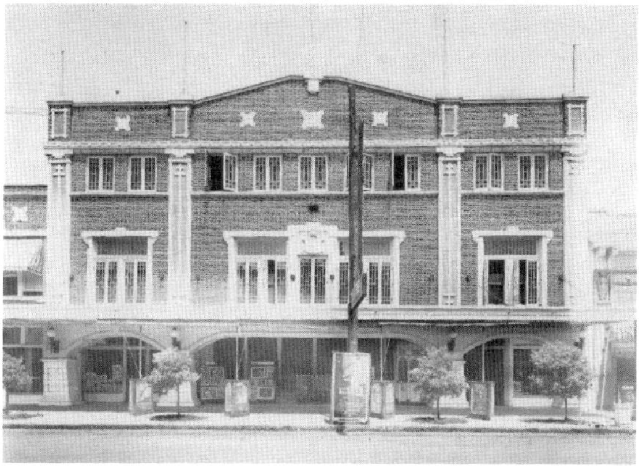

The newly renovated Strand, with "every new device in the theatrical world," opened as the Paramount Theatre. *Shaw Design Group collection.*

was unchanged, with a set of stairs leading up from each side of the lobby. The large restrooms remained on the second floor.

A raffle conducted during the Christmas holidays was the most significant event held annually at the Paramount during the '50s. The local merchants gave entry tickets to their customers for every dollar of items purchased. At the stroke of midnight on New Year's Eve, a drawing was held on stage at the Paramount. The person whose name was on the ticket won the prize of a new Chevrolet from Jay-Jay Chevrolet.

THE ANDERSON THEATRE (L-106)

This building was originally the Anderson Theatre, owned and operated by a Gulfport merchant, Vassar Anderson. The architects were Shaw and Woleben, who had also designed the new Strand Theatre on 26th Avenue, the Gulf and Ship Island Railroad Building on 13th Street and other prominent buildings in downtown Gulfport. The Anderson Theatre had a

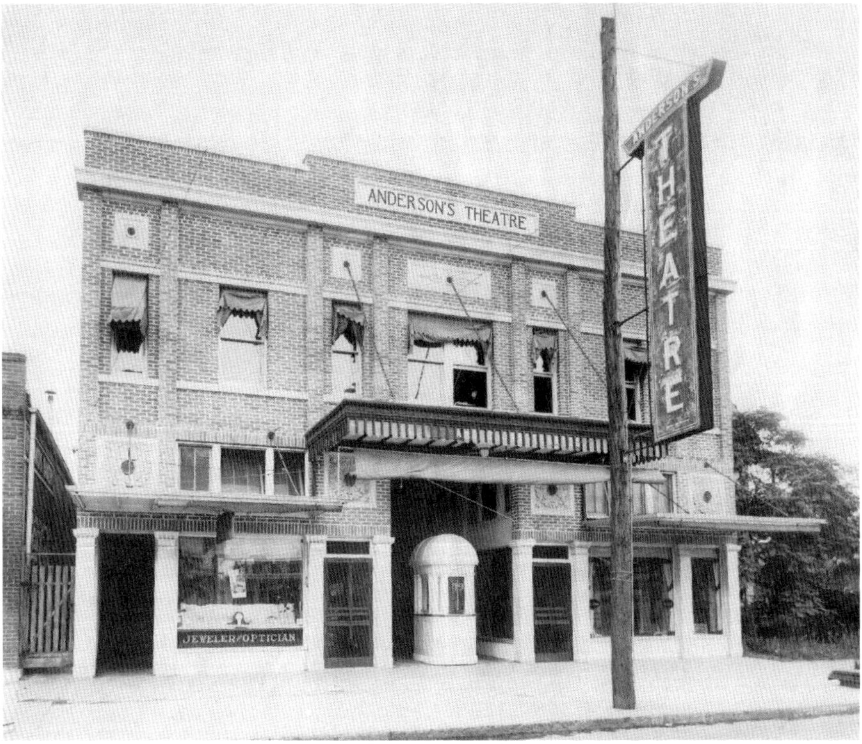

The Anderson Theatre opened on December 23, 1921. The name was changed to the Gulf Theatre in the 1930s. *Paul Jermyn Collection.*

capacity of 844. Stairs leading to the second floor were on the north side of the entrance. At the front of the building on the second floor were four offices and retail store suites. Downstairs on the west side of the entrance, the elder Karl Fasold had a jewelry store, having moved the business from his first location in the Bouslog Building on the corner of 14th Street and 27th Avenue. A beauty shop was on the south side of the entrance.

The Anderson's Theatre opened on December 23, 1921. The opening feature was *A Man's Home*, starring Harry T. Morey, Kathlyn Williams and Faire Binney. There was also a Harry Semon comedy and a newsreel. A four-piece orchestra provided music.

Vassar Anderson sold the theater a year later to the Saenger Amusement Company of New Orleans. The name was changed to the Gulf Theatre sometime in the 1930s, and it remained the name until the theater closed in 1952. Not many of us were old enough to remember watching movies at the Anderson, but some of us have vague memories of the original Gulf Theatre.

After the Gulf Theatre closed and moved to 27th Avenue across from the L&N train station, the Anderson Theatre building became Coast Hardware. Coast Hardware was a family-run hardware store throughout the '50s.

The First Legion Theatre (P-138)

Leroy McWhite's Fruit Store was the original business at this location across from the L&N train depot on 27th Avenue. After that came the Union Café. When these two businesses closed, the American Legion Joe Graham Post 119 opened the first Legion Theatre in this building.

The American Legion had been hosting annual Christmas parties for area children at the Strand (later called the Paramount) on 26th Avenue for several years. After successful use of the Strand, they decided to open their own theater. The American Legion, along with a partner, theater operator Ed Ortte, built the first Legion Theatre here in the old Union Hotel building. The first Legion Theatre opened here on March 5, 1941.

The Two Gulf Theatres (L-106; P-138)

Vassar Anderson sold the Anderson Theatre on 25th Avenue to the Saenger Amusement Company of New Orleans in 1922, only a year after the Anderson had opened. The name was changed to the Gulf Theatre sometime in the 1930s and remained the name until the theater closed in 1952. Coast Hardware took over the building when the Gulf Theatre closed.

When the Anderson Theatre closed, the Gulf Theatre's name and neon sign were sold to the owners of the Legion Theatre on 27th Avenue. When the American Legion opened its new larger Legion Theatre on 13th Street in 1951, it changed the name of the old Legion Theatre to the Gulf Theatre, using the name and marquee sign that had been purchased from the old Anderson Theatre (P-138).

The Gulf Theatre regularly showed double features, a cartoon and a serial. One of the favorite serials was *Commando Cody: "The Rocket Man."* Other favorites were westerns like *Lash Larue* and *Red Ryder*.

When this second Gulf Theatre was demolished in the 1970s, the original black-and-white tiles of the Union Café, as well as the anchors for the counter stools, were still visible in the floor of the theater's box office and general office area.

THE ROYAL THEATRE (P-148)

Lloyd Royal of Meridian opened the Royal Theatre here on 26th Avenue in 1940. It was the first theater in Gulfport to have stadium-style seats. The first ten to fifteen rows of seats were on a normal slanted floor made of wood. After these front seats, the remainder were stadium style all the way to the back. The Royal Theatre closed in 1949 and reopened under the new name, the Don Theatre.

THE DON THEATRE (P-148)

The Royal Theatre closed in 1949 and reopened as the Don Theatre. The Don was the least expensive theater in Gulfport, charging only ten cents for a child's ticket, five cents less than the others. One of the earliest movies shown at the newly opened Don Theatre was the 1949 version of the film *The Secret Garden*, starring Fred Wilcox and Margaret O'Brien.

The Don closed in 1955, just as the Don Drive Inn Theatre opened on the service drive east of the Friendship House on Highway 90.

THE DOME THEATRE (R-193)

In the 1970s, the American Legion opened the Dome Theatre on 25th Avenue in the old Firestone Tire location to replace its Gulf Theatre on 27th Avenue. The booth and projection equipment were purchased from the Lobe Theatre in Long Beach on Jeff Davis Avenue. The Lobe closed after Camille. The name was a contraction of the city's name Long (LO) Beach (BE), or Lobe.

Sports

Brown's Sporting Goods (G-25)
Brown's Sporting Goods store was at the corner of 30th Avenue and 13th Street. The store was mostly known for hunting and fishing equipment. There was a wide array of rifles, shotguns and hunting bows. The store also featured boats, motors and boating accessories.

Sportsman's Corner (G-25)
In the mid- to late '50s, Henry Haller bought Brown's Sporting Goods and changed the name of the store to Sportsman's Corner. The new store also changed the merchandise from hunting and fishing equipment to athletic equipment and supplies. After a few years, Sportsman's Corner moved to 24th Avenue, a block from the railroad tracks.

American Legion Wrestling Arena (H-34)
In the '50s, professional wrestling was experiencing its golden age. It began with the growth of television, when pro wrestling became a popular attraction. Wrestling fit in perfectly with the new medium of television because it had drama and colorful characters and was inexpensive to produce. Since television was so new and had never been seen before, people all over the country were eager to watch anything that was broadcast regardless of content.

Professional wrestling was one of the first programs to be broadcast, so it is understandable that it would become so popular. Wrestling stars like the first champion, Lou Thez; scowling wild men like Dick "The Bruiser"; and more mainstream wrestlers like Duke Keomuka, Stu Hart, Joe Dusek, Pat O'Connor, Billy Goelz, Dory Funk Sr., "Iron" Mike DiBiase, Rito Romero, Blackie Guzman and Ray Gunkel were hits with every member of the family.

In the beginning, the wrestling matches were pretty much straightforward, with good athletes competing more or less by the rules…until the advent of Gorgeous George. George Raymond Wagner (1915–1963), aka "Gorgeous George," is credited with shaping the look of professional wrestling from that time on. In his heyday, Gorgeous George was so popular that it is often said he sold more television sets than Milton Berle.

Those of us who enjoyed the spectacle tuned in every week to see the flamboyant Gorgeous George. He would stroll into the arena under a purple spotlight while the music played "Pomp and Circumstance." His personal valet, Jeffries, spread rose petals in front of George as the wrestler walked down a red carpet rolled out just for him. George made his spectacular entrance wearing elegant robes covered with sequins and gold-plated bobby pins in his long bleach-blond hair. He referred to the pins as "Georgie pins," which he distributing to the cheering audience. As he walked the red carpet, he would stop occasionally to admire himself in a silver handheld mirror. Before Gorgeous George, wrestling had never been like this—after Gorgeous George, wrestling was never the same.

Wrestling was just as popular in Gulfport as it was throughout the country. Many of the fans were excited when, in 1936, the Joe Graham Post 119 of the American Legion announced that it had purchased this property on 29th Avenue to the rear of the Lane Hotel to build a wrestling arena. H.S. "Tony" Everts, the Legion's wrestling promoter, announced plans to bring professional wrestling to Gulfport for the first time. The new arena was an open-air facility surrounded by cinderblock walls with eight hundred "modern" bleacher seats around the center ring.

None of the pros made famous on early television appeared at the arena, with one notable exception. Gorgeous George supposedly made an appearance at the arena near the end of his career when he was relegated to playing small venues, although his visit has not been verified. This did not mean that there weren't wrestlers who took advantage of television's effect on the sport. For example, there was a wrestler calling himself "Davy Crockett" who was obviously cashing in on the Walt Disney television series that was extremely popular at that time.

Although we did not see really big stars at the Legion arena, there was one Gulfport wrestler, Pat Newman, who was as popular with the local crowd as any of the big-name wrestlers we saw on television. Newman packed the American Legion arena every time he was on the card for the evening. In one memorable match in 1954, Pat defeated the wrestler "Wolf Man" at the Gulfport arena in eighteen minutes in two out of three falls. Pat also fought Gorgeous George, although not at the Gulfport arena. According to the wrestling site wrestlingdata.com, Pat won his only match with the famous wrestler.

H&J Sports (L-115)

H&J Sports was next to Smart Shoes on 14th Street. H&J handled a range of sports equipment.

Gulfport Bowling Center (P-139)
In the late '40s, Gulf Savings and Loan was located here, but in the early '50s, the Gulfport Bowling Center took over the space. It was a small, two-lane, manually operated bowling alley. Unlike the large, glitzy bowling alleys of today, this one still used "pinsetters." These were teenage boys, behind the pins, who would manually reset the bowling pins to the correct position and clear out fallen pins. About the time that Gulfport Bowling Center closed, AMF (American Machine and Foundry) introduced the automatic pin setting equipment, eliminating the need for pin boys. This innovation caused the sport of bowling to explode. The '50s became known as the golden age of bowling. Through the exposure on national television, professional players received salaries as large as the players of the other major sports of baseball, football and hockey.

Fun Things to Do

The *Lysistrata* (Ship Island Excursion Boat) (J-63)
In 1933, the American Legion, Joe Graham Post 119, of Gulfport purchased Ship Island. Dr. Lee B. Daron was chairman of the Legion's transportation committee and began operating the first excursion boat, the *Cavalier*, from Gulfport to Ship Island. Dr. Daron ran the boat through the 1940s and early 1950s, when he replaced the *Cavalier* with a new boat called the *Lysistrata*. The *Lysistrata* ran until about 1954. He sold the boat to Edward Ortte in 1955. Ortte continued to run the *Lysistrata* until about 1965, when the Pan American Clipper from Biloxi took over the Ship Island excursion trips from both Gulfport and Biloxi.

Dixie Amusement Company (P-160)
In the early '50s, the Dixie Amusement Company was in this location next to Chuck's Bar on 14th Street. The company leased jukeboxes, pinball machines and slot machines at a period when illegal gambling was wide open on the coast. When Dixie Amusement moved, the space was converted to the Palace Restaurant in the later '50s.

Gulfport Recreation Center (U-234)
The GRC (Gulfport Recreation Center) was a one-story, hollow, tile and stucco building that contained a social hall with a stage, a reading room, a study lounge and a snack bar. Many of us spent hours playing ping-pong

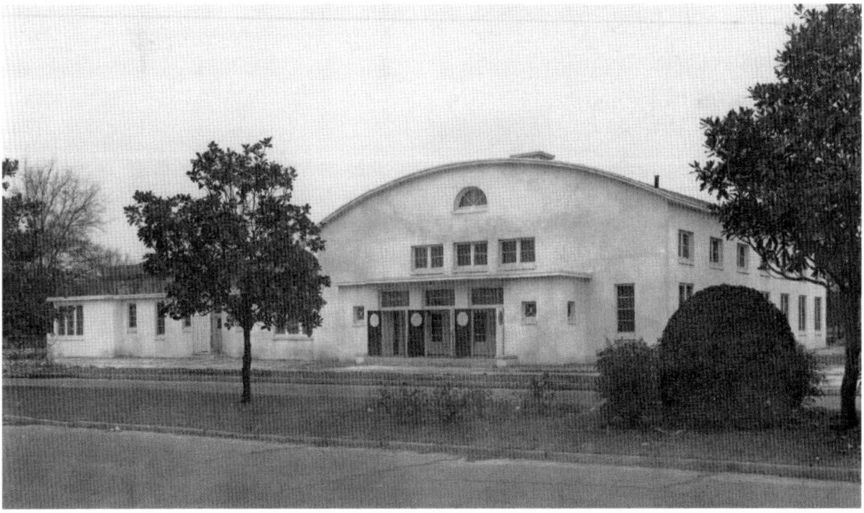

The GRC was a one-story, hollow, tile and stucco building containing a social hall, a stage, a reading room, a study lounge and a snack bar. *Paul Jermyn Collection.*

and bumper pool or jumping on the trampolines. Some of us had the great honor to study art and painting under one of Gulfport's special citizens, Miss Effie Gridley.

Miss Gridley was from Syracuse, New York, and had studied art in Paris until 1915, just after the First World War broke out. She and her husband lived in several places throughout the country before finally settling in Gulfport. She taught art at the GRC throughout the '50s and early '60s. As the vitality of the GRC began to fade, Miss Effie retired to teach private art classes in her home. As she advanced in age, she left Gulfport and returned to Syracuse to live with her only son.

Many will also remember Jacqueline "Jackie" Fontaine Hines, who taught gymnastics, acrobatics and dancing at the GRC for decades. She had studied dance since she was five years old and opened her own dance studio in the Crystal Ballroom of the Markham Hotel while in her teens. She later took over the gym programs at the GRC, where she affected the lives of the hundreds of children who studied under her. She was an ideal role model who not only taught the virtues of good sportsmanship but also tutored those students who needed help in math, English and other subjects.

Jackie's family had moved to the coast from Pontotoc County, Mississippi, in 1919 from Lochnivar, their antebellum plantation. She married her husband, Leon Hines, and they made a wonderful life together on the Gulf Coast.

Biloxi-Gulfport Amusement Park

The Biloxi-Gulfport Amusement Park was fun. Located on the south side of Highway 90 at Pat Harrison Avenue, everyone loved the carnival atmosphere, the small-scale mom and pop rides, the games of chance and the calliope music blaring from large speakers attached to telephone poles high above the midway. A small Ferris wheel ran continuously, taking us high above the beach. The colorful characters who ran the games would let us win just enough to keep us coming back. The prizes were mostly cheap figurines made of plaster of Paris dressed with silver or gold glitter.

The park had opened in 1955 but was destroyed by Hurricane Camille in 1969. It was reopened under new owners and ran until the early '80s, when it closed for good.

Eight Flags Deer Ranch

One of the most unique attractions on the coast was an entertaining attraction called Eight Flags Deer Ranch. Started in 1962, it was actually not part of the '50s, although many of us remember it fondly. It was a petting zoo that allowed the visitors to feed and pet the tame deer that had been brought in from other parts of the world. Other attractions included a bird act featuring trained parrots and other exotic birds. The most exciting part of the deer ranch was the Red Dog Saloon, which was a replica of an old western saloon complete with dancing girls. The saloon was part of a bigger set known as Six Gun Junction, where cowboys staged realistic gunfights, shooting one another down in the streets as well as dramatically off the old buildings.

Marine Life

The Marine Life Oceanarium opened in Jones Park in 1956 with interactive exhibits that featured many forms of marine life. Marine Life was dedicated to the conservation and protection of the animals' environment, as well as educating the public. The experienced staff gave interesting information during the thrilling porpoise shows and other spectacles that centered on some of the other animals, several species of which were endangered in some way. Guests could ride a quaint tour train that would take them around the harbor area. Sheltered pavilions protected most of the attractions, allowing Marine Life to remain open year-round.

Pass Road Speedway

Stock car racing was very popular on the coast with the opening of the Pass Road Speedway. It was located halfway between Gulfport and Biloxi on the south side of Pass Road, approximately where the Great Southern Golf Course is today. The track was opened in February 1954 on what had been a greyhound dog racing track. The owners were Pete Omas and Raymond C. Barry. There were several popular drivers in Gulfport. Among the more popular were Walter Johnson in car no. 252, Charley Meyers in no. 32, Joe Cospelich in no. 8, Ralph McMurray in no. 64, Joe Fascio in no. 39, Joe Booker in no. 42, Lamar Griffing in no. 91, Gene Allen in no. 16, Bobby Herring in no. 8 and Horace Crane driving car no. 26. Horace Crane was known as "Pappy" Crane because he was the oldest driver on the circuit, continuing to race well into his sixties. Pappy loved racing and raced all over the state. It was said that Pappy felt his way through the turns by bouncing off the other cars.

"Bouncing off of the other cars" was part of the appeal of stock car racing. We went to watch not only the races but also the wrecks, which were inevitable. It wasn't the same as demolition derby, but it was close.

The Pass Road Speedway closed in 1956.

RIPPY'S SKATING RINK

Almost everyone who lived in the '50s has fond memories of Mrs. Eva Rippy's skating rink on the corner of 17th Street and 26th Avenue. Every Saturday, we would go zooming around the rink, hand in hand, moving with the rhythm of the organ music—music we would have never listen to on our radios but which was the perfect accompaniment for the skaters. Ma Rippy's grandson, Bill, managed the pacing of the music from slow to party time, playing music from Eva's stack of 78rpm records. The rink was festively decorated with colorful balloons floating up to the ceiling. Special events kept the atmosphere hopping while we did the hokey pokey or the limbo. How low can you go? That was the question.

SPACE STATION KITES

For more than twenty-five years, Mr. Bev Alt made and sold one of the more recognizable products along the beach, rivaling only Bobbie's String Bikinis in later years. Starting in the late '50s, Bev designed and made a special beach toy he called his Space Station Kite. They could be seen twirling on the end of a long string from Gulfport to Biloxi every year beginning in March and going through September.

Mr. Alt was an inspiration to the many high school and college students who worked for him over the years selling the kites during their summer breaks. Mr. Bev, as everyone called him, had survived polio as a child and was confined to a wheelchair for the rest of his life. His shop was directly behind Wet Willys on Highway 90. He worked from a three-wheeled wheelchair that he used to move back and forth from his shop to the beach.

Mr. Bev was born and raised in Ohio and moved to Gulfport in 1959. He got the idea for his kites after observing a World War II tow target. Using large sheets of coated paper, wooden dowels and plastic tabs, he made the kites by hand using a modified printing press to cut out each kite. He had as many as five or six students selling the kites at locations on the beach between Long Beach and Biloxi. The kites sold for $3.75 in the 1950s up to $7.50 through the years. Later, he also sold his kites in Miami and Galveston, Texas.

Mr. Alt stopped selling the kites in the late '80s when the market declined. As the kite business began to slow, he invested in a jet ski/sailboat rental business across Highway 90 in front of Wet Willys and Fun Time. Beginning in 1982–83, his was the second company to rent jet skis on the Gulf Coast.

TRIANGLE LANES

The Triangle Lanes on 25th Avenue was the first modern bowling facility in Gulfport. The sport of bowling exploded in popularity during the late '50s and early '60s, mainly due to the emergence of television and the development of automatic pin setting equipment. Just like televised wrestling matches helped to bring national attention to professional wrestling, bowling programs like *Jack Pot Bowling*, the first national televised bowling show, led to the immediate popularity of the sport.

The Triangle Lanes opened with great fanfare and immediately became a popular place for friends to hang out and have fun together. The development of bowling leagues more than doubled across the country from 1955 to 1963, according to HighBeam Business research. Leagues formed on the coast were typically made up of four or five players who competed over a specified period of time, usually about a thirty-week period. Women's leagues in Gulfport competed at the Triangle Lanes weekday mornings, substituting bowling for their regular card games of bridge and canasta. Midnight bowling on Friday nights was also popular.

MUSIC, PHOTOGRAPHERS AND TELEVISION SHOPS

MUSIC STORES

BROUSSARD'S MUSIC STORE (J-50)

Broussard's Music Store took over this space from Karl Joseph Fasold and his partner, Mr. Harlass. Those who remember downtown might recall those warm summer evenings when Mr. Otis Broussard would open the doors of his music store and play some of the most wonderful piano music for all to hear. As the day shifted to twilight, the sounds of classical music that filled the streets of Gulfport were a wonderful end to the day.

Otis and his wife, Amida, opened their first music store in Houma, Louisiana, in 1945. They soon moved their business from their original location in the Evangeline Hotel in Houma to downtown Gulfport. As the business expanded, they moved to a new building on Pass Road.

ZOLLMAN'S MUSIC (J-64)

Zollman's Music was basically a sheet music store. In 1946, owner Lee J. Zollman and his wife, Betty, along with Ethelynd Baxley, drama teacher at Gulfport High School, formed the popular Gulfport Little Theatre.

HOUSE OF MUSIC (Q-176)

The House of Music was located on 26th Avenue. The store not only sold a full range of musical instruments and sheet music but also provided sound equipment for various public and private functions. The House of Music was only in business for a short time.

PHOTOGRAPHERS

SALE STUDIO (K-84)

Harvey and Mallie Sale owned Sale Studio, a full-service photography store with cameras and supplies. Sale was the main outlet for the popular View-Master viewer and slides. View-Master was a handheld stereoscope that used cardboard disks of fourteen small color photographs on film to produce a very real 3-D effect. The View-Master was a modern version of the Stereopticon of the late 1800s. The most popular slides were travel related or tourist attractions such as the Grand Canyon. View-Master allowed people to see the world from their living rooms. In much the same way as the Stereopticon, the three-dimensional images were the next best thing to being there. Although the slides were originally produced for people of all ages, today children are the major market, with images of popular storybook and cartoon characters.

FULTON PHOTOGRAPHY STUDIO (P-149)
Fulton Photography Studio took over the space once occupied by Sew 'n' Save. Everyone who went to school in Gulfport during the '50s will remember Lawrence Fulton, the school photographer. He took the yearbook photos, and I can only imagine the number of flashbulbs he had to use in the course of his career. Fulton provided a full range of photography services. In addition to his contract with the Gulfport school, Lawrence specialized in photographing weddings and other special occasions all along the coast.

RADIO, RECORDS AND TELEVISION SHOPS

OBERLIES RADIO REPAIR (J-71)
E.K. Oberlies started a radio repair shop above Quality Bakery in 1939. He later expanded and moved to the Hatten Building on the corner of 27th Avenue and 14th Street.

In the 1950s, Oberlies Radio and Television was located in the western front corner of the Hatten Building (S-224). Those who grew up in the '50s remember going through the stacks of 45s at Oberlies looking for favorite

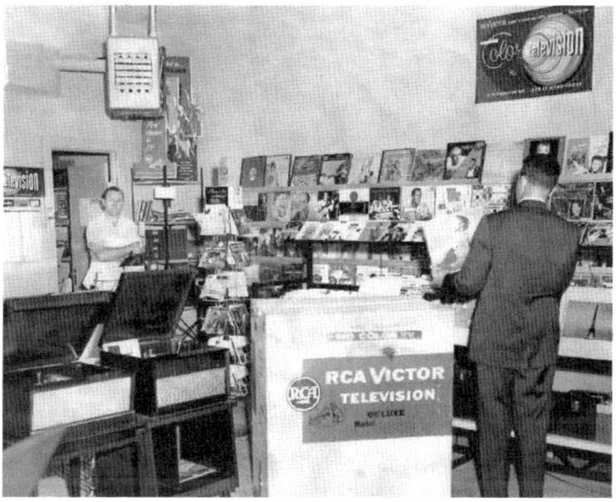

E.K. Oberlies started a radio repair shop above Quality Bakery in the 1950s. He later expanded and moved to the Hatten Building. *Television Shop, Clayton Rand Papers, Manuscripts Division, Special Collections Department, Mississippi State University Libraries.*

records. The company was started in 1939 by E.K. Oberlies as a radio repair shop on 13th Street above Quality Bakery. Later, the shop was moved to the corner of 27th Avenue and 14th Street, where it expanded to include records and stereos. When black-and-white television came on the market in the '50s, he also sold and repaired television sets. Oberlies moved to the Hatten Building in the mid-'50s and expanded his record sales.

HELWICK RADIO & TV (J-72)
(Later) BRUMFIELD DRUGS
Helwick Radio and Television occupied this store in the early 1950s. The store did not survive the competition from Western Auto, Oberlies, Pecoul's and other radio and TV outlets. Brumfield Drugs took over this space in the later 1950s.

PECOUL'S TV (N-131)
F.A. "Flick" Pecoul started Pecoul's TV, a radio and television repair shop, in the '40s on 25th Avenue. As his business grew, he moved here on 14th Street to a larger shop next to the Stone Ice Cream Company. He shared the space with Pete the Top Man, another growing Gulfport company. In 1957, Pecoul's son, Jo Jo, joined Flick, and they moved the television repair shop to 1425 25th Avenue to the Palace Restaurant location.

NEWSPAPERS AND PRINTING COMPANIES

NEWSPAPER

THE *DAILY HERALD* (N-129)
The *Daily Herald* building, located on the corner of 14th Street and 23rd Avenue across the street from the Markham Hotel, was constructed in 1922 and remained the paper's headquarters until Hurricane Camille hit the coast in 1969. After Camille, the company built a new plant and headquarters on the dividing line between Gulfport and Biloxi. The original building on 14th Street was sold to a group of lawyers. The old building was damaged beyond repair during Hurricane Katrina in 2005 and was not rebuilt.

George Wilkes and M.B. Richmond originally started the *Daily Herald* in Biloxi in 1884 as the *Weekly Herald*. The paper began serving Gulfport in 1905 and ultimately moved its headquarters to Gulfport in 1912. Sometime within the next twenty years, the name was changed to the *SunHerald*. In 1985, the paper became a seven-day morning and evening paper. The evening edition was dropped in 1986. George Wilkes's son, Eugene, eventually took over as editor and ran the paper for years, even after it was sold in 1968.

PRINTING COMPANIES

GULFPORT PRINTING COMPANY (Q-177)

Gulfport Printing Company was on 25th Avenue next to the Holmes Barbershop. It was a small printing shop that specialized in business cards, letterheads and envelopes. It also printed brochures and fliers for political campaigns and promotional advertising.

FENTISS PRINTING COMPANY (Q-181)

Fentiss was one of a few printing companies in downtown Gulfport. Located on 25th Avenue, this company specialized in printing small jobs like business cards, envelopes and letterhead. Later, when Fentiss closed, Western Auto expanded into this space.

DIXIE PRESS PRINTING COMPANY (R-208)

Dixie Press Printing Company was owned and operated by Clayton Thomas Rand and was a full-service printing and publishing company. Rand graduated from Mississippi A&M College (Mississippi State University). After winning a state oratorical contest, he received a scholarship to Harvard University, from which he graduated in 1913 with a second BS degree. Afterward, he entered Harvard Law School but dropped out to pursue various business ventures. He came back to Mississippi and studied law in Jackson, passing the Mississippi bar exam in 1918. He later purchased and ran the *Neshoba Democrat* newspaper in Philadelphia, Mississippi, and soon the *DeKalb Independent* in neighboring Kemper County.

In 1925, Rand sold his two papers and bought the Dixie Press in Gulfport. There he started the popular *Dixie Guide*. The paper was the first in Mississippi to hire photographers and have engraving capabilities and the ability to include pictures with its stories.

Over the next few years, Clayton Rand developed a national reputation with his syndicated column, "Crossroads Scribe." In 1936, he was elected the president of the National Press Association and became a popular lecturer and after-dinner speaker. He was also the author of several books and articles crusading against such groups as the Ku Klux Klan and also against liberal government.

Clayton Rand died on February 26, 1971.

RESTAURANTS, BARS AND HAMBURGER STANDS

Restaurants

Katie's Café (H-43)

Almost every "old-timer" remembers Katie's Café. Katie's was open twenty-four hours a day, allowing downtown workers to enjoy a wonderful breakfast before heading off to work regardless of their work schedule. The atmosphere was homey and appealing and the staff warm and friendly. Arguably, it had some of the best-tasting, greasiest food on the coast, but people couldn't get enough of it. One of the most requested items on the menu was the veal cutlet with biscuits and gravy. As an added service, a customer could place an order, and for a fee, a Yellow Cab driver would deliver it. The café remained a favorite of downtown long after other businesses had closed.

Southern Restaurant (J-75)

The Southern Restaurant was on 13th Street next door to the Quality Bakery. It served good old southern food, like fried chicken and biscuits. When the restaurant closed in the '50s, the space was taken over by Russell Finance.

Charcoal Grill (J-66)

The Charcoal Grill was famous for the smell of smothered onions that wafted out onto the sidewalk. The spot served delicious hamburgers, fries and BLTs among other favorites like grilled cheese sandwiches and minute fried steaks. It was a great go-to place for the lunchtime crowd of businessmen and downtown shoppers.

The Splendid Café (K-76)

The Splendid Café first opened in 1920 but was bought by John and Salvadore Bertucci in 1922. Salvadore soon took over sole ownership,

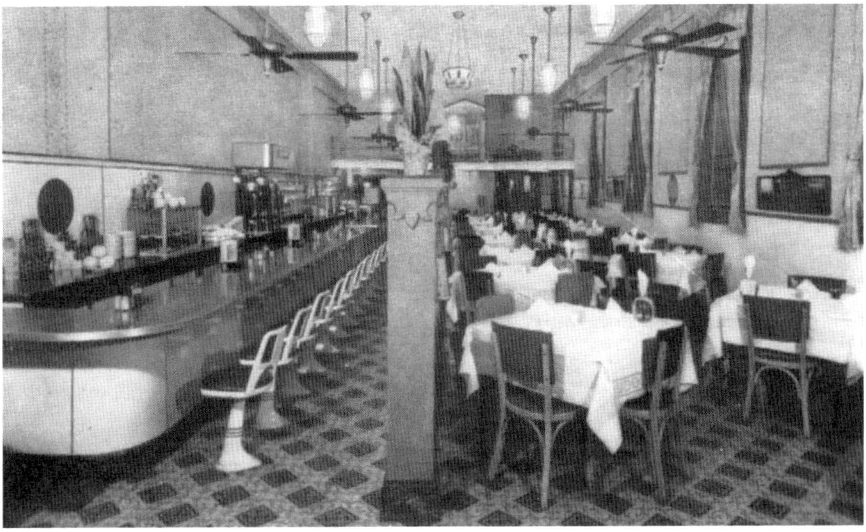

The Splendid Café advertised as "A Restaurant with Individuality." Owner Salvadore Bertucci promised to make it "the best in the state." *Paul Jermyn Collection.*

promising to make it "the best in the state." The Splendid's menu featured steaks and seafood, with a large scrumptious square of strawberry shortcake as a dessert.

The Splendid Café is best known for serving breakfast to Arthur W. Lang Sr. and Harold Metz before they left on a promotion trip to spotlight tourism and commerce on the Gulf Coast. They left Gulfport on April 20, 1925, on a nonstop forty-hour, one-thousand-mile endurance road trip to Chicago along the now famous Magnolia Route. The idea was to connect the Gulf Coast with Chicago and to show that transportation by car was as beneficial as travel by rail between states.

The Splendid Café, advertised as "A Restaurant with Individuality," closed in 1947.

MERCHANT'S RESTAURANT (K-81)
(Later) PARAMOUNT RESTAURANT (K-81)
(Later) RAUL'S RESTAURANT (K-81)
(Later) COMMODORE RESTAURANT (K-81)
(Later) PALACE RESTAURANT (K-81)

The Paramount Restaurant, located between the Paramount Theatre and Jones Brothers' Drug Store, remained a popular diner through the years, although it had several owners and names. In the '50s, it was the Merchant's Restaurant before it was the Paramount. After the Paramount, it was called Raul's Restaurant and then the Commodore Restaurant, named for the Gulfport High School mascot. Finally, it was the Palace Restaurant before the restaurant closed. The Palace had moved to this location from its original building on 14th Street when that building was torn down as part of the 1960s urban renewal project in downtown Gulfport.

HOLDER'S CAFÉ (M-125)

Holder's Café was on 14th Street across the alley next to the Markham Hotel. The Holders, who also owned a small boardinghouse on the corner of 22nd Avenue and 18th Street, owned this popular café. Holder's Café was a favorite stop at lunch for the workers in the downtown area. It featured hot and cold sandwiches, including chicken salad and tuna.

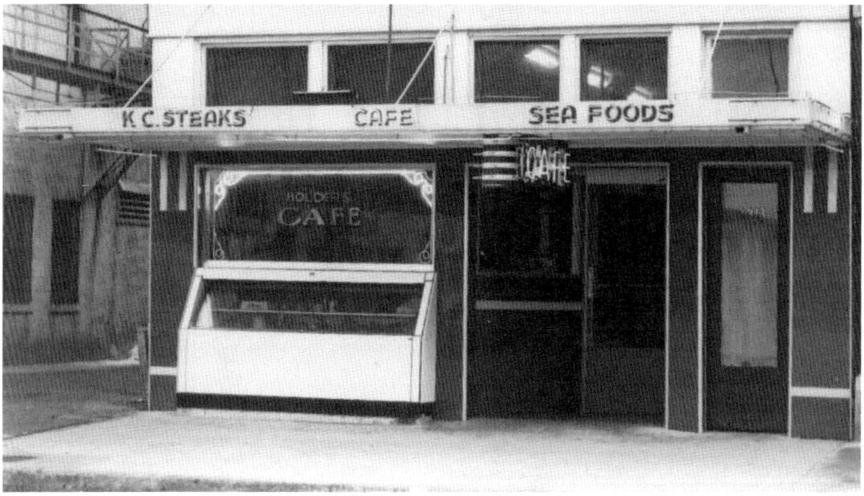

Holder's Café was a favorite stop at lunch for the workers in the downtown area. It featured hot and cold sandwiches, including chicken salad and tuna. *Paul Jermyn Collection.*

LANDER'S CAFÉ (P-142)

(Later) BILL'S PLACE

Lander's Café was located on the corner of 16th Street and 26th Avenue from the early to mid-'50s. After it closed, the restaurant became Bill's Place from the late 1950s to the 1960s.

Ernie's Hamburgers (P-157)

Ernie Duvall and his wife opened Ernie's Hamburgers in this space formerly occupied by Central Barber Shop. Ernie had worked as a salesman for M. Salloum's for years. At night, he would work at the Dog House Jr. on 14th Street. When urban renewal closed 26th Avenue, Ernie moved across the street to the H&H Hotel, renaming his new place Ernie's Corral. Unfortunately, the H&H Hotel was also taken down, so Ernie's Corral was closed for good. Afterward, Duvall changed the name to Ernie's Hamburgers and moved to a new location on 13th Street.

The Dog House Jr. (P-158)

Standing in front of the Dog House Jr., one could smell the onions cooking on the grill. The chili cheeseburgers were the best on the coast. Mr. T.J. "Jack" Simmons owned the Dog House Jr. here on 14th Street and also the original Dog House on Pass Road. His brother, E.A. Simmons, ran the Dog House Jr., which was really just a small hamburger stand. The distinctive sign on top of the building was in the shape of a doghouse, with two eyes peeking out from inside, and the name "Dog House Jr." was plastered across the front. The entrance was to the left of the building, with a large picture window to the right. A sign stretched across the front below the window that read "Hamburgers." Inside the small building, there was a counter that could only accommodate two or three barstools. There was a walk-up window on the side of the store in the alley for pickup orders. Wayne May and Ernie Duvall got their start in the hamburger business working at the Dog House Jr. They later opened their own hamburger restaurants down the street.

Ernie's Corral (P-160)

There were several businesses that rented storefronts in the H&H Hotel building. Ernie Duvall operated his restaurant, Ernie's Corral, in the south end of the lobby inside the hotel. When urban renewal closed the block of 26th Avenue, Ernie Duvall was forced to close his Ernie's Hamburgers shop. He moved down the street to the H&H Hotel, renaming his new place Ernie's Corral. Unfortunately, the H&H Hotel was also eventually taken down, so Ernie's Corral was closed for good.

Dixie Lunch Room (P-162)

Next to the Dog House Jr. on 14th Street was a small restaurant called the Dixie Lunch Room. There were several small eateries in downtown Gulfport during the '50s. Some have stood out, while others seem to have faded from our memories. The Dixie Lunch Room was one of those restaurants that has faded over time.

Anthony's Grill (Q-167)
Anthony's Grill was another small café that occupied space in the H&H Hotel building. It remained there for a few years in the late '50s. Urban renewal ultimately took the hotel.

Rebel Grill (Q-173)
(Later) Palace Grill (Q-173)
(Later) Turan's Corner House Café (Q-173)
Don Parks and his wife opened Turan's Corner House Café in the late '50s. The Corner House Café was a standalone structure with a drive on the south side and the east side of the building. In the early '50s, this had been the Rebel Grill, later becoming the Palace Grill before the Parks took over. The Parks family later opened the Palace Restaurant on 14th Street, leaving Turan's Corner House Café to their son, Don, and his wife to run.

H&H Hotel Café (Q-187)
Most hotels have a café and coffee shop, and the H&H Hotel was no exception. The H&H Hotel Café was one of several businesses in the old H&H Hotel.

Cottage Grill (R-190)
The Cottage Grill occupied the store next to the Ideal Shop on 25th Avenue. This sandwich shop was popular with the lunch crowd in downtown Gulfport. Whether it was cold cuts or steaming patty melts, the Cottage Grill served up the most delicious variety of luncheon items.

Angelo's Place
Angelo's Place on Highway 90 in Gulfport was probably the most recognized restaurant on the Gulf Coast. It was owned and operated by Angelo Xidis, who emigrated from Greece at the age of sixteen. After moving to Gulfport in 1935, he started a small diner. As his business grew, so did the diner, until it became the fine building made of steel and glass that became the familiar Angelo's Place.

Angelo was not sure if his restaurant would survive the numerous hurricanes that were possible on the coast, so as his business grew over the years, he chose to build his additions around the large oak trees that were on

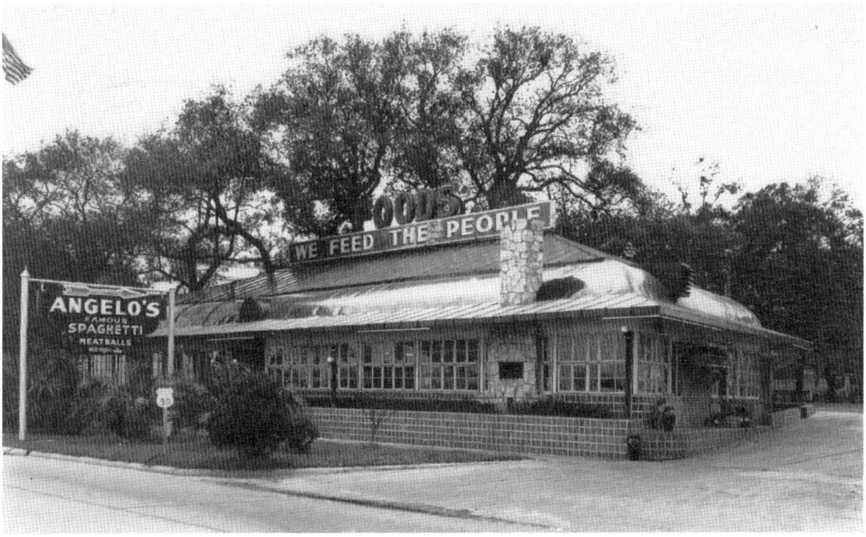

The novel décor of Angelo's Place became a landmark on the coast. Only at Angelo's could you dine while sitting inside under live oak trees. *Paul Jermyn Collection.*

the property rather than cut them down. His decision to save the trees was a brilliant marketing move. The novel décor became a landmark on the coast. Only at Angelo's Place could you relish your meal inside while sitting under live oak trees.

People from New Orleans and Mobile would regularly come to dine on such delicacies as Italian Spaghetti á la Caruso, Pan Roasted Scallops and Oysters, Broiled Flounder with Angelo's Special Lemon Oil Sauce, Chicken Livers á la Milanaise and spaghetti with meatballs. One of the specialties was stuffed flounder covered in Mr. Xidis's special garlic tomato sauce. Angelo guarded his unique recipes closely, even keeping the formulas secret from his employees.

There was a large sign on the building that proclaimed, "Foods…We Feed the People," and that is exactly what Angelo Xidis did. Sadly, Hurricane Camille destroyed the building in 1969. It was eventually rebuilt but finally closed for good in 1985.

DOG HOUSE RESTAURANT

Mr. T.J. "Jack" Simmons owned the original Dog House Restaurant on Pass Road and 14th Avenue near the National Muffler Shop. Charlie Sinopoli leased the restaurant from Jack Simmons, continuing to build a tradition of great dining places in Gulfport and on the coast run by the popular Sinopoli brothers. The Dog House featured shrimp gumbo for $0.45, meatballs and spaghetti for $0.65, the "World's Best" hamburger and French fries for only $0.25, genuine hickory-smoked barbecue (your choice of beef, ham or pork) for only $0.45 and a shrimp, oyster or crab po'boy for just $0.40, to name just a few of the great items at unbelievable prices by today's standards. For $0.15 each, you could add your choice of sides, including barbecue beans, coleslaw, potato salad or French fries. For dessert, the Dog House featured its own apple or cherry pie for $0.20 or delicious thick malts for $0.25. There was also a hot fudge sundae to die for. Other entrées featured breaded veal cutlets for $0.85, broiled calf liver with two vegetables for a whopping $0.75 and its special steak served with a salad and French fries for only $1.25.

In addition to the sit-down restaurant, the Dog House was also a drive-in that included carhops who were eager to serve you in the comfort of your car. The Dog House was one of the unique restaurants in Gulfport.

FALK'S WAFFLE SHOP

Falk's Waffle Shop was a wonderful little diner located at 1601 25th Avenue. Jimmy Falk originally opened the small eatery with space for only twelve barstools at the counter and curb service in the rear. Curb service was a must-have for any small restaurant with limited seating. There was just room enough behind the counter for Mr. Falk and one helper to

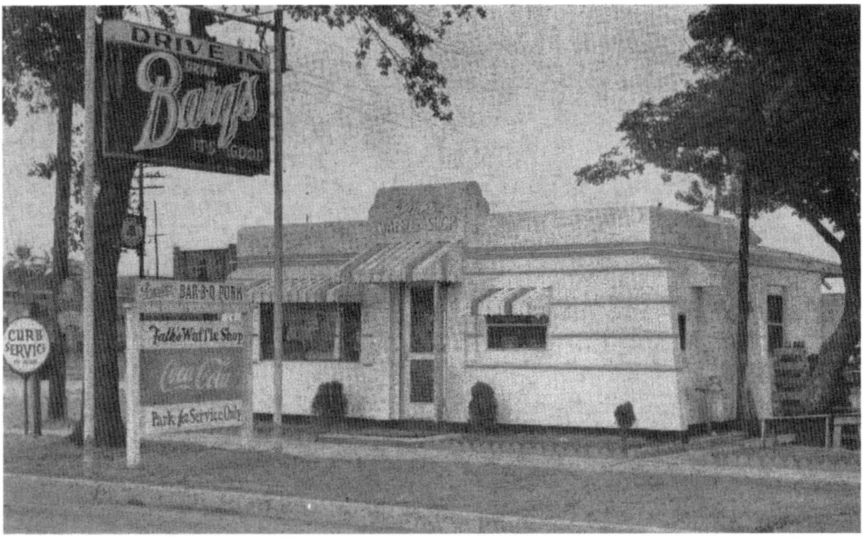

Jimmy Falk originally opened the small eatery with space for only twelve barstools at the counter, as well as curb service in the rear. *Paul Jermyn Collection.*

serve up his famous roast beef po'boys and delicious hamburgers. The hamburgers were made with chili, mustard and a slice of pickle. For those who wanted their hamburger dressed with mayonnaise, lettuce and tomato, he offered his "Aristocrat" hamburger. He also served a small variety of ice cream flavors. The orange sherbet and the strawberry were perfect for the hot summer days in Gulfport. Eventually, Mr. Falk expanded his diner by opening a new section that allowed him to add an additional eight booths. There was even enough room in the new space to include two pinball machines, which seemed to be a must in many of the eating places on the coast.

FLAME DRIVE-IN

Although this would not be considered a date place, it definitely needs to be added to the list of great hangouts. It was located southeast of Gulfport High School within a half block walking distance. Some of us were looking for a change from the regular school cafeteria food, so we would leave the school grounds to find alternatives. The Flame Drive-In was one of the top choices because it was close, it was quick and the po'boy sandwiches were delicious. The Flame was also a great oyster bar. In the evening after work, men would stop by on their way home for fresh oysters straight off of the boats.

FRIENDSHIP HOUSE RESTAURANT

Jim and Mary Meyers opened the Friendship House Restaurant in 1949. Mr. Meyers's daughter, Susie Wilson, told the story that her father had been to the horse tracks in New Orleans and had won a large sum of money. He came back to Biloxi after his good fortune and bought the old Dinty Moore restaurant on the corner of DeBuys Road and Highway 90. He and Mary converted Dinty Moore into the Friendship House. Whether the story is true or not we may never know, but we do know that Jim and Mary turned the Friendship House into one of the most popular restaurants on the Gulf Coast. Located midway between Gulfport and Biloxi, it was advertised to be exactly six miles east of Gulfport and six miles west of Biloxi. The Friendship House Restaurant became known as the "Hosts of the Gulf Coast."

It was a great place for breakfast, served by waitresses in starched white uniforms with red trim and at tables overlooking the beach. The Friendship House was known as much for its great cup of coffee as any of its delicious items on the menu. Along with the basket of biscuits that was served at each table, Mary included her trademark plum jelly. Many of us still remember its catchy advertising jingle that captured the flavor of the restaurant: "Heave Ho the anchor now, and call out the captain and the crew. We're off to eat at the Friendship House where the flounder is so fresh and shrimp are too. And, the steaks are great, and the chicken is the same, and the lobster and the crab have their very own name. We're off to eat at the Friendship House. Friendship (toot, toot, toot) is their middle name."

The Friendship House featured a "Hospitality Menu" every day from 11:30 a.m. to 3:00 p.m. Prices during that time were reduced on specialty items. Among the items offered was a cup of seafood gumbo for $0.35 and a flounder plate that included a flounder steak fried in corn meal, French fried potatoes, green beans or peas, lettuce and tomato salad for only $1.25. For dessert, there was chocolate ice box pie covered with whipped cream or fresh baked apple pie for only $0.25. Other choices of entrées included broiled lobster, veal cutlet, short rib of beef, stuffed deviled crab, spaghetti, creamed chicken, Swiss steak and roast loin of pork. All included delicious sides, like candied sweet potatoes, homemade dressing, mashed potatoes with gravy and others.

The regular menu featured much of the same. Entrées included boneless sirloin, loin steak prepared to choice, veal cutlet, fried chicken, Swiss steak with wine gravy, short rib of beef, spaghetti, creamed chicken and beef stew. The prices ranged from $1.25 to no more than $1.95, with the exception of the boneless sirloin, which was $5.75. A children's menu was available with most items.

Everyone was surprised when the Friendship House was sold to the Brennan family from New Orleans in 1963. The Brennans ran the restaurant successfully until it finally closed in 1980.

Shortly after the Meyerses sold the Friendship House, they opened the Log Cabin restaurant a little bit north on DeBuys Road. It soon became just as popular, thanks to the great hospitality and good food served up by Jim and Mary Meyers.

PALM DRIVE-IN

The Palm Drive-In was a white masonry block building on the southwest corner of 22nd Avenue and 22nd Street. It got its name from the few palm trees that surrounded the lot. The interior was plain with only a few booths and a few of the most popular pinball machines on the coast. Some would argue that the pinball machines kept the Palm Drive-In in business. Players had a better than even chance to win, and they would. The machines would regularly pay a nickel for every game won. It was not unusual for someone to make a few bucks.

Although the food was not particularly outstanding, it was good enough for many of us to keep going back for more. The oyster and shrimp po'boys were good, especially the roast beef po'boys. Some preferred the chili dogs, while others liked the Palm hamburgers. The beer was cold and inexpensive. For curb service, we would blink our headlights to signal for a carhop. Anything we wanted would be delivered directly to our cars.

PARKSIDE DRIVE-IN

In the late '50s, E.A. Simmons and Himbert Sinopoli took over Pam's Drive-In from the owner, Jack Beattle. Pam's was located at the intersection of 38th Avenue and Highway 90. The drive-in had been named after Beattle's sister, Pam. Sinopoli changed the name to Parkside and made the drive-in similar to Jack Simmon's Park 'n Eat on the beach in Gulfport. One of the unique features of Parkside were the curbside speakers, which allowed customers to order from their cars by simply pushing a button. This was the forerunner of the ordering system common in Sonic Drive-In restaurants today.

POPPS FERRY RESTAURANT

Popps Ferry was one of the best restaurants for informal dining on the Gulf Coast, not only recognized for its delicious menu but also the picturesque setting overlooking Biloxi's Back Bay. Located at the foot of the Popps Ferry Bridge, this popular eatery was owned by the Sinopoli brothers. Charlie Sinopoli had started in the restaurant business with the Dog House on Pass Road, which he had leased from well-known coast restaurateur Jack Simmons. Later, Charlie and his brother Himbert took over the Parkside Drive-In Restaurant on the beach, also from Simmons. Their brother Raymond joined them, and the three bought the Popps Ferry Restaurant from J.N. Randall Sr.

The restaurant was known for its excellent food at reasonable prices. The Tuesday night "all you can eat" chicken special served family style was a favorite. Steak night was on Thursdays, featuring ten different kinds of steaks, broiled any way the customer requested. On Friday nights, you could "eat your fill" of fried fish with salad, French fries and homemade buttermilk biscuits with plum preserves. On Sundays, the special was a turkey dinner including cornbread dressing, giblet gravy, candied yams and cranberry sauce. All of these specials were only $1.25 per person and $0.75 for a child's plate. These were real bargains even in the '50s.

There were several well-known personalities who enjoyed dining at Popps Ferry. The J. Giles Band was a popular group that would stop by on its way home after a gig or a tour. Sports figures like Archie Manning were also regulars at the restaurant. Archie and his wife would sometimes eat at Popps Ferry after attending church services on Sunday morning.

After graduating from college, Gary Sinopoli joined his three brothers in their restaurant business, opening a Colonel Dixie in Picayune (1965) and on Courthouse Road in Gulfport (1966). Many remember the hamburgers and fries at Colonel Dixie that were only fifteen cents, as well as the popular hot dogs, which were served with chili and sauerkraut. The average check was usually less than seventy cents.

Later, the brothers opened the extremely successful Catfish Charlie's, which featured fried catfish and the same buttermilk biscuits that were so popular at Popps Ferry Restaurant. You could be assured that if it was a Sinopoli restaurant, you would receive the best food at the best price.

SIMMON'S PARK AND EAT

After World War II, American servicemen came home to a world that was much different from the one they left. For the first time, families found themselves with an abundance of leisure time and discretionary cash. This new environment offered an atmosphere of infinite possibilities. Teenagers no longer had to work to help support their families, so they fell right in with this new prosperity. The automobile, more than anything else, contributed to this new mood in the country. Cars became a symbol of American freedom that allowed us to feel as though we could do anything, have anything and go anywhere. With our cars we took to the open roads, visiting sites and places we had only dreamed of but never imagined we would ever be able to visit.

We developed personal attachments to our cars, surpassing our houses for the first time as a status statement. To own a Cadillac was the ultimate dream. For teenagers, their cars were like apartments on wheels. They were convenient places to make out without fear of parents interrupting. Our cars were an integral part of our lives; we no longer went inside theaters to watch our favorite movies since we could watch them from the privacy of our cars. Drive-in movies were the result of our love affair with our cars. This led to other activities we enjoyed in our cars, including dining out. The drive-in developed out of our passions for speed and efficiency. The drive-in concept was not only convenient for the customers, allowing them to remain in their cars, but it was also a financial boon to restaurateurs. The rectangular or circular shape of the buildings allowed for the maximum number of cars on all sides of the building. Drive-ins

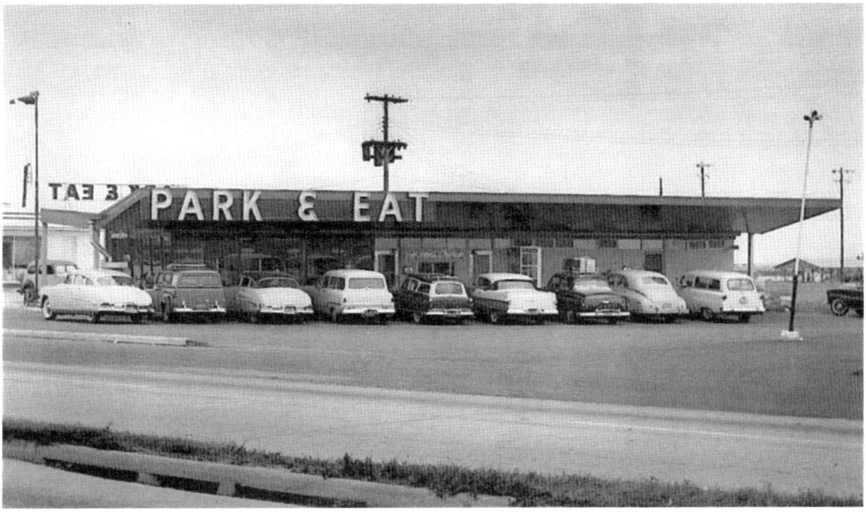

Simmon's Park & Eat was a popular hangout for teenagers. *Park & Eat Restaurant, Clayton Rand Papers, Manuscripts Division, Special Collections Department, Mississippi State University Libraries.*

focused on curb service. We would pull up and park with our music blaring and were quickly greeted by a carhop to take our orders.

T.J. "Jack" Simmons opened the popular drive-in Park and Eat. Because of its convenient location at the intersection of Highway 49 and beach drive, it became a popular hangout for high school kids in the 1950s and early 1960s. We all met there after football games to enjoy a hamburger and Barq's root beer.

HOT TAMALES AND POPCORN

LOPEZ TAMALE CART (J-68)

Señor Antonio "Tony" Lopez did not have a storefront, but he was as much a part of the downtown merchants as any other business in Gulfport during the '50s. His pushcart could be seen on street corners all around downtown. His made-from-scratch hot tamales at five cents apiece or fifty cents per dozen were a bargain by today's standards. He kept his tamales warm in his cart with a small butane gas burner under a large pot that he kept covered with a heavy quilted top.

Making tamales was not a simple task for Señor Lopez. Every day he would begin by simmering some pork. He would then put cornhusks in a bowl over which he poured warm water. While letting them sit for twenty minutes, he would blend masa harina (corn flour) with lard. Filling the cornhusks with the right amount of filling is an art that takes practice. Everyone would agree that Señor Lopez had mastered the art.

The Pop Corn King (K-98)

The Pop Corn King was located in a small store he built in the alley between Gryder's Shoes and the Auto-Lec store (later Shamis and, finally, Marshall's Books and Gifts). Almost everyone in Gulfport knew Clarence Welch, the "Pop Corn King," but few may know how through hard work, a great business sense and his religious faith Clarence built a business that became a classic in the city's history.

Clarence Welch was a Gulfport city employee during the early years of the Great Depression. He had always dreamed of owning his own business, but times were hard and money was in short supply. In 1933, his uncle opened a popcorn stand selling popcorn to the businesspeople and shoppers in downtown Gulfport. It wasn't long before the uncle wanted to move on to something else and decided to close his popcorn stand. Mr. Welch, then in his early twenties, was looking for a commercial opportunity and saw the potential in this little stand. He bought out his uncle for thirty-five dollars. After renting a popcorn machine and adding roasted peanuts to his initial list of products, Clarence Welch was excited to have his own business.

Initially, he moved his little stand to various street corners around town, but he soon realized that to be really successful he needed a permanent location. He went to the city and negotiated for a spot on the sidewalk in front of Coast Hardware Company on 25th Avenue. Coast Hardware agreed to let him build a permanent stand on the sidewalk after Clarence promised that it would be a "nifty" store that Coast Hardware would be proud of. He then enlisted the help of his father, Nathan G. Welch, a local carpenter, to build a stand for him that would become his first permanent business location.

His little stand, measuring only five by eight feet, was the only sidewalk store in Gulfport and probably the smallest store on the coast. The compact building was made of rustproof and fireproof copper alloy sheet iron that he painted silver and enclosed in glass for sanitation purposes. A new electric popcorn popper and peanut roaster were installed. Jolly Time Pop Corn was the only brand he used because it was considered to be the "choicest." He popped corn all throughout the day to ensure that it was always fresh.

He called himself the "Pop Corn King," a name that stuck throughout his long career. In addition to his signature popcorn and peanuts, he also sold

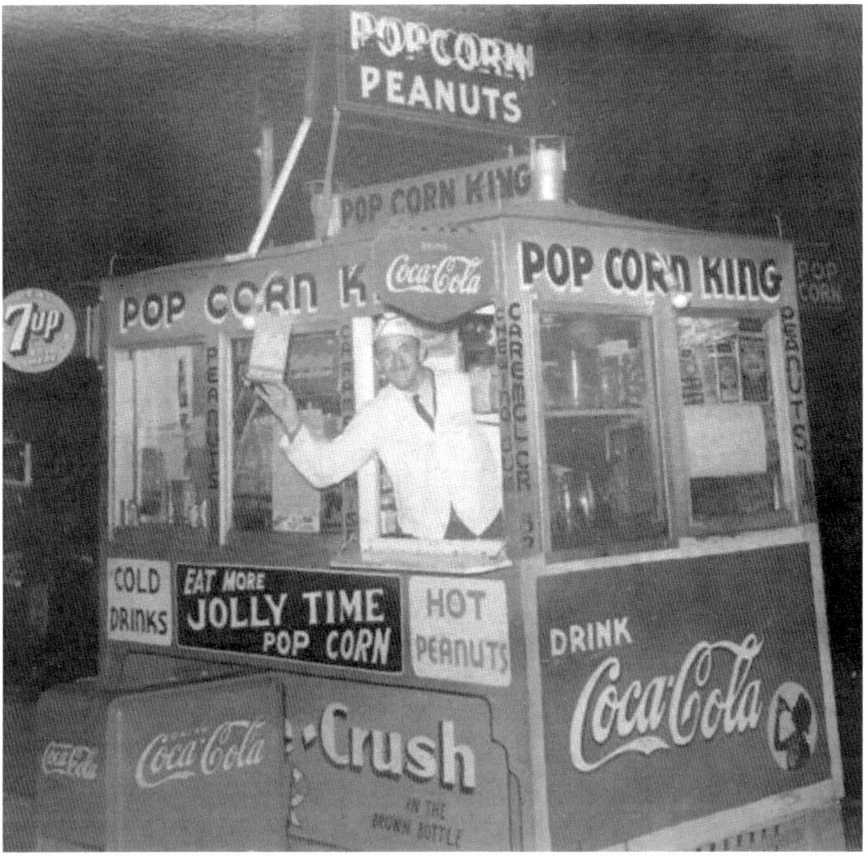

Clarence Welch's first significant stand, measuring only five by eight feet, was located in front of Coast Hardware. It was the smallest store in Gulfport. *From Debra Reyer Hilton.*

soft drinks—Coca-Cola, Orange Crush and 7 Up. He later manufactured his own brand of popcorn candy, which he called Korn-Kandy. As he improved his Korn-Kandy formula, he added new flavors, including peanut molasses, coconut, peppermint, maple, orange, lemon, black walnut and vanilla.

His business in front of Coast Hardware continued to grow, but after a few years, the hardware store asked him to move. He was able to relocate on the corner a few yards north near Triplett-Day Drug Store. This move made him realize that he could no longer rely on a sidewalk business and needed a storefront location. He searched around town but found no spaces to rent that were small enough for his needs. A normal storefront would have had too much overhead to be profitable. After much thought, he came

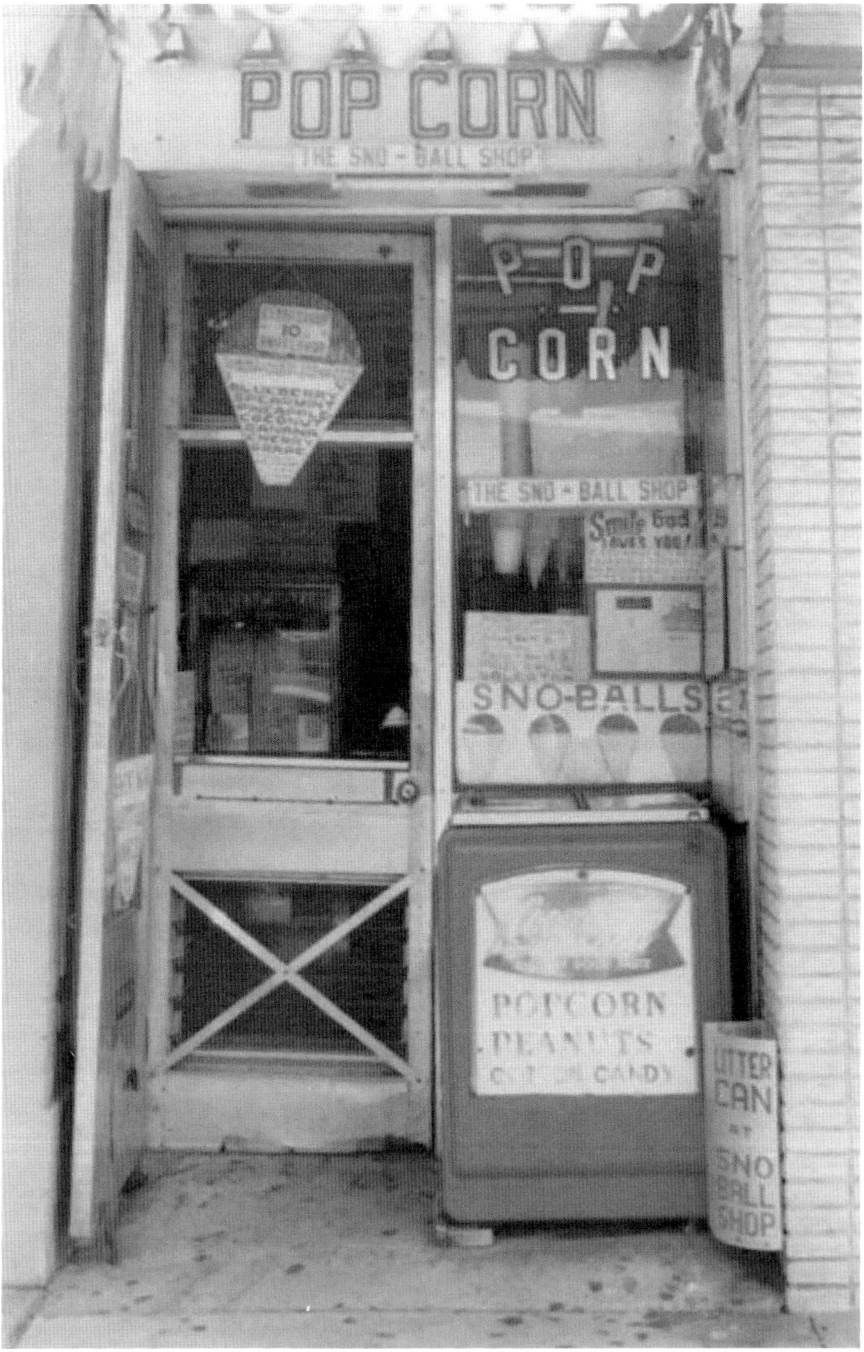

After much thought, Welch came up with the idea that an unused space between two buildings would be the perfect size for his permanent store. *From Debra Reyer Hilton.*

up with the idea that an unused space between two buildings would be the perfect size. He chose a high-profile spot between Gryder's Shoes and Auto-Lec and negotiated a permit with the city to build a store in the alley. He began construction in his spare time, using the exterior walls of the stores for the walls of his shop. He enclosed a five-foot-wide space going back only fourteen feet deep so as not to cover the windows of the existing buildings on each side. He added an aluminum door at the entrance with a built-in serving window. He painted the interior walls white and added worktables. He hung stainless steel shelves from chains in the ceiling to hold his supplies. After adding plumbing, electrical wiring and ventilation for the small space, he installed the machines necessary to make all of his products. In the beginning, his brother, Emmitt, worked with him, and as the business grew, Clarence was joined by his wife and children.

In 1948, Milner Stadium opened, and the city was looking for a concessionaire to sell peanuts, popcorn and drinks at the various sporting events. Clarence negotiated a deal with Gulfport to sell his products at the stadium. This also included rights to the small craft harbor. To accommodate this additional business, Welch bought a panel truck and equipped it with the same machines that he had in his shop on 13th Street. The familiar truck was a traveling store and became a familiar sight at the stadium and at Jones Park on the beach.

Although he was widely known as the "Pop Corn King," Clarence became equally identified as the "Sno-Ball King." He was the first on the coast to offer those wonderful cups of frozen delight. He took great care in preparing all of his products, but the way he delicately shaved the ice for his Sno-Balls was never duplicated. He served the Sno-Balls in a paper cone-shaped cup over which he poured the most wonderful flavors of syrup. There was strawberry, grape, blueberry, banana, cherry and the crowd favorite, spearmint. Many would agree that his spearmint Sno-Balls were the best. I have bought spearmint Sno-Balls from other vendors over the years, but I have never found any that could compare to Mr. Welch's unique spearmint flavor.

From time to time, several vendors tried to compete (Do you remember, "Beat the heat with Sno-Ball Pete"?). They vowed to put Clarence out of business, but with no success. As their businesses failed, they would ask Mr. Welch to buy out their products, which he did. No one could beat the Pop Corn King.

More than thirty years after he bought out his uncle's little popcorn stand, and almost twenty years after operating his little alley store downtown, the Pop Corn King closed. A special era in Gulfport history came to an end.

BARS AND POOL HALLS

FRANK'S PLACE (K-100)
Frank's Place was one of the small bars in downtown Gulfport. In the 1950s, it was located in the Splendid Hotel building and was one of the favorite hangouts for the locals.

JOE'S POOL HALL (GULFPORT AMUSEMENTS) (P-137)
Everyone in Gulfport knew this as "Joe's Pool Hall," although the actual name was Gulfport Amusements. Joe Numnum (real name, so they say) was the manager there for so many years that people thought he was the owner. After such a long time, the pool hall was simply known as Joe's. Before the pool hall, there was a café in this location. The pool hall wrapped around the Purple Lantern on the corner in somewhat of an "L" shape, so that there was an entrance on 27th Avenue as well as a side entrance on 14th Street.

TOTSY'S POOL HALL (P-139)
When the Gulfport Bowling Center closed, the space was taken over by Totsy D'Angelo. Totsy's Pool Hall was a dimly lit room with a less than sanitary-looking bathroom to the right of the entry. Totsy was strict. He would not allow anyone to try trick shots for fear of tearing the felt on the tables. Jump shots were our favorite, although we never quite mastered the technique. But even with his stern oversight, we liked Totsy's better than Joe's Pool Hall just two doors down.

GUS'S BAR (P-159)
There was a number of small bars in downtown Gulfport. Gus's Bar was one of them. Located on 14th Street, there was nothing unusual about Gus's Bar. It was a typical small-time tavern where businessmen would congregate almost daily to discuss everything, including politics and religion.

H&H HOTEL BAR (Q-165)
(Later) MATT'S BAR (Q-165)
(Later) BLUE MIRROR GIFTS (Q-165)
(Later) CHUCK'S BAR (Q-165)
This space in the H&H Hotel was originally opened as the H&H Hotel Bar, but that was eventually closed and Matt's Bar opened here. After Matt's Bar closed, there was a short period of time when the space was leased to a retail store called Blue Mirror Gifts. Apparently the location was better suited for a bar, so when Blue Mirror Gifts closed, Chuck's Bar opened in its place.

ELSIE'S BAR

Elsie's was a small bar just south of the railroad tracks on the west side of Cowan Road. Spider's Bar, located on the beach, catered to the same crowd. Spider's was a tavern much like the neighborhood bar featured on the television show *Cheers*, while Elsie's was the bar couples would drop by to visit friends before going out for the evening. Both bars featured twenty-five-cent mixed drinks during happy hour. Elsie's happy hour was between 6:00 p.m. and 9:00 p.m. The cheap mixed drinks ensured the bars would be packed. In fact, the people would start at Elsie's and then move to Spider's and then come back to Elsie's for more of the same. Elsie and her husband, Lanny, and her son-in-law, Bob, kept the mixed drinks coming at a speed that was incredible. The regulars had to only get Bob's attention and hold up their fingers to let Bob know how many more drinks were needed, and within seconds, he would have them at the table.

On the inside of Elsie's was a long bar along the left wall, with the rest of the space filled with small tables. On the right wall were three pinball machines, with bells ringing and lights flashing and guys crowded around keeping the machines hot, and the nearby jukebox grinded out the hits.

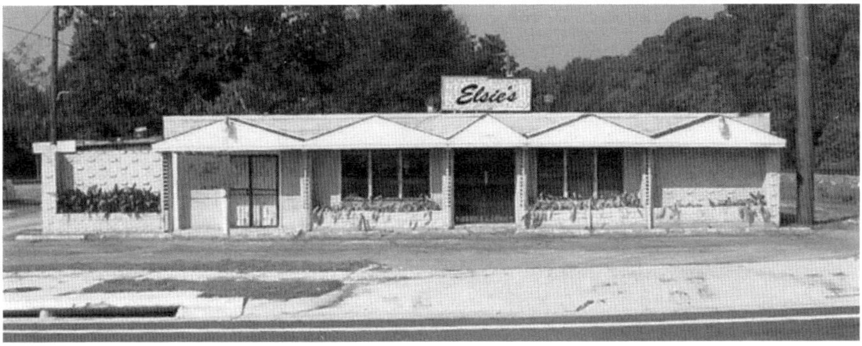

Elsie, along with her husband, Lanny, and their son-in-law, Bob, kept the mixed drinks coming at Elsie's with an incredible speed. *Author's collection.*

SPIDER'S BAR

Spider's Bar was located on East Beach Boulevard at Dolan Avenue. Parking for Spider's was at the Standard Oil station across the street. The station was closed at night, giving bar customers a place to park. The entrance to Spider's was on the left side of the building. The interior décor was typical of a beach bar, with neon beer signs adding a colorful glow to the walls. Above the bar, a Schlitz sign flickered as if the neon bulb was about to blow. The bar was "U" shaped, although most of the guys crowded around the left side near the restrooms so they could check out the girls going by and possibly strike up conversations. On the east side of the bar, two pinball machines were always in play.

Spider's served twenty-five-cent mixed drinks during happy hour, which started at five o'clock, a full hour before any other bar on the coast. Spider's also had good food. Many people came just for its house special: the Wheelburger, a hamburger to die for. There were also other great items on the menu that ensured a good lunch business.

On New Year's Day 1963, the original Spider's was destroyed by fire. It reopened on the lot where the Standard Oil Station once stood. Spider's continued on as a popular watering hole for several years after it was rebuilt.

Food and Drink

The Merchants Company (A-2)

The Merchants Company was a large food distributor that supplied a wide range of traditional brands of food and ingredients in bulk to restaurants, schools and other food service outlets. Among the products offered were baked goods, baking supplies, marinades, tenderizers, cooking wines, processed meats and beef, canned meats and seafood, beverages, water, candies, snacks, nuts, chips, cookies, salad toppings, cones, cereals, dried foods, grains, cheese, cheese sauce, cleaning products, coffee and tea, condiments, crackers, bread crumbs, stuffing mixes, cups, lids and straws.

Gulfport Ice Company (B-4)

The Gulfport Ice Company provided ice for homes and restaurants. With the advent of iceboxes in the mid-1800s, families took advantage of regular home delivery by ice providers like the Gulfport Ice Company. People no longer had to go to the grocery store daily for fresh meat and vegetables. Food could be stored for several days and kept fresh in the icebox. The iceman from the Gulfport Ice Company and other ice providers like the Crystal Ice Company would deliver large blocks of ice on a regular basis to their customers to fill their icebox. A large cardboard sign placed on the family's screen door would let the iceman know whether to leave one or two twenty-five-pound blocks of ice.

Iceboxes were an incredible improvement over the past, although the boxes did have their problems. If the door were opened too often, the ice would melt too fast. If the odor of any of the stored food seeped into the sides of the box, the smell would affect all of the other foods. This often would get so bad that the icebox had to be replaced. Also, if the wrong products were placed together, one smell could affect the other.

Iceboxes virtually disappeared during the '50s as electric refrigerators became more affordable.

HARDY MEAT COMPANY (H-32)

The Hardy Meat Company processed meat for local farmers. It not only handled the slaughtering of cattle, pigs and other livestock for human consumption, but it also produced byproducts, including hides, bone meal and other useful commodities.

THE COAST COCA-COLA BOTTLING COMPANY (G-30)

Captain Joseph T. Jones founded the Coast Coca-Cola Bottling Company in 1906. Two years later, J.K. "John" Milner and Walter Bellingrath purchased the company from Jones. Milner bought out Bellingrath in 1912 and moved the company from its original location on 24th Avenue just north of the L&N railroad tracks to a building on 29th Avenue. Milner moved to this location in the Arcade Building in about 1938. The building featured a large front window through which pedestrians could watch a conveyor belt carrying empty bottles along the line to be filled with Coca-Cola syrup. In 1964, the Coca-Cola Bottling Company moved to its current location on U.S. Highway 49.

THE WASHINGTON PECAN COMPANY (H-31)

The Washington Pecan Company was a local company that processed and packaged pecans.

GROCERY STORES

BE-WISE FOOD STORE (E-21)

Be-Wise was a new and innovative grocery store when it opened here in the early '50s. It featured the only self-opening electric doors in Gulfport that are common on many of our buildings today. For several years, it was a very popular food market for the people in the downtown area. In the early '60s, the food store closed, and the Purple Lantern expanded into this space when the exotic gift store moved from its original location on the corner of 27th Avenue and 14th Street.

A&P SUPERMARKET (J-45)
The A&P Supermarket was a downtown fixture for many years. During the late '50s, Ted Hawkins was the manager, with Leroy Ladner the assistant. As with other grocery stores in town, many students found work after school and on the weekends as bagboys at an unbelievable wage of twenty-five cents per hour. Although that might seem like a meager amount to us today, in the '50s this was a decent wage for temporary work.

ASHTON'S FOOD STORE (L-118)
Ashton's Food Store was one of several downtown grocery stores in the early '50s. Gulfport was not spread out like it is today, so grocery stores in town were convenient for most of the people. As the town grew and the population moved north, the grocery stores gradually left downtown. When Ashton's closed, the Standard Furniture Company took over the space and was a major furniture store in Gulfport during the late '50s.

GULFPORT COFFEE STORE (Q-177)
The Gulfport Coffee store was next to André Appliances on 25th Avenue. It sold freshly ground coffee of various types. Some Gulfport residents might remember Standard Coffee, a brand of coffee that was delivered right to their homes and offices. Mr. William B. Riley first established the Luzianne brand coffee and tea company in New Orleans. Several years later, he started Standard Coffee, also in New Orleans, to offer coffee delivery. By the late 1940s, he had more than nine hundred routes. The company dropped home delivery in the 1960s and kept the focus on business outlets.

H.G. HILL FOOD STORE (S-221)
At the entrance to the H.G. Hill Food Store, there was a large display of Maxwell House Coffee. The sign over the shelves reads, "Good to the last drop." This popular slogan, still well known today, is a reminder of how the H.G. Hill store came to be. The story begins in 1884, when Joel Cheek, a coffee broker, moved to Nashville and met a British coffee broker, Roger Nolley Smith. Smith claimed that he could tell the origin of a coffee simply by smelling the green coffee beans. Cheek and Smith teamed up to try and develop the perfect coffee blend. Prominent businessman Charles Nelson encouraged Cheek to take his coffee to the Maxwell House Hotel in Nashville. Cheek approached the hotel and gave twenty pounds of his special blend to the food buyer to try. The coffee proved to be such a success that the hotel bought the exclusive

rights to the blend. It was at the hotel that the coffee was proclaimed to be "Good to the last drop."

After such a great success, Cheek and a new partner, John Neal, formed a new company called the Nashville Coffee and Manufacturing Company to sell his blend of coffee, which came to be known as Maxwell House Coffee. Charles Nelson also encouraged his butcher, Horace G. Hill, to start his own grocery store. Hill took his advice and started the H.G. Hill Food Stores. The Winn-Dixie stores bought this store, becoming the Winn-Dixie-Hill Food Store in the late '50s.

MISCELLANEOUS BUSINESSES

NATIONAL CASH REGISTER COMPANY (H-42)

The National Cash Register Company, more commonly known as NCR, developed and sold cash registers in the beginning. The company expanded its products after the war, developing new computing and communications technology. In 1953, it invented NCR Paper, a carbonless copy paper. It was the first company to develop a successful electric cash register.

GULF TYPEWRITER & EQUIPMENT (L-116)

Gulf Typewriter and Equipment Company sold the major brands of typewriters, adding machines and other office equipment. The store also carried office books and business manuals. The books used in the Gulfport High School typing class were available from Gulf Typewriter & Equipment so students could practice their typing skills at home.

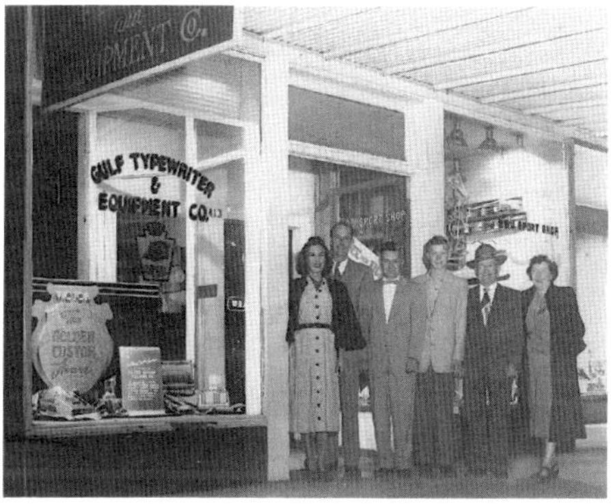

Gulf Typewriter and Equipment Company sold the major brands of typewriters, adding machines and other office equipment. *Gulfport Small Business, Clayton Rand Papers, Manuscripts Division, Special Collections Department, Mississippi State University Libraries.*

WAYNE FEED STORE

Wayne Feed Store was located on 25th Avenue next to Moses Department Store. The store offered a variety of gardening products, including seeds, fertilizers, mulch, potting soil and tools. It had a state-certified chicken hatchery where many of the local farmers purchased their stock of baby chicks. Ten thousand per month were hatched in large incubators at the store. Wayne's was particularly known for the colorful biddies that were dyed for Easter. The store was purchased in later years, and the name was changed to Wayne Farm & Garden Supply Company, although people in Gulfport still remembered it as Wayne Feed Store.

BUSINESSES ON 29TH AVENUE, NORTH OF THE RAILROAD TRACKS

For the purpose of this tour, the area of 29th Avenue past the railroad tracks is not considered part of the downtown business district. Although the buildings are not shown on the map, going north on the west side of 29th Avenue across the railroad tracks you could find the SWIFT COMPANY and the COTTAM COMPANY. Going farther north on the west side of 29th Avenue past the 15th Street intersection, you could see GULF AMUSEMENT, BARIA SALES, WIGLEY & CULP WHOLESALE and several warehouses. On the east side of 29th Avenue was the FEB DISTRIBUTION COMPANY and more warehouses. In addition to the commercial buildings, there were also two private homes on the west side of the street, the GEORGE SAUCIER HOME and the LLOYD EUBANKS HOME.

EPILOGUE

It appears that in our modern society, the biggest problem we face is not the lack of change but rather the incredible speed at which it sometimes happens. The most significant thing about it seems to be our lack of memory about the way things were before the changes took place. How many of us have had the experience of driving down the same street for a period of time, and one day we notice that one of the buildings is suddenly gone and a new building is in its place. We try to recall what was there before but can't seem to remember, although we may have passed it for years. The same is true with the whole town of Gulfport. We might remember the name of some of the stores, but we can't remember exactly where they were located.

When we were growing up on the coast during the '50s and '60s, the pace of life was slower, and change went almost unnoticed. We never had the sense that anything about the town would ever change. But within the blink of an eye, Hurricane Camille came blowing through, and things were dramatically changed. It was 1969, and we were shocked at the devastation that the coast experienced. At the time, it was the most powerful storm that had ever hit the continental United States. But the town survived. We pulled together, and over the next thirty-plus years, Gulfport and the other cities along the coast gradually recovered. In 2005, however, Katrina, a second and more devastating hurricane, struck the area. It was a one-two punch that proved to be disastrous. Much of the city was virtually destroyed. Not only were most of the businesses damaged, but also entire buildings were completely washed away.

After Katrina, Gulfport was never the same. Downtown was no longer the hustling, bustling center of commercial activity. Only a few of the businesses returned, and the whole character of the city began to change. Gradually, the storm-damaged city began a transformation into a mecca of upscale restaurants and quaint seaside bars. Before old Gulfport had been completely replaced, we never imagined that one day Gerald Holmes would no longer be around to keep our flattop haircuts standing at attention or that the Woolworth lunch counter would no longer be serving up those mouthwatering BLTs. Change has come to Gulfport, not in the slow and imperceptible way that change usually occurs, but in one powerful blast. No longer was M. Salloum's on the corner, no longer was Jones Brothers' Drug Store across the street and no longer did the lights of the Paramount Theatre marquee flash its headline movie of the day.

The Gulfport we knew and loved is just a distant memory. Some of us now have difficulty remembering the details of the downtown area. Hopefully this tour has helped the reader recall some of the people and places that were a part of lost Gulfport.

BIBLIOGRAPHY

Bechtel, Stefan. *Roar of Heavens: Surviving Hurricane Camille, the Worst Storm in American History*. New York: Kensington Pub, 2006.

Belfrage, Sally. *Un-American Activities: A Memoir of the Fifties.* New York: HarperPerennial, 1995.

Black, Henry W. *Gulfport—Beginnings and Growth*. Bowling Green, KY: Riverdell Publications, 1986.

Carter, Hodding, and Anthony Ragusin. *Gulf Coast Country*. New York: Duell, Sloan & Pearce, 1961.

Clark, Dick, Jim Mones and Vincent Alabiso. *The Fantastic '50s: When Fads, Fun and Flying Saucers Ruled the World*. New York: Times Books, 2009.

Cohen, Lizabeth, Thomas W. Hanchett and Kenneth T. Jackson. "AHR Forum: Shopping Malls in America." *American Historical Review* 101 (1996): 1,049–1,121. Three articles discuss aspects of the postwar shopping center boom.

Derks, Scott. *This Is Who We Were: In the 1950s*. Amenia, NY: Grey House Publishing, 2013.

Dunar, Andrew J. *America in the Fifties*. Syracuse, NY: Syracuse University Press, 2006.

Ellis, Dan. *All About Camille*. Eureka Springs, AR: Dan Ellis, 2010.

———. *Gold Coast Watering Places: Grand Hotels*. Pass Christian, MS: self-published, 2002.

———. *The Great Gulf Coast: Sails, Trails and Rails*. Pass Christian, MS: self-published, 2005.

———. *Gulfport: "Celebration City."* Gulfport, MS: self-published, 2016.

———. *Gulfport Discovered.* Gulfport, MS: self-published, 1997.

———. *Pass Christian: Historic District & Lost Mansions.* Pass Christian, MS: self-published, 2000.

Ellis, Dan, and Jessie Heitzmann. *Mississippi Gulf Coast: A Panorama of History and Culture.* Pass Christian, MS: self-published, 1998.

Erickson, Lynne Martin, and Kathryn Leide. *Remembering the Fifties.* Madison, WI: Bi-Folkal Productions, 2006.

Facts About the Gulf Coast of Harrison County, Mississippi. Gulfport, MS: Harrison County Observer, 1985.

Fraiser, Jim, and Rick Guy. *Vanished Mississippi Gulf Coast.* Gretna, LA: Pelican Pub. Company, 2006.

Gillette, Howard. "The Evolution of the Planned Shopping Center in Suburb and City." *Journal of the American Planning Association* 51 (1985).

Gulfport Area Chamber of Commerce. *Gulfport, Mississippi.* Lubbock, TX: Impact Map Company, 1977.

Gulfport Army Air Field. Baton Rouge, LA: Army and Navy Pub. Company, 1944.

Gulfport Field: Army Air Forces Training Command. Baton Rouge, LA: Army and Navy Pub. Company, 1943.

Gulfport, Mississippi City Directory. Richmond, VA: R.L. Polk & Company, 1900.

Gulfport, Mississippi: The Gateway to Panama. N.p.: Nabu Press, 2010.

Hancock Bank, Gulfport. *The Coast of Mississippi: Its Past and Progress.* Baton Rouge, LA: Moran Publishing Corporation, 1982.

Harris, Neil. "Spaced Out at the Shopping Center." *Cultural Excursions: Marketing Appetites and Cultural Tastes in Modern America.* Chicago: University of Chicago Press, 1990.

Harrison County Development Committee (Miss.). *Harrison County Overall Economic Development Plan.* Gulfport, MS: Harrison County Development Committee, 1964.

Hearn, Philip D. *Hurricane Camille: Monster Storm of the Gulf Coast.* Jackson: University Press of Mississippi, 2004.

Holt, Hazel. *History of Biloxi.* Biloxi, MS: First National Bank of Biloxi, 1968.

Hurricane Katrina: The Storm that Changed America. Introduction by Wynton Marsalis. New York: Time Books, 2005.

Keylin, Arleen. *The Fabulous Fifties.* New York: Arno Press, 1978.

Kowinski, William Severini. *The Malling of America: An Inside Look at the Great Consumer Paradise.* New York: William Morrow and Company, 1985.

Levin, Philip L. *Mississippi Gulf Coast and Neighboring Sites.* Long Beach, MS: Doctor's Dreams Publishing, 2013.

Oliver, Nola Nance. *The Gulf Coast of Mississippi.* New York: Hastings House, 1941.

Owen, William. *Gulfport Blues.* Jackson, MS: Town Square Books, 2001.

Pearce, Christopher. *Fifties Source Book.* Kent, UK: Grange Books, 1998.

Pfister, Sally, and Melody Golding. *Katrina: Mississippi Women Remember.* Jackson: University Press of Mississippi, 2007.

Shaw, Betty Hancock. *Gulfport.* Charleston, SC: Arcadia Publishing, 2011.

Sullivan, Charles L. *Down South with the Dixie Press.* Gulfport: Mississippi Gulf Coast Community College, 2008.

———. *Gulf Coast Album: A Journey in Historic Photographs, 1899–2011 from New Orleans Across the Mississippi Gulf Coast to Mobile.* Perkinston: Mississippi Gulf Coast Community College Press, 2011.

Sullivan, Charles L., and Murella Hebert Powell. *The Mississippi Gulf Coast: Portrait of a People.* Sun Valley, CA: American Historical Press, 1999.

Trethewey, Natasha D. *Beyond Katrina: A Meditation on the Mississippi Gulf Coast.* London: University of Georgia Press, 2012.

Ward, Kelly, Stephen Tyler and Phil Johnson. *Gulf Coast Memories.* New Orleans, LA: Greater New Orleans Educational Television Foundation, 2002.

INDEX

A

Abstract Building 32, 121
A.E. Morlan Jewelry and Watch Repair 28, 34, 70, 71, 72
Agar Realty 29, 72, 112
Albright & Wood Drugs 26, 50, 59, 60
American Discount Store (ADS) 34, 109
American Legion Building 120
American Legion Wrestling Arena 27, 127
American Plan Corporation 26, 59
Anderson's Men's Wear 20, 31, 39, 60, 71
Anderson Theatre 31, 39, 60, 69, 70, 72, 124, 125
André Appliances 34, 110, 158
Angelo's Place 142, 143
Anthony's Grill 34, 116, 142
A&P Supermarket 28, 158
Arrow Grill 30
Ashton's Food Store 31, 158
Atkinson Brokerage 33
Austin's Style Shop 35, 69
Auto-Lec 30, 47, 150, 153
Avis Car Rental Company 34, 44

B

Barber and Thatcher Books 30, 49, 60
Barber's Hardware 28, 29, 40, 54, 111
Baria Sales 27, 160
Barnett Cleaners 33, 60
Be-Wise Food Store 26, 54, 110, 157
B.F. Goodrich Company 35, 49
B. Havard Insurance 35, 42
Bill's Place 33, 140
Billups Service Station 25, 46
Biloxi-Gulfport Amusement Park 131

Bomar's Shoe Store 31
Bourgeois Building Supplies 27
Bradley Jewelry 30, 70
Broach Finance 33
Broussard's Music Store 28, 39, 72, 134
Brown's Sporting Goods 27, 127
Brumfield Drugs 29, 51, 66, 136
Brumfield's Bargain Annex 34, 47, 67, 110
Brumfield's Department Store 31, 90
Buena Vista Hotel 19
Busch Jewelry Store 26, 70
Butler's Shoes 26, 74

C

Cabibi and Son Shoe Service 34, 62
Cahill Mansion 96, 98, 99
Campbell Appliance Company 26, 54, 110
Candy Company 30, 52, 79
Cardinal Flower Shop 35, 69
Central Barber Shop 33, 64, 71, 141
Charcoal Grill 29, 49, 51, 138
Chuck's Bar 34, 116, 129, 154
city bus service 25, 104
C.L. Bullock Jewelry 34, 71
Coast Coca-Cola Bottling Company 27, 157
Coast Co-op Farm Store & Farm Bureau Insurance 25, 41
Coast Federal Savings and Loan 36, 120
Coast Hardware 31, 125, 150, 151
Coast Inn 36
Coast Printing Company 33
Coca-Cola Company's storage building 27
Colonial Bakery 77, 78
Commerce Building 120
Commodore Restaurant 30, 139, 140
Confederate Monument 32, 106
Cooper's Jewelry 30, 50, 71
Cottage Grill 35, 142
Cottam Company 27, 160
Crescent Jewelry 33

D

Daily Herald 32, 40, 67, 77, 82, 92, 99, 106, 136
Dairy Queen 36, 82
D'Angelo, Totsy 154
Darling Shop 30, 51, 66
Day Drug Store 30, 31, 39, 52, 53, 60, 151
Deluxe Shoeshine and Hat Cleaning 30, 59
Dixie Amusement Company 33, 34, 67, 129
Dixie Lunch Room 33, 141, 142
Dixie Press Printing Company 35, 137
Dixie Theatre 30, 93, 122
Dog House 143, 144
Dog House Jr. 14, 20, 33, 141, 147
Dome Theatre 35, 126
Don Theatre 33, 126
Dr. Lee B. Daron & Dr. Starr, Optometrists 29, 40

E

Ear, Nose and Throat Clinic 29, 40
Edgewater Gulf Hotel 12, 13
Edgewater Mall 13, 88, 89
Edgewater Plaza Shopping City 12, 13
Ed Salloum's Women's Wear 31, 66, 71
Eight Flags Deer Ranch 131
E.J. Younghans Novelty Shop 29, 54
Elite Shop 35, 69
Ellis Salloum's Men's Wear 35, 62
El Mecca Hotel and Café 19, 29, 64, 70, 113
Elmer's Men's Wear 34, 58, 59, 67, 75
Elsie's Bar 155
Ernie's Corral 33, 116, 141
Ernie's Hamburgers 33, 141

F

Falk's Waffle Shop 144
Fasold, Karl 9, 31, 39, 70, 72, 112, 125
Fasold's Jewelry 20, 29, 31, 35, 39, 69, 70, 72
Fasold's Optometry 29, 72, 112
Fayard Moving and Transportation Corporation 27, 43
FEB Distribution Company 27, 160
Fentiss Printing Company 34, 137
Firestone Store 35, 48
First National Bank 29, 34, 45, 116, 118, 120
First Presbyterian Church of Gulfport 26, 55
First United Methodist Church 36, 56, 57, 97
Fisher Office Building 35, 121
Flame Drive-In 145
Flying Saucer House 99, 100
4-H Market 30, 55
Frank's Place 30, 154
Frazier Hotel 33, 115
Friendship House Restaurant 126, 145, 146
Fulton Photography Studio 33, 135

G

George Saucier home 27, 160
Gillis Furniture Company 33, 92
Glass Women's Wear 33
Glenn's Drug Store 31, 52
Goodyear Store 34, 48
Grand Prize Stamp Redemption Center 33
Grant Drugs 30, 51
Great Southern Golf Club 18, 132
Great Southern Hotel 17, 19, 108, 109
Gremillion's Barber Shop 27, 64
Greyhound Bus Station and Snack Bar 31, 43, 44, 121
Gryder's Shoes 47, 66, 74, 118, 150, 153
Gulf Amusement 27, 160
Gulf and Ship Island Railroad Building 25, 120, 124
Gulf National Bank 26, 30, 74, 116, 118
Gulf Paint & Glass Company 35, 111
Gulfport Amusements 154

Gulfport Battery Company 35, 49
Gulfport Bowling Center 33, 129, 154
Gulfport Business Machines 33
Gulfport Carnegie Library 32, 105, 106
Gulfport City Hall 37, 107
Gulfport Coffee Store 34, 158
Gulfport Fire Department 37, 108
Gulfport Hat Cleaning & Shoe Shine Shop 33, 60
Gulfport Ice Company 25, 156
Gulfport Laundry Building 27
Gulfport Police Station and City Jail 37, 108
Gulfport Post Office 26, 104
Gulfport Printing Company 34, 137
Gulfport Recreation Center 37, 129
Gulfport Yacht Club 18
Gulf Savings and Loan 33, 129
Gulf Service Station 32, 36
Gulf Theatre 31, 33, 115, 122, 125, 126
Gulf Typewriter & Equipment 31, 159
Gus's Bar 33, 154

H

Hamilton Brothers Plumbing 25, 41
Hancock Bank 19, 24, 34, 35, 59, 68, 94, 116, 118, 120
Hardy Meat Company 27, 157
Hardy, William H. 120
Harp's Bakery 26, 28, 75
Harrison County Courthouse 106
Harry, Jason "Jay-Jay" 45
Hatten Building 36, 43, 44, 110, 121, 135, 136
Helwick Radio and Television 29, 64, 136
Hewes Brothers Department Store 31, 90
Hewes Office Building 30, 120
H.G. Hill Food Store 36, 158, 159
H&H Hotel 34, 67, 68, 94, 109, 116, 141, 142, 154
H&H Hotel Bar 34, 116, 154
H&H Hotel Café 34, 142
H&J Sports 31, 128
Holder's Café 32, 140
Holmes Barber Shop 34, 65
Home Furniture 35
Household Finance Corporation 30, 118
House of Music 34, 65, 134
Huber Jewelry Store 31, 71
Hurd's Style Shop 20, 31, 66, 67, 68, 94

I

Ideal Shop 35, 67, 68, 142

J

Jack's Barber Shop 29, 64
Jay-Jay Chevrolet 37, 45, 124
Jay's Barber Shop 29, 64
J.C. Clower 28, 29, 88, 91, 92
J.C. Clower Furniture Company 20, 92
J.C. Penney 13, 29, 40, 88, 91

Joe's Pool Hall 33, 90, 154
Johnson's Auto Repair 27, 43
Jones Brothers' Drug Store 14, 30, 51, 59, 139, 162
Jones, Joseph T. 17, 18, 96, 105, 108, 109, 120, 157
Jordan's Newsstand 29, 49, 71

K

Karl's Jewelry 30, 70
Katie's Café 27, 138
Kean's Children's Wear 33
Keith Jewelry 26, 70
Kerr Real Estate 30, 112
King's Dollar Store 34, 116
Kinney Shoes 26, 74
Koury, Foaud C. 62
Koury's Men's Wear 35, 62

L

Lander's Café 33, 140
Lane Hotel 27, 64, 112, 113, 128
Lane Hotel Coffee Shop 27, 113
Lang, Arthur Wallace "Buzzy" 41, 71
Lang, Arthur W., Sr. 41, 139
Lang Funeral Home 35, 41, 62
Larson's Men's Wear 33, 60, 62
Legion Hotel 33, 115
Legion Theatre 25, 33, 122, 125
Lenwood Sawyer Realty and Insurance 33, 42
Lerner Shop 65
Leroy McWhite's Fruit Store 33, 125
Life of Georgia Insurance 28, 42
Lloyd Eubanks Home 27
L&N Railroad Freight Building & Yard 27, 44, 157
L&N Train Depot 32, 43, 75, 115, 122, 125
Lopez, Antonio "Tony" 14, 149, 150
Lopez Tamale Cart 14, 29, 149
Luther Maple Attorney 33, 40
Lyle, John Lewis 39, 94, 95
Lyle's Variety Store 39, 94, 95
Lyon Jewelry Store 29, 70

M

Mack's Barber Supply Company 27, 64
Marine Life Oceanarium 131
Markham Hotel 32, 56, 106, 113, 114, 130, 136, 140
Marshall's Books and Gifts 20, 30, 49, 50, 60, 71, 150
Master Brake and Tire Company 27, 46
Matt's Bar 34, 116, 154
Maxie Broadus Furniture Store 32, 92
McCrory's Five and Dime 13, 20, 25, 74, 92, 104
McDaniel Refrigeration Sales & Service 36, 110
McKnight, James Alfred "Mack," Sr. 39, 75, 76
Merchants Company 25, 156
Merchant's Restaurant 30, 139, 140
Merry Mansion 101, 103
Mill End Fabric 34, 106
Mississippi Power Company 30, 55, 109

Mississippi State Employment Office 36, 107, 120
Moses Department Store 63, 160
Moses' Mens Wear 63
M. Salloum Department Store 19, 20, 29, 39, 59, 63, 67, 68, 69, 72, 87, 88, 112, 141, 162
M. Salloum Toggery 60
Myrick Real Estate 28, 112

N

National Cash Register Company 27, 159
Nelson Hotel 33, 115
Northrop's 20, 29, 35, 68, 69, 87
Nunnally Ford 25, 45

O

Oberlies Radio and Television 29, 36, 121, 135, 136
Office Supply Store 30
O.K. Transfer Company 27, 43
Our Barber Shop 34, 65
Owen Palmer Attorney 32, 40
oyster shell roads 20

P

Palace Grill 34, 142
Palace Pool Hall 33
Palace Restaurant 30, 33, 129, 136, 139, 140, 142
Palm Drive-In 146
Paramount Restaurant 30, 139
Paramount Theatre 20, 30, 70, 71, 72, 94, 122, 123, 139, 162
Pecoul's TV 32, 47, 136
Pete's Electric Service 27, 43
Pete the Top Man 32, 34, 47, 67, 136
Pop Corn King 14, 20, 30, 39, 150, 153
Popps Ferry 147, 148
power plant, the 17, 25, 108, 109
Purple Lantern 26, 33, 53, 75, 110, 154, 157

Q

Quality Bakery 29, 39, 75, 76, 77, 135, 136, 138

R

Raul's Restaurant 30, 139, 140
Rayner Hotel 33, 115
Rebel Grill 34, 142
Reed's Dress Shop 29, 66
Rex Hats 26, 59
Riemann, Dr. E.T. 35, 40, 41
Riemann's Funeral Home 41
Rippy's Skating Rink 14, 132
Robertson's Men's Wear 29, 59
R.O. Besse Jewelers 30, 71
Rosenblum's Women's Wear 34, 67, 94, 116
Ross, Donald 18
Royal Jewelry Store 33, 60, 71, 122
Royal Theatre 33, 126
Roy Anderson Real Estate & Insurance 33, 42
Russell Finance 29, 138

S

Sale Studio 30, 59, 134
Salloum, Mansour 39, 63, 88
Sally's Beauty Shop 34
Sand Theatre 122
Schwobilt's Men's Wear 26, 58
Scottie Discount Store 31, 67, 68, 94, 116
Sears 13, 20, 31, 43, 88, 89, 90, 110, 111
Sew 'n' Save Fabric 33, 67, 135
Shamis Ladies Fashion 30, 50, 66, 150
Shannon Motors 37, 45
Sherwin-Williams Paint 35, 112
Shoe Hospital 30, 33, 49, 60
Simpson and Company 33
Singer Sewing Machine Company 26, 65
Smart Shoes 31, 128
Smith Alteration Shop 34, 67
Smith-Todd Hardware 30, 111
Standard Furniture Company 31, 35, 68, 92, 158
Stewart-Sneed-Hewes Insurance Office 35, 42
Stone, Dan 39, 40, 79, 80, 82, 83, 84, 85, 86, 87
Stone Ice Cream 14, 32, 39, 40, 47, 67, 79, 80, 82, 83, 84, 85, 86, 87, 136
Stone, Ruth 87
Strand Theatre 30, 122, 123, 124, 125
Sunlite Bakery 28, 75
Swift Company 27, 160

T

Toggery, The 30, 52, 59, 60, 88, 109
Toomer's Gift Shop 30, 55, 112
Totsy's Pool Hall 33, 92, 154
Town & Country Shop 28, 66, 112
Town House Restaurant 35
Trailways Bus Depot 36, 44, 121
Triangle Barber Shop 31, 64
Triangle Lanes 133
Tripplet-Day Drug Store 31, 39, 53
Turan's Corner House Café 34, 142

U

U-Haul 34, 44
Union Café 33, 125, 126
Union Hotel 33, 115, 125
United Gas Company Office 34, 37, 109, 116
United Stores 34, 67

W

Walgreen Drugs 30, 51, 122
Ward's Fisk Tire and Appliances 35, 48
Washington Pecan Company 27, 157
Wayne Feed Store 160
Welch, Clarence 39, 150
Western Auto 20, 34, 47, 48, 136, 137
Western Union Office 35, 109

Wharton Furniture Company 33, 92
Wigley & Culp Wholesale 27, 160
Women's Club of Gulfport 32, 56, 114
Woolworth 20, 30, 51, 74, 93, 94, 95, 122, 162

Y

Yellow Cab Company 34, 44, 138
Young Ages Children Wear 31, 69

Z

Zollman's Music 29, 49, 134

ABOUT THE AUTHOR

John Cuevas was born and raised in Gulfport and has been researching coast history since the 1950s. His family is one of the oldest pioneer families between Mobile and New Orleans. As creative director of his own advertising firm in Atlanta for more than twenty-five years, he has worked with some of the nation's top companies, winning gold awards in radio, television and print advertising. Cuevas has written articles and books about the coast. His book *Cat Island* (McFarland, 2011) is considered to be the definitive history of that Gulf Coast barrier island. His latest book, *Discovering Cat Island: Photographs and History* (University Press of Mississippi, 2018), is a coffee-table photographic guide to the historic sites of the island.